"the Little Book"; Key To The Bible And Heaven

Larsen, Ludwig B., 1864-1929

Nabu Public Domain Reprints:

You are holding a reproduction of an original work published before 1923 that is in the public domain in the United States of America, and possibly other countries. You may freely copy and distribute this work as no entity (individual or corporate) has a copyright on the body of the work. This book may contain prior copyright references, and library stamps (as most of these works were scanned from library copies). These have been scanned and retained as part of the historical artifact.

This book may have occasional imperfections such as missing or blurred pages, poor pictures, errant marks, etc. that were either part of the original artifact, or were introduced by the scanning process. We believe this work is culturally important, and despite the imperfections, have elected to bring it back into print as part of our continuing commitment to the preservation of printed works worldwide. We appreciate your understanding of the imperfections in the preservation process, and hope you enjoy this valuable book.

LUDWIG B. LARSEN.

"The Little Book"
Key
TO THE
Bible and Heaven

BY

LUDWIG B. LARSEN.

The Mystery of The Ages Revealed.

Describing What the Bible Contains Regarding God; Heaven; Earth; Christ; Holy Ghost; Angels; Satan; Dragon; Religion; Patriarchs; Houses in Heaven; Cycles of Time; The United States; The Twelve Tribes of Israel; The Bull, Goat, Lion and Lamb, and the Time of the End of the World.

Illustrated.

PUBLISHED BY THE AUTHOR.
PORTLAND, OREGON.

PRINTED BY HAUSER PRINTING CO.
NEW ORLEANS, LA.

COPYRIGHT 1919
BY
LUDWIG B. LARSEN.
ALL TRANSLATIONS AND RIGHTS RESERVED.

Dedicated

to the

Memory of the Author's son,

Angeleo W. Larsen,

Seventeen years and six months old,
October 7, 1917.
Portland, Oregon.

CONTENTS.

Preface

PART I

CREATION AND PHILOSOPHY OF THE UNIVERSE

Chapter	Page
1. God's Laws	13
2. Religion	16
3. End of Time	20
4. Great Trinity	22
5. Patriarchs	25
6. Lost Law	29

PART II

THE AGES OF HEAVEN AND EARTH

Chapter	Page
7. The Heavens	35
8. Houses in Heaven	43
9. Nature of Houses	49
10. Houses and Tribes	52
11. Finished Mystery	55

PART III

RECORDED HISTORY FOR 6,000 YEARS

Chapter	Page
12. Beginning of History	61
13. Adam and Eve	68
14. Genesis	70
(a) Noah.	
(b) Abraham.	
(c) Isaac and Jacob.	
(d) Joseph.	
15. Exodus	90
16. Leviticus	94
17. Numbers	95
18. Deuteronomy	96
19. Joshua	99
20. Repetitions of Cycles	102
21. Solomon's Empire	108
22. Nebuchadnezzar's Dream	111
23. Alexander's Empire	112
24. The Savior	114

PART IV

BIBLE PROPHECIES

Chapter	Page
25. Earth Life Compared	120
26. Historical Events	123
27. The Life of Jesus	129
28. Crucifying Christ	134
29. Isaiah	137
30. Ezekiel	141
31. Revelation	146
32. The United States	153
33. Millenium and New World	161
34. The Mormons	164
35. Reincarnation and Evolution	166
36. The Acts	167

PART V

HEAVENLY CONDITIONS ON EARTH

Chapter	Page
37. Twelve Tribes in United States	171
38. Egypt, The Pyramids, and Sphinx	179
39. The Great Planets	183
40. Description of the Tribes	186
41. Head of Man	199
42. Astrology	202
43. Meaning of Bible Names	205

PART VI

THE UNIVERSAL LAW

Chapter	Page
44. Science of The Heavens	209
45. Equinoctial Influence	216
46. The Heavens and Earth	226
47. Time and Space in The Heavens	237
48. Constellations	242
49. Astronomy	252
50. Location of Suns and Stars	272

LIST OF CHARTS

Chapter	Page
1. Author's Photo	Frontispiece
2. The Heavens	35
3. Houses in The Heavens	44
4. Man as a Universe	47
5. Three Cycles	63
6. End of Time	142
7. Pacific Coast States Tribes	175
8. Nations as Tribes	179
9. The Tribes of Israel	187
10. Heaven Within Man	199
11. Astrological Houses	202
12. Space, Time and Cycles	215
13. Precessional Zones	237
14-15-16. Polar Constellations	244 to 247
17 to 25. Constellations	253 to 279

PREFACE.

In making a brief statement of what the Bible contains, we will say that the Bible is an astronomical, astrological and geographical book, describing a condition of existence in the heavens and on earth. The conditions as described in the heavens have been illustrated and applied to life on earth, and individual names of the human race have been applied to the elements of the heavens, to show that: "as it is in heaven so is it on earth."

The only information we have regarding the history of the Bible is, that, all the ancient writings refer to it as history of the pre-historic periods. The main points regarding the history of the Bible and the study of the heavens are that in all the "Sacred Books," "Inscriptions on Stones," and in the Pyramids, is found the evidence that the study was of a religious nature and considered sacred.

It is suffiicient for us to know that the study of the heavens is pre-historic and that the ancient writers had a detailed knowledge of the operation of the universe. The Bible is the best book to study; in fact, it is the only book to read to get any information regarding this law. Scientists and Bible students have tried for centuries to get the key to the Bible. They knew that part of the Bible is a mystery and that it has been impossible to explain it or use reason in its study.

It is so, also, with the scientific study of the heavens. The original method of the study is lost and all forms of guesswork have resulted. The fact is, that the key to the secrets of the heavens will be found in the Bible, and it is a very simple study after getting the first lesson.

The Bible contains the study of Astrology, Astronomy and Geography, from which a deduction is made and a philosophy produced. The earth is described as globular and the continents as well as each nation and race are described according to location in degrees. The Bible describes the surface of the earth and the measurements were made the same as they are now, in degrees of longitude and latitude, with Greenwich and Equator as dividing centers.

The dividing of the earth into continents, nations and specified localities is illustrated as the ages or cycles of time, and are represented as the children of the patriarchs or races.

It is evident that the Bible was, and is not understood by the exponents of Bible theories according to the ancients. The

Bible proves positively that the ancient writers knew that the earth was globular and that the law of evolution was the fundamental principle of creation. It is furthermore shown by the system illustrated in the Bible, that the earth revolves on its axis eastward, whereby all cycles of time are calculated in degrees of longitude westward and around the earth; which is also a positive proof that the Bible writers knew the law of creation as a God-given principle.

The Bible illustrates the principle of creation and the philosophy of life in the three planets Uranus, Neptune and Saturn; in the movement of these planets in the heavens the law of God is expressed. These planets represent a principle as a God-given power and illustrate the trinity of creation. The space in heaven corresponds to the space on our earth, and when the planets pass through the heavens a given condition is produced and this condition is reproduced on the earth. The God-given principle or nature of the planets is according to the will of God, and we have no comment or excuse to make.

In order to make our study more clear we will give an outline of the study as illustrated in the Bible and spoken of as the origin of man and the creation of the earth.

The beginning of time is figured from the meridian degree west, around the earth. The time spoken of is in degrees of longitude figured in years. The different ages are calculated westward in cycles of a given number of degrees. The three great cycles consist of 120 degrees each and are called the ages of the patriarchs.

The naming of the continents and dividing of the surface of the earth by the degrees of longitude is the naming of the races, tribes and children of the ages.

The first illustration of the division of the continent is represented in Adam, Eve and the children. The first cycle of 120 degrees represents Adam, the second cycle, Eve, and the third cycle, Abel and Cain, covering a period of 360 degrees. The children of Noah are Shem, Ham and Japheth and represent the dividing of the earth into three great divisions; Ham represents the American continent; Japheth, the European continent, and Shem, the Asiatic continent.

The description of the beginning of the race takes place about 5000 years ago, at the time of Noah. The real beginning of all the races of Bible time is figured from the descendants of Noah, in the dividing of Asia and Europe.

Preface. 9

The patriarchs as described represent a cycle of time; figured from the planet Uranus, when he makes a complete circuit of the twelve houses of the heaven in 1000 years. The travels of the patriarchs are described as an age and are the description of the earth as countries and nations.

In Genesis is described the first or actual beginning of the cycles or ages from which to figure time. The family of Abraham is the first described and includes the United States. Up to this age, the description had been general, but after this time, the description is that of an individual family, which is illustrated by Abraham. The age of Abraham as we figure time was at 1921 B. C. prior to the Chaldean period of the East. The actual space of Abraham was figured from Greenwich to 120 degrees west, which is the Pacific Coast States.

The next description is of the life of Isaac, which is for the period from the 120-degree west to the 120-degree east of Greenwich, which is in China.

The third age represents the life of Jacob and is a detailed description of Asia-Europe; and at the end of the age at Greenwich is where Jacob dies and is the end of the cycle.

The ages or cycles of time have been represented by others known as patriarchs. The life of Moses, Joshua, the Judges, including David, covers the same field and is figured in 120 degree cycles.

The last three cycles are figured from Solomon and the Empires up to the present time.

The circuit of Uranus is of twelve houses, which are divided into three periods of four houses each. Each group of four houses constitute an age. The end of each cycle is when the three leading planets, Uranus, Neptune and Saturn, pass from one 120-degree cycle in the heavens to another; then a condition is produced which causes war and pestilence on the earth.

The cycle of time for each patriarch or age is 336 years (degrees), and three divisions to the circuit makes 1008 years to a complete age.

The beginning of the first cycle as recorded was in 4004 B. C. Covering four 1000-year cycles to the beginning of the Roman Empire age.

The real cause or foundation for the apparent worship which is described in the Bible is the change in the cycles of time called the passover, caused by the changing of polarity in the precession of the equinoxes for the heavens and earth. This event was considered religiously sacred and very important as all life in the heavens and on earth became affected by it. The ancients saw in this event the intelligent will and power of God and that the law of the heavens was the words spoken by God to man on earth. From this can be seen what is meant by the God power who rules in the heavens and on earth.

That part of the Bible which deals with future conditions called prophecy as given in the books of Isaiah, Ezekiel, Daniel and the Revelations, is the most disputed and misunderstood part of the Bible. It may be permissible here to state that when parables regarding God's laws are used, that is has reference to the workings of the laws of the universe, and is called astronomy. When these explanations deal with the future it is commonly known as astrology.

The contents of the Bible, so far as they refer to the material or earthly conditions, are a simple study of the planets and houses of the Zodiac. This is a strong statement to make, but the object of writing this book is to give a key and to prove by the Bible what these mystery writings are. The reason for putting forth this book is to show the right way and correct a misleading knowledge of God; consequently the opinion of individuals will be disregarded.

It has been known for many years that the Bible contained an astronomical study, but to what extent or how to read it has not been known. One who is somewhat familiar with the study of astrology will, when he gets the key or idea of this book, read the Bible and see the most harmonious scientific teachings. And for those not familiar with the study, a little application will give an inclination to know more and the study will become so interesting that it will take care of itself. The knowledge of being able to read and discern the truth of the greatest book in existence is worth the effort made to learn to read the Bible correctly.

To the students of the Bible, the illustrations as pictured there are the teachings of perfect character, and not as it may appear to the untutored, immoral and the language considered filthy. The coarse and vulgar terms as used in the Bible are applied to nations, the signs of the Zodiac and planets; to illustrate characters and not applied to any human being, consequently the immoral meaning as generally understood is lost.

From this it will be seen that when the Bible is rightly understood, the reading of the Bible will be a pleasure and a satisfaction.

There is another very important question which each individual has to decide for himself, and that is: Do we survive after the so-called death? Today the Bible is our fundamental textbook, teaching us what the future life is; or as we term it, the life in the next world. Now, if there is something in the Bible, which is not understood, the student will be misled into a false belief. If this knowledge can be obtained by yourself, to your own satisfaction, you can look toward the future life without fear. In the study of the Bible this knowledge can be obtained, and it is a knowledge and not merely a belief. A law will be found in the universe of God, so good, great, and just that the fear of a devil and hell will disappear. The satisfaction of this knowledge alone is worth the time spent in this study.

The scientific study of the Bible, without the idea of worship included in it will show to the conscientious student that the ancient writers knew that the human race continues to live after the so-called death. Anyone who wants to get this knowledge can get it out of the Bible, but this information cannot be obtained as long as the student maintains the idea of a personal or individual God or Devil.

LUDWIG B. LARSEN.

Portland, Oregon, April, 1919.

Part I.

Chapter 1.

God's Laws.

God and the Universe are One.

"In the beginning was the word and the word was with God, and the word was God." John I.

God's laws are the operation or movements of the creative Universe, from the smallest molecule to the greatest Solar Systems.

The Holy Spirit or Word of God is the life-giving principle which permeates the entire creation. It is the reproductive element in the grain of wheat, in the power of sunlight or in the influence of atmosphere. Its operation is caused by the action of the elements of nature from all sources.

God's children constitute every living atom, regardless of form or degree of development; whether it may be a human being, the earth, or a planet or part of some other solar system, in any part of the Universe.

God and the Universe are one; are all, and in all; and the creative principle as expressed in what we call natural laws, are the expressions of God's will. The Universe was not made for the benefit of the human race, but they are only part, and a very small part, of a great unit of all.

To worship God is to know his will, which is to study the operation or manifestation of the laws of nature, and to live accordingly.

To sin is to disregard God's laws, or to live and act contrary to nature, whether it be intentionally or by ignorance of the law.

Heaven is the space or place wherein the different solar systems exist and operate as an eternal Universe. Heaven is not a specific location in the Universe, where the souls of the human race go after they pass out of the body; neither is it a place of reward for a certain class of people to live in after death.

Hell is supposed to be a place where the Devil exists and is outside of the jurisdiction of God. There is no place in the Universe where hell is located. Neither is there a Devil or Satan as a being, whose aim is to eternally torture human beings. Heaven and hell refer to conditions of existence spoken of in the Bible as a reward or punishment.

To live according to the law is to obey God and the reward is heaven here and hereafter. To disobey God is to act contrary to nature and be punished with disease and hell conditions.

The law of nature or God does not stop when the human being passes out of the body. The being is the same, with the same traits of character and individuality, living and existing as others who have passed out of the body of flesh. These beings enter into a life on a higher atmospheric condition. They are subject to the conditions of this earth in its motion around the sun, the planets and elements of nature, as well as to the local condition of each individual.

Life is eternal whether it is expressed in a human being or in any other form. The expression of life changes form at certain given periods of existence. For instance, as expressed through the flesh, the living life principle at birth takes on the form of a human being in the shape of a child and maintains this form until the functions of the body of flesh cease. When the human being or life principle passes out of the flesh it takes on the form which is known as spirit and lives in an atmosphere of spirits.

The manifestation of all life in the flesh is compulsory and is part of God's laws, for it is impossible for any being to stop living. The life principle called nature, which eminates from God, is indestructible and after it takes on the form of a human being it maintains a memory throughout eternity. As it is impossible to prevent or stop the manifestation of life in the flesh, so is it impossible to maintain the spirit in the flesh indefinitely. There is a law which governs all things and the law makes it impossible to stop the spirit from passing out of the flesh whether the human being desires it or not.

The life in what is known as the spirit world is similar to the life in the flesh; only some of the forms and functions of nature are different. It is the same universe and the same natural laws to contend with. The fact is, it is the continuation of the same life. First Corinthians 15:35-55.

The existence as a being in the spiritual form is also limited to a given period of time. The soul passes out of the body of the spirit and takes on another living form again. The spirit body after separation of the soul is disintegrated by the elements on the plain of the spirit, the same as the flesh is disintegrated by the material elements here.

These are the fundamental principles of the laws of the universe affecting the existence of the human being now and hereafter.

In order to live according to the laws of God, we should study the laws and know how to live both now and in the future. As God is a living God and includes the entire universe, the study of God's laws must be the study of the laws of the universe.

The next most important question is, what constitutes the universe and what is known of it that can be studied? Our knowledge of the great universe is very limited. The Bible and some other ancient writings give us some information concerning the universe, and the modern science of astronomy has verified and confirmed some of the teachings found in the Bible. The fact is that the study of astronomy is the actual study of God's laws. Astronomers observe the heavens and measure space and the movements of the different solar systems. They have found that our earth, together with seven other planets, make a regular and systematic circuit around the sun, making our sun a center for this planetary unit. They have also found that other solar systems exist, and that other planets make circuits around other suns, and that there is no limit to space, and that space may be considered as eternity. The modern science of astronomy gives us the cold figures and facts of the actual physical manifestation of some of the operation of God's laws, and we take it for granted that it is absolutely correct. The Christian Bible and some other ancient writings give us the same information and much more. The Bible shows that our solar system goes round another solar system and the length of time in years it takes to make a circuit.

The Bible is the best book published, giving detailed information of the operation of the universe. It shows that there are sixty seconds in a minute, sixty minutes in the hour and twenty-four hours in the day. It also shows that a circle consists of three hundred and sixty degrees, and that the entire creation is operated in cycles. It shows that the manifestation and operation of the universe as described in the Bible is the same as the science of astronomy, which gives figures and measurements and dates of time.

The teachings of other ancient writings when reference is

made to God and the worship of God, is the same as in the Bible. They speak of God as the great power, which rules the universe.

The "Book of the Dead," which is the translation of the writings found in the pyramids, shows that the heavens have been divided, and that names have been given the different sections; that the same fundamental rule was used in their time as now. They speak of Isis corresponding to the East or Sunrise, "as a Hymn of Praise when rising in the horizon" God is in his glory at Midday in the south, proclaiming exaltation and Osiris is the west or "sunset with lamentation" as the elements of nature pass to the "underworld," under the earth at night. The first part of the "Book of the Dead" contains the meaning of what the twelve signs of the Zodiac give in the four cardinal points, North, East, South and West, and the rest of the book describes details. Much may be said about these writings but let it be said that they contain a natural explanation of the universe.

Chapter 2.

RELIGION.

In all ages the philosophy of life has been the problem that the human race has tried to solve. The writings regarding this study as handed down to us from the different tribes and nations, show that the human race has existed on this earth for the past six thousand years. These writings, whether they have been preserved in the Bible or other religious documents, or found carved on stones in the Pyramids, or the tombs of Egypt or India, show that the fundamental principles of all writings are from the same origin. The doctrine of the writings, is the study of the operation of the universe; the relation of our earth to the planets of our solar system; illustrating a philosophy which is applied to all life. It is unnecessary to mention the different religious doctrines of the past and their teachings. We have today three great organizations, which are the outgrowth of teachings of the time previous to the Christian age. The three great organizations are the Buddhists, Christians and Mohammedans.

The original center of population and civilization before our age was east of the Mediterranean Sea, in Babylonia, Asyria and Egypt. Many books have been published giving the details of the origin and history of these religious organizations, so it will be necessary only to mention here, that they all originated from the same place, and that their law and philosophy of life come from the same root and their doctrine originally was the same. The promulgation of each doctrine in the last two thousand years has conformed to the natural growth of the nations and the advancement caused by civilization. The Brahman and the Buddhist religion has answered the purpose for the Japanese, Chinese and for nations of the far east in Asia; the Christian religion for the European and American nations, and the Mohammedan religion for the Balkans, Turkey, India and Northern Africa. It is apparent that each has a mission to perform; a life to live; or period of existence.

When we look back over the history of Nations and religious organizations, we find that from their formation they grow to their zenith, then they decline and finally change form of existence or die. The history of the three great religions of today is no exception, and by observation we now know that the great churches or religious organizations will be compelled to change.

The reason why the author refers to religious organizations is that the same law which governs nations, also governs the religious or spiritual laws of God. The churches represent a principle of a spiritual life, and teach the continuation of life after death. The priests or teachers of a spiritual life must know the laws of God in order to teach others this principle. Many of the teachers of this spiritual knowledge do not know the laws of God and are teaching a substitute philosophy which adheres to a personal God instead of a universal God. It is at this time, God's will, that the truth shall be known and we feel it a privilege to present this law as it is written in the Bible, knowing, as we do, that the time has now come, when the truth shall be known and will become a blessing to future generations.

The correct interpretation of the Bible as well as the Vedas and the Koran is very simple. Read it as it is written and forget the personal teachings of the Romans or any of the other churches and study it as any other book. The language and form used in the Bible is apparently put there for a purpose, for the writers of the Bible did know of the dark ages which the Bible had to survive and if it had been written differently, there might not have been a Bible in existence today.

The Talmud is the original manuscript upon which the Jewish and Christian religions are based. It is the root from which the Christian religion originated. The Hebrew religion, as a world's teaching, cannot be considered. It has passed its cycle of time in its present form and has now become the Christian religion.

The new age is scientifically called the age of the Universal Republic. It is the beginning of "God's Sunday," or "Seventh Day." The new age will be the beginning of a new dispensation for the Hebrew race, as well as for all others.

We aim to prove that the study of the Bible is a science and that the laws of the universe are the key which unlocks the door to this knowledge. We have explained part of the Bible and proved by actual figures and facts, that the mystery of the Bible is solved. The study of the heaven is as much of a lost science as the study of the Bible and as we intend only to give the key to the study and not go into detail of its operations, this short and conscise explanation is all that is necessary.

The Bible is an astronomical book. It contains the study of the heavens and the movements of the planets through the different houses. It teaches the science of the heavens, as it is studied today and gives full instruction how to set up a figure of the heaven and measure time, space and degrees. The Bible contains nothing but wisdom of the heavens and explains the philosophy of life to be God's laws. The God as spoken of is the Universal God, the law of creation. God is not individualized, but the son of God is an independent personality as illustrated by the story of Jesus. The writings about Jesus are facts; his life history as pictured in the Bible shows that Christ has lived in the flesh during the Christian age. Jesus the Christ, as an actual being is living with his father in heaven today. He rules and has great power, is merciful, loving and tolerant, illustrating a perfect character as a God-given principle.

We will accept and take for granted as facts the story about Jesus as written in the Bible, all the characteristics, the individuality, the beautiful history of the Savior, that he is the only begotten son of God, that he has lived as Christ and that he was crucified.

The illustrations, as pictured in the Bible as the Life of Christ is the Christian Age, which begins at the age or year 40 B. C. and ends in 1918. It is a misconception of truth to think that Christ was a man who lived thirty-two years. Christ has lived as a period of time and his life's history is not as a human being but it is the planet Uranus which the ancient Bible writers called the Son of God. He is the one who has the power in heaven and on earth.

The cycle or period of time known as the Christian age, is the time when our solar system has passed through the house of Pisces, and as the life of the Christians or Christ was thirty-two years, (thirty-two degrees). The ending of the Christian Age took place October, 1918, when Christianity gave up its spirit and was crucified. From this it will be seen that Jesus and Christianity are two different topics. Jesus, the Christ is the planet Uranus; but Christianity is the life of Christ or age. The Holy Ghost is the spirit or influence which the planet Neptune produces, as represented by the Church. Satan, the devil, is the planet Saturn. From this brief statement will be seen what the study of the Bible is.

The Catholic Church has promulgated the theory of a place in the universe called purgatory, but there is nothing written in the Bible describing this place. It is supposed to be a place where the human race, as spiritual entities are tortured for not taking an active part in church organizations. The doctrines of the Bible and also the writings of Emanuel Swedenborg describes, that the same conditions prevail in the spiritual world as here in the flesh, it is however a condition and not a place. The life as spiritual beings is the continuation of the life which inhabited the flesh and as the laws of the universe also govern the life of spirits, we will find that conditions must arise to cause a difference of opinions there as well as here. The elements of nature and disposition of man produces a condition which would be a hell to one and a heaven to another. To live in environments and places contrary to one's nature is to be in hell and with congenial company and climatic conditions is heaven both now and hereafter.

When the ego or spirit of man separates from the body of flesh, he lives in the realms of spirits. The place and conditions wherein man exists as spirits is called by different names. The Catholics call it Purgatory; the theosophists, the astral plain; the spiritualists, a spiritual life; the Indians call it the happy hunting grounds, but most of the churches call it heaven and hell.

These different churches or doctrines teach only of one life where the spirit of man lives, and forget that the spirit or soul of man continues to die and live. The spirit dies on the plains of spirits and the soul or ego goes into a higher life in a higher etherial atmospheric condition and continues to do so throughout eternity.

The question of the Sabbath or Sunday and the first day of the week has been made an important issue in church organizations and worthy of consideration. In the old testament the "Sabbath" means "the passover;" that is, the solar system passing from one cycle into another. At the time of this passover as described, the children of Israel were numbered. In the new testament this passover is called the Sabbath or Lord's day and illustrated as the first day of the week. This Sabbath is the first day of the new dispensation and is figured from the day that Jesus rose from the grave; which is the third day after he was crucified. Jesus died in the fall of 1918 and he will rise again in the third year or in the fall of 1920, as the evening before the morning of the first day or Sabbath. The passover or Sabbath for the present cycle begins in September, 1920, as the evening before 1921.

"And the evening and the morning were the first day." Gen. 1:5. "From even unto even, shall ye celebrate your Sabbath." Lev. 23:32.

The real Sabbath or passover is the seventh day whether it is figured for a week, year or a thousand years. From this can be seen that the Sabbath and the first day of the week are two different topics.

The reformed Christian churches have disclaimed any and all connections with the Catholic Church but continue to teach the Christian doctrines of the Catholic Church. This includes the Mormans, Seventh Day Adventists, Christian Scientists, and all Bible societies formed from the outgrowth of the Roman Church. Church worship and Catholic holidays are part of their religion, inherited from the mother church but they dishonor the giver and worship the gift. From this can be seen that the Sunday worship of God, as now used, is a Catholic Church day and used for the promulgation of Church organizations.

CHAPTER 3.
THE END OF TIME.

In the Bible, the Books of Isaiah, Ezekiel and Revelations have been considered a mystery. They deal with a period of time in the future and the prophecies made there are for the end of time. Students of the Bible have figured out that the time to which the Bible refers is the present time. They calculate from certain given years, when a change of condition is due to take place. It is apparent that the Bible students have figured correctly, but they do not know the cause or reason for such changes or what the end of time means. They look at God as a personal God or individual being and as the Bible says that "A Savior will appear to make a new earth and a new heaven." So they look at this prophecy from a personal and material standpoint, instead of a change in the cycles of time, which is the actual meaning of the prophecy.

It is not the intention to argue with Bible students regarding a religious belief or teachings but to correct a wrong interpretation of the Bible as explained by Bible students. We aim to prove positively that the Savior as spoken of is not going to destroy this earth or make a new heaven, but we aim to show by facts and figures, from the Bible, what the correct interpretation is.

We have known for a number of years, that the Bible refers to the planets and the signs of the Zodiac, but it was not until we found a complete explanation of the Zodiacal signs in the "Book of the Dead," which is the writing found in the Pryamids, that we obtained the key to this study.

The "Book of the Dead" contains nothing, absolutely nothing, but the explanation of the Zodiacal signs and the planets. The teachings of Zoroaster, Buddha and all ancient religions, contain the study of the heavens. The Babylonian, Assyrian, Jewish, and Mohammedan teachings show that the Zodiac was the foundation for the study of God's laws.

It may be permissible to state that Zoroaster, Buddha, Adam and Eve, Abraham, Isaac and Jacob, and also Noah, Moses and Jesus, are characters used for the illustration of a condition or a period of time, as applied to this human race. This is a strong statement to make in face of the teachings of the different religions of today, but we are happy to say that we can prove it and aim to illustrate it, so that others can read the different Bibles and understand what they are reading. We also say that from the first chapter of Genesis to the last chapter of Revelations, the Bible contains the study of the planets in the heavens. We do not say that it contains nothing else, as in the case of the "Book of the Dead," but it is a fact that the Zodiac is referred to in the Bible from cover to cover. We can honestly state that every book and chapter in the Bible contains teachings of the Zodiac and the planets. The philosophy of the Bible is to illustrate the condition in the heavens as manifested by the planets, and that this philosophy of the heavens is to be applied to the conditions of our earth life. The Bible informs us that "as it is in heaven, so is it on earth." From this alone is shown that the philosophy of the Bible is to teach us of a heavenly or future life. In no place in the Bible does it say that the human race lives after the so-called death. It does, however, illustrate that the spirit and body separate at death, and that the spirit continues to live in a new form of existence. This is an indisputable evidence of the philosophy of life as illustrated by the planets.

CHAPTER 4.

THE GREAT TRINITY.

The study of the Bible is the study of our solar system and its movement around another central sun, suns or center. It has been proved that during the periods of 25,920 years which it takes for our earth to make a revolution, that the conditions of education, living, health, religion, and forms of government of this earth are effected. The earth has passed through dark periods or ages and also ages of progress. It has been found that the Bible has stated in a mysterious way that this was to be so, and it states also that in the future certain conditions would take place at given periods of time, some prophecies dating as far ahead as 2000 years or more. It has now been proven by Bible students that these prophecies or predictions which have taken place in the last 2000 years are correct, to the very year. These Bible students differ in opinion as to what was the original cause and what the result of these prophecies would be.

According to the Bible we are now living in an age, (1918), when a change of condition is to take place. War, pestilence, revolutions, changes in form of government and religion, in fact a new age or a new cycle of time is to begin. The Bible has prophesied the place and condition of the present war and the result. This has proven to the Bible students that the predictions for the present time are also correct.

Now the question is, have the Bible students throughout

Part I—Chapter 4.

the world found the right system which explains these prophecies, or are they guessing or arguing among themselves as to the cause and effects of the prophecies? The class of students who have made a business of studying these prophecies in the Bible are not in the true sense of the word students. They are a class of religious worshipers, blinded by the teachings from the dark centuries, worshiping an individualized God made in Rome.

The writers of the Bible were students of the laws of the universe and were advanced in learning and enlightened similar to the present generation. The study as spoken of in the Bible is the study of the Zodiac and the planets. It explains how to calculate time, measure space and distance, calculate angles, squares and circles. It instructs how to locate the equator and figure longitudes and latitudes, and it explains how to estimate degrees, days, hours, minutes and seconds.

The Bible also shows the location of the planets in special houses at the present time. It gives the location of the larger planets such as Neptune, Uranus and Saturn, and how long they are to stay in each house. The Bible teaches that these planets, when in a certain location at a given time will produce an effect on this earth peculiar to its own nature, that is: Neptune, Uranus and Saturn produce a condition or influence which effects the life and governing powers on this earth.

We will prove that the study of Bible prophecies are not a study of a personal God, who lived as a man and returned as a God; one who will utterly destroy this earth and most of the human race and save a few belonging to a sectarian organization. The Bible says that this "Son of God," "Savior" or "Lord of the heaven" will return in all his glory and power to establish a new cycle of time, a new kingdom, yes, everything the Bible students say, he will do. Now, let it be clear in everyone's mind that this "Savior" is the planet Uranus. That he has come back the same way as they saw him depart years ago in the clouds. Uranus will tear down and destroy before building better, and is in fact a Savior and reformer. We should look to him as a friend, even if he is a planet, as he is the beloved "Son of God" and has eternal power.

The Bible says that Saturn or the devil has great power over the earth at the time of the end of this age. He is to fight with the Lord but he is to be put into a burning furnace of fire to be tortured and destroyed. Saturn is to be assisted and have the help of a feminine element in torturing the people of the earth at the time of the end of the world.

We take it for granted that everyone knows the name and works of the devil and those who help him suffice it to say that the Devil or Satan is the planet "Saturn," with all his evil qualities. The one spoken of in the Bible who is to help Satan, is the planet Neptune. She is helping Saturn at the present time. From this can be seen what the entire mystery is about.

The trinity of the Father, Son and Holy Ghost with Satan, are the fundamental characters of Bible study. The father is the God power which rules the universe. The Son of God is the planet Uranus. The Holy Ghost is the planet Neptune. Satan is the planet Saturn. There are no other characters described in the Bible having individual power other than these planets who can influence the human race. The great trinity of Father, Son and Holy Spirit is clearly shown to influence the human race for good, acting in harmony to produce heavenly conditions on this earth. We find that Satan is spoken of in the Bible from Genesis to Revelations. His home is in Gehennah, which means "on the north." Satan's influence is for evil and produces evil for those with whom he comes in contact. Satan is also spoken of as a snake and the home of the snake is in the north. We find the constellations "Draco" and "Hydra" illustrated as snakes in the north in the ancients' pictures of the heavens. From this it will be seen that Satan and the snake give the same influence.

In the middle of the constellation Hydra is a picture of a crater. This is the center of all evil. From this crater a hell condition is produced. When a planet is passing this place in the heavens he is in darkness and produces darkness. This crater is represented as a place to destroy or cremate. The term "fiery furnace" has been applied to it. The house of the lion is in this part of the heavens and this house is a barren, fiery place. At the end of all cycles of time Satan and the Holy Ghost are in this place in the heavens. At the same time Jesus, as Uranus, the Son of God, is directly in the opposite side of the heaven, in the house of Aquarius. In this house is the picture of a man with an urn pouring out water. From this it will be seen that Jesus is pouring out the water of life from his urn and Satan is destroying them from his position in the heavens.

If a hell should be pictured or a statement made that such

a place existed in the universe, it would be from 10° of Cancer to 12° of Libra with the 25th degree of Leo as a center and this would be the Hell spoken of in the Bible.

If we should look for the home of the Lord of Heaven, we would find it in 25 degrees of the house of Aquarius, for here is the place where the Son of God is crucified and where he takes possession of the heavenly kingdom.

When we can realize what the Trinity of God is, and what the influence of Satan means, we will have learned the first lesson of the laws of the universe. If we do not understand who God is, we cannot know his laws and if we do not know his laws, we cannot follow the law and teach others what the word of God is. The Bible says that the "Word was God," and as the word of God is in the heavens we will have to look in the heavens to find the word of God. As God is in the heavens, we look to the trinity of God in heaven for the power which rules the world.

CHAPTER 5.

THE PATRIARCHS.

The Bible says that the Christ has lived in the flesh and those who say he did not are speaking falsely. In the first place there is a distinction between Jesus and Christ as explained in the Bible. "Jesus is the Savior," He is the Lord of Heaven," "God's Son." In other words Jesus is the planet Uranus. The Christ is the Christian Age. It is Christianity which was established when Uranus was in the same heavenly place years ago, that he is now.

The Christ, or Christianity as an age, has lived in the flesh, which means that Christ has actually lived in the flesh for the last two thousand years. This goes to show that the statement in the Bible is correct.

Jesus was not an individual man who was crucified, for he represents an age. It is the same illustration as used about Buddha as being born of a virgin and sacrificed. The fact is, these stories are an explanation of the Zodiacal houses. It will be seen from illustration that the watery house of Pisces is the water that the Savior had to be born from, in order to be born again when he enters the new kingdom.

The Virgin who was the Saviors mother is Neptune in the house opposite to Pisces, which is Virgo. This is just another illustration of the same story. It is the same principle which is represented as the mother of Buddha, in fact the same principle is represented in the maiden who met the lovers at the well and watered the sheep and the camels in olden times.

This virgin is the mother of all the generations of the past ages. This same virgin is now watching her Christian children being crucified in Europe; that is, she is now in pain and agony to see her child die, but it must be done; the killing has to take place as it is God's will. The Savior knew beforehand that this horrible agony would come and he has told his disciples so long ago.

We hope that every student of the Bible realizes what this means, for it is the Key Stone and also the foundation of everything that the Christian religion is based on. We will, however, say that before a natural death comes, suffering must take place. The reason why the Lord had to suffer death was that the human race should live and live eternally.

The Savior is now in his last dying struggle (in the year 1918). He will remain dead, or in the tomb, for nearly three days (years), when he will raise from the dead and speak and prove to his disciples that he is not dead.

Uranus who is the Lord and Savior, entered into his own house, Aquarius in 1912. He will stay in this house for seven years or during the period that the nations of Europe are unsettled. The actual dying of the Christian age will last for seven years. Read in Revelations, where every day or year is shown, even that Europe had to be ruined and that revolutions will take place.

As Uranus is in Aquarius so is Saturn or Satan directly opposite in the house of Leo, representing the heart of things, and is a house of fire, or fiery furnace.

This means that the Lord and Satan are now fighting a life and death struggle, and it shows clearly when the end will come. Uranus is in direct opposition to Saturn on October 1st, 1918, being also in parallel position, so this is the end of the life of Christianity. Bible students should now read the life of Christ from beginning to end; they will realize that the life of Christ is the actual life of the Roman Age. The last few years show the trial of Christ before Pilate and all the excuses he made that he was not guilty of taking the life of Christ. From this illustration we see who started the war. The people said crucify, and he is crucified. The Bible says that the Lord will overcome Satan and that Satan shall be burned to death in the most fearful manner.

The place of the present struggle is shown to be where it is actually taking place and Italy is especially mentioned as the home of the woman of the "seven mountains." The Catholic Church with all her daughters, that is all the Christian Churches of all denominations, are shown to be illustrated as the planet Neptune. Now Neptune is in the house of Leo or the Lion with Saturn, and the Bible says, that they are both going to their doom and destruction. They are to be killed by the Lord when he enters the new heaven or age. It has not been generally known what the planet Neptune represents but read Revelations 19, and it is all there. Neptune illustrates the principle of church religion and morals. She is the Holy Ghost. In other words in order to know what the elements of Neptune are, compare her with the church. She is called the mother of harlots. From this it will be seen that the churches at the present time are not teaching the words of the Lord. The fact is that Neptune, or the church, is now in company with Saturn or Satan in the burning fiery house of the Lion. She is in company with Satan and dying. Satan and the Holy Ghost will be burned to death before September, 1920, in the great furnace of the lions.

The war today is in the Christian countries and the Catholic Church is in the midst of the fire, in every sense of the word. Neptune represents the Church and her children, and when it says in the Bible they will be destroyed and killed, we take it for granted that the Bible means the same as when reference is made to the destruction of the earth and heavens, which means that the old methods and conditions will be killed. The Christian Church, as well as all other churches of the entire world, will undergo a change. They will all be born again into the new age, with new life and new principles and a great reform movement will take place.

Saturn, or Satan, and Neptune or the Church, as they now are, will be killed, when the Savior or Uranus rules in the new heaven. He is giving his life that the new generation may live with him in the Kingdom of Heaven which is the coming age.

We should adopt the explanation of the planet Uranus as used in the Bible and not use the terms as used in astrological books. Everyone knows the terms as applied to the character of Jesus, which is the character of Uranus, a Lord and Savior, great, good, loving, and willing to die for a principle. Take the life of Jesus and the teachings of the Christian Churches as a whole, which is the character and life work of Uranus. Let it be understood that he kills in order to build up anew, and that he destroys for the sake of doing good.

Saturn is what the astrological books say he is, Saturn is Satan and we find in the Bible that Satan is not always bad but he can adapt himself to the place he is in. If he is in a good place he is good and beneficent. But in a dark place or with bad elements he is bad. Saturn's worst place is in the house of Leo, in the north, which is his home, but he does not have to act bad even at home in hell. Always remember that Saturn is Satan wherever he is. Satan is now with the Holy Ghost, Neptune, in Leo, killing nations, churches and religion.

The planet Neptune is not explained in astrological books and for good reasons. She has not been known as a planet of our solar system very long and there are no books published which tell of her nature. Neptune is the "Holy Ghost" of old. She works on theories and arguments. She is the spirit of principle, which is being promulgated. If her teachings are good she must get it from the Lord, Uranus, otherwise from Saturn. She is killed with Saturn every one thousand years.

Neptune becomes a prophet after leaving the company of Saturn. She was the many prophets of old. The spirit of Neptune will be good in the New Age. The Holy Spirit will manifest that Jesus is not dead but that the Lord now rules in heaven. After 1921, when the Lord or Uranus enters the new kingdom all of the people (or degrees) of the old generation will have passed away. The Lord of Heaven will manifest through the Holy Spirit that Christ lives, that he is risen from the dead and that his kingdom is of the new heaven and the new earth. This is the dispensation spoken of by later day churches. It is the glorious age which begins in 1921.

Before going further we will find out "why." God's days or years are a thousand days or years with the Lord.

Uranus makes his circuit around the sun in nearly eighty-four years. He makes twelve revolutions in one thousand and eight years, which means Uranus is in the house of Aquarius every one thousand years. He is also in the same house every five hundred years, or six revolutions of eighty-four years each, which makes five hundred years.

It takes one hundred and sixty-four years for Neptune to

make a revolution around the sun. Neptune makes six revolutions in nine hundred and eighty-four years and three revolutions in four hundred and ninety-two years.

This shows that Neptune returns to the same place in the heavens every one thousand years. When Uranus is in Aquarius every one thousand years, is the time when Neptune is in Leo. This holds good also for every five hundred years, but at no other periods. That is, Uranus and Neptune are in opposition every five hundred years at the end of all cycles.

Saturn makes his revolution in nearly thirty years and thirty-three revolutions brings him in Leo, when he will be in conjunction with Neptune within thirty years, of the one thousand-year period. This means that Saturn and Neptune will be in the house of Leo every one thousand years when the Lord of Heaven is in Aquarius. This is the time spoken of in the Bible when Satan is to be let loose for a short time. It depends on the houses how much damage Satan can do. If he is in the middle of the house or cycle he does not destroy as much, but if it is when he changes from one house or cycle to another he will make war and destroy. We realize that God's days are as a year or a thousand years, half a day as five hundred years. We find that in the time as history has recorded events, a change takes place in religious organizations every five hundred years. This record compares favorably with the ages as given in Bible history. The cycle of Uranus is 1008 years and is as one day with the Lord.

CHAPTER 6.

THE LOST LAW.

The Bible contains a knowledge of the universe which is lost to the human race, and as we have obtained the key to this study we feel it is our duty to let others know of this law. The fact is that the Bible was written by astrologers and is a text book of heaven.

The Bible contains a description of the globular formation of the earth, and the dividing of the entire surface of the earth into degrees of longitude and latitude in the same manner as is used today. It describes the great solar system and the earth's relation to the three great planets Uranus, Neptune and Saturn; illustrating the principle of creation and the philosophy of life. The earth's circuit in its orbit around the sun demonstrates the principle that the universe is operated in cycles of time, having a beginning and an ending within a measured space. The revolution of the earth on its axis eastward produces a condition whereby all life moves westward around the earth in a given time and space.

The Bible demonstrates that the laws of the universe apply to the entire creation and the laws of the heavens are also the laws of the earth.

The Bible illustrates a philosophy of life in the operation of the solar system; for by the earth, and the three planets are pictured the operating principles of the universe. The Bible stories illustrating the patriarchs as human beings are really stories of the three great planets, Uranus, Neptune and Saturn. The names of these planets are changed with each cycle of time to correspond to the certain number of degrees of the earth of each location described.

The laws of Moses, as described in the Bible, are the universal laws which govern creation. The Jewish people had this law handed down to them and from them it has been passed to the Christian nations.

The laws of Moses are the laws which govern the earth and the relation of the earth to the sun and the three planets in the heavens. These laws do not represent the history of one man's life, living in the flesh for a few years. The laws of Moses are the text book for the study of the sun and the three planets and describes how the planets will affect the earth. There is very little known at the present time about what these laws mean, even as seen from an astronomical point of view. Information of the Moon's time is about all that is left from the original laws of Moses, as a science The time of the earth has been changed from 360 to 365 days for a year, and the rest of the law has been discovered by astronomers at great effort. The law as laid down by Moses represented by the planet Uranus is not a Jewish religion but a law of God for the people to follow and live by. From this it will be seen that the Laws of Moses are the laws of heaven and earth. The law spoken of in the Bible is the law of the heavens. It is the operation of our sun, moon and stars, in their respective orbits, and our solar system's operation in relation to other solar systems, constellations or centers.

The fundamental principle of this law is applied to the entire creation. The system and measurement as applied to our earth in its relation to other planets are the Laws of Moses. The heavens, with all their myriads of constellations and solar systems are measured to the second, minute and degree. The space in the heaven is as eternity, as there is no limit to space. The heavens represent eternal life and God is the power of the entire creation and is the universe. The law of the universe is the operation of all elements in cycles or circles of time and space. Each cycle of time or space has a beginning and an ending.

The first principle of this material universe is that all elements are formed globular. The second principle is that all elements are formed dual or opposite to each other, as light and darkness; good and evil; male and female; spiritual and material. The third principle is the dividing of the operating force of nature into four elements; fire, earth, air and water; and north, east, south and west. The fourth principle is the dividing of each of the main elements, force or power into twelve detailed characters, showing their nature and relation to the universe as a life-giving principle.

The entire universe is made globular and operated in cycles. So is our earth made and operated on the same principle. The earth is divided and measured from north to south by degrees of latitude with the equator as the dividing line; west and east are measured by degrees of longitude with the dividing line known as Greenwich time.

The earth moves in its orbit around the sun in a cycle of 360 degrees (or days). The beginning and the ending of this 360-degree cycle is measured from the time our earth enters the house of Aries on March 21st every year, the measurement being taken at Greenwich longitude. This is what the old Bible writers called the passover, and is in the precession of the equinoxes.

The cycles begin and end at the first degree of Aries, but the great solar cycle begins and ends at the sixth degree of Pisces.

It takes the earth one year of twelve months to pass through the twelve houses of the heavens.

It takes our solar system, which consists of the sun and eight planets, 2160 years (or degrees) to pass through one house, and 25,920 years to make a complete cycle or circuit of the twelve houses in the great cycle.

The beginning and ending of the cycle for the earth is at

the beginning and ending of the first degrees of longitude west and east, known as Greenwich time. The moon's cycle corresponds to the solar cycle, and begins and ends at the same time and place.

The earth's cycle beginning March 21st is divided into two periods of six months each, from March 21st to September 23rd and from September 23rd to March 21st. The first period is from Aries to Libra, which is the north cycle when the earth's position to the sun is north of the equator and is the positive division of the earth. The second period of six months is the division from Libra to Aries, the southern or negative division.

The dividing of the earth into time and space and into west and east is also figured from longitude Greenwich time. The degrees west of Greenwich to 180 degrees are one division and the other division is east from Greenwich to 180 degrees longitude completing the cycle. As the earth is divided north and south by the equator, so is it divided west and east into four quarters by the degrees of longitude from 1 to 180 degrees east and west. The west degrees of longitude from Greenwich represents the male principle called the Occident, and the east degrees, the female principle, which is termed the Orient. It takes the earth twelve months to travel in its orbit around the sun. Each month has 30 days (or degrees). The first month begins at the first degree of Aries on March 21st every year and the sixth month ends at 30 degrees Virgo. The second, or female division begins on September 23rd at the first degree of Libra, 180 degrees east of Greenwich and ends at Aries, March 21st, Greenwich time.

The fundamental law of the universe is first the globular or rounded form of expression; second the male and female principle; the third the elements of nature, fire, earth, air and water; and fourth the dividing of space and time.

The law or principle as here described and applied to the earth, is the law of the entire creation. It is the law upon which the sun, stars, planets and also the earth operate.

It is also applied to countries, nations, forms of government and religion, as well as to man. When applied to man the head is the beginning and the feet the ending, with 180 degrees in the solar plexus. Man is divided into upper and lower portions; right and left; corresponding to north and south, east and west.

This principle is also expressed by the movements of the

Part I—Chapter 6.

moon, as a complete cycle or age. The moon's phases are full moon, half moon, and first and last quarters; the moon making twelve revolutions of 30 degrees each, in a cycle.

The beginning of a 120-degree cycle or age, is the beginning of the measurement of time and space, in longitude Greenwich time. The earth is now, in the year 1918, within three degrees of the end of the cycle and as we count one degree for each year, the new cycle will begin 1920-1921. The old Bible and ancient writers called this the passover and it was considered very important. The Bible contains, as we know, a full description of what would take place at the time of this event. This is dealt with fully elsewhere.

We have explained that the world is operated on a scientific principle and that the same law which governs this earth is the law of heaven.

The movement of the heavenly bodies in space is in cycles of time, through a measured area and in a given locality. Each planet or star has a period or cycle of its own, governing the distance and location of its circuit. The sun and each planet represents a creative principle and demonstrates the operation of God's laws. As each star in the heavens represents a living principle or character of its own nature, so do the planets of our solar system represent a complete unit of a whole and part of God.

In the Bible we find certain characters spoken of as human beings, these characters represent a period of time. They are spoken of as men who talk with God giving orders and advice. Their personality represents the houses of heaven.

There is also another type of characters who represent or show the nature of the planets in relation to our earth, and are spoken of in such terms as, "The servants of God," "Prophets," "Son of God," and "The leaders of Israel," etc. Each of these characters are represented as an individual and correspond to the nature of the planet they represent.

Part 2.

THE AGES OF HEAVEN AND EARTH.

CHAPTER 7.

THE HEAVENS.

The ancients divided the heavens into sections of four divisions, corresponding to north, east, south and west. The different parts of the heavens were again divided into constellations, which are groups or clusters of stars, operating as solar systems. These groups are illustrated by animals such as a bear, bird, horse or snake, and by other symbols. The nature

THE HEAVENS.

of the groups of stars correspond to the nature of the animals in illustrations. It was as necessary to name the clusters of stars and illustrate them in olden times as it is today and astronomers use the same illustrations now as the ancients did. The illustrations were used for the convenience of memorizing these groups.

Regardless of the positions of the fixed stars or groups of stars in the heavens, the ancients divided heaven into twelve equal parts or spaces and called them houses or mansions. To each of these houses was attributed a peculiar characteristic of its own. Each house was named and illustrated by an animal or by some other symbol to correspond to the nature of the house. This division of the heavens is what we today call the twelve signs of the Zodiac.

The ancients also knew that our solar system consisted of the sun and the seven planets, besides our earth; and that our solar system travels through the space of the heavens in systematic and regular periods.

The Bible shows that the ancients knew how long it would take the earth, moon and each of the planets to make the circuit around the sun, and when the planets would be in certain parts of the heavens.

After having divided the heavens into twelve divisions, each division being named, our solar system was then observed when it passed through the twelve houses.

As the moon revolves around the earth, so do the seven planets and the earth revolve around the sun. The time required for each to make a circuit depends on the distance the planets are from the sun.

As the earth and the planets make their revolution around the sun, so does our solar system revolve around other centers or suns. It must be distinctly understood that the ancient writers knew that our sun was not considered to be a final center and that they did not worship the sun as a power or God, but that they knew of a higher power than our solar system which governs the suns and planets, which they called God.

The movements of our solar system in the heavens becomes a matter of calculation, that is, the figuring out of the length of time that it takes the sun and each planet to make its revolution. Thus there becomes a period of time, a cycle or circle, for each. The measurements of the heavens and the movements of our solar system through space in circuits have been demonstrated to be a scientific fact and the beginning and the ending of all cycles must be at a given place in space.

Part II—Chapter 7.

The following explanation will show how the ancients figured time and the periods of cycles, ages or generations:

The heavens were divided into twelve divisions called houses, and these twelve divisions were again divided into two groups of six divisions each, thus making six northern and six southern houses. The point in the heavens where the sun appears to be, when it crosses the equator on its journey northward in March, is taken as a fixed point from which to count for both space and time and is called Aries. This passover, the sun's entering Aries, takes place in March, when the sun goes north; and in September, when the sun goes south.

A further division of the heavens were made by dividing the heavens into two divisions from the center of the south division to the center of the north division, thus forming the east and west divisions. This gives the four cardinal points of the heavens calculated from the equator.

This may not seem to be important to the present day student, but it is of ancient origin and the foundation of all Bible study. It must be considered, for thereby is shown that north, east, south and west become established localities.

The space of the heaven which we call the twelve houses was calculated by the ancients to contain 360 degrees; each house, or one-twelfth division, containing 30 degrees, making 360 degrees in the twelve houses. This constitutes practically all of the fundamental principles of the study of astronomy.

We now come to the study of astrology and will show the method used by the ancient Bible writers and their system of applying this knowledge of the heavens to the earth, nations, and individuals.

The heavens, which consist of twelve divisions, the sun and planets, were considered as a complete miniature universe. The ancient Bible writers saw in it all the elements of nature in every conceivable form. The universal condition as they saw it in the heavens was applied to the earth and to their local conditions.

We are informed that the Arabians and the Egyptians were among the first to adopt this system, but unverified claims are made that India and China had this knowledge about the period of 3000 B. C. From calculations we are now able to make, this knowledge was known thousands of years ago, and every two thousand years it has been rediscovered, at the end of every 2000-year cycle.

The Babylonians applied the condition of the heaven to Babylon. The Egyptians applied it to Egypt and so on. They established the four cardinal points at four cities or places within their country, corresponding to north, east, south and west. They applied the names of the houses of the heaven to the different parts of the country; the nature and location of the houses corresponding to the nature of the land, whether it be desert or fruitful; applications were also made to water or to mountainous country. The special places of interest such as cities, cross-roads and shrines of lakes and rivers were used to illustrate the constellations or fixed stars of the heavens.

It will be observed that every tribe or nation, as then existing, consisted of twelve tribes. The country was also divided and named to correspond to the tribes. This principle of dividing the country and the naming of the people is best illustrated by the twelve tribes of Israel, so well known to all, which illustrate this idea completely.

The next point to consider will be the generations or ages; we may call them cycles, a lifetime or a term of years.

In the early Bible history period called the pre-historic time, the cycle of 360 degrees or years was used. It was divided into twelve months or houses of 30 degrees or days each. This was changed during the dark age of our present era to the globular method, when the earth was known to revolve around the sun in 365 days of our calendar time. It may be said here that this changing of time from 360 to 365 days has brought on a conflict among Bible students. They knew that 360 degrees means Zodiacal years, but they have tried to prove that the 365-day period as well as the moon's periods correspond to Bible years, and fit the events of the Bible but they have failed. They have neglected to reason that at no time in the Bible is the sun's or moon's time of 365 days used. The 365-day period was established after the Bible was written, in the Christian era, and of no use in Bible study.

The period of time spoken of in the Bible was calculated for 360 degrees or days, for this is for Zodiacal years and has reference to the houses or tribes.

When the Bible says that so and so remained so long in this or that country, or that this or that person lived a certain length of time, the only figures to use are the 30 degrees or the 360 degrees. This will positively give the time or age. For instance, a certain partiarch lived to be 960 years old; by dividing the 960 by 30 degrees gives 32 degrees or years; the time of this patriarch's age as a distance.

If the student finds examples in the Bible where all the years or degrees are added together, he should use the 30 degrees in figuring for the house and 360 degrees for a complete cycle. The rule will also apply where it is stated that a certain number of people were congregated at a given place. It means that they were so many degrees in that specified house in the heavens. The people represent the degrees.

In order to review our statements concerning the degrees, time and space, we shall briefly show what each one contains. 60 seconds to 1 prime minute; 60 prime minutes to 1 hour, or 1 degree; 30 degrees to a house; 12 houses to a cycle. This gives 360 degrees as a basic number for a complete cycle. 90 degrees is one-fourth of a cycle of 360 degrees; 120 degrees is one-third; 180 is one-half of 360 degrees. The circle of 360 degrees is a complete cycle which is used for our earth and the planets in their circuit around the sun.

CYCLES.

The study of our solar system's great cycle is the study of the measurement of the heavens, and the measurements for the constellations and fixed stars. The solar system travels in the heavens within a given space in cycles of time, beginning with the point called the vernal equinox, in Pisces, which is the Meridian of the heavens.

The great cycle is the measurement of space which our solar system passes through, consisting of 25,920°. This great period is divided into three cycles of 8,640° each, and this cycle is again subdivided into three lesser cycles or periods of time and corresponds to the degrees as measured around the earth. the great cycle of 8,640° corresponds to the earth's cycle of 120° and is the period of time as figured in the Bible, as 72 times 120 equals 8,640.

The cycle of 2,880° corresponds to an age of 120°, a third of the Zodiacal circle, which contains 40° of 72 years each.

The cycle of 2,160° is a twelfth part of a complete heavenly cycle and is also divided into an age of 30° of 72 years each, making 2,160°.

The solar system complete cycle consists of 72 times 360, which equals 25,920°.

The same rule applies to the measurement of time, space

and degrees; that is, degrees of space or distance around the earth in miles is measured by the same rule as the measurements for hours, days, months and years. The terms days, years, degrees, miles, etc., can be used interchangeably according to the requirements of any desired illustration.

The following table of measurements will be found helpful: There are 30 days (degrees, miles) to the month; 60 seconds to 1 minute; 60 minutes to 1 hour; 1 hour also contains 360°; one-half hour contains 180°; one-quarter hour 90°; 1 cycle of the earth contains 360°; and 12 houses of 30° each.

The sun's cycle corresponds to the distance around the earth, which is 25,920 degrees (miles). This space of 25,920 degrees is divided into 72 divisions of 360 degrees each, that is, the earth's cycle is contained in the sun's cycle 72 times.

Each of the 72-degree divisions is used as a unit, as 30 degrees are used as a unit in figuring the earth's cycle.

Thirty degrees are one-twelfth of the earth's cycle; 2,160 degrees are one-twelfth of the sun's cycle.

The 72 degrees are divided into units of time as follows: 72 degrees equals 24 hours; 36 degrees equals 12 hours; 18 degrees equals 6 hours; 9 degrees equals 3 hours; 4½ degrees equals 1½ hours; and 1½ degrees equals ½ hour.

Any student who is a little familiar with the study will readily see the method used in the calculation of time and space. It takes the solar system nearly 26,000 years to make a complete revolution through the twelve houses of the heavens; so the earth is subject to the condition of each of the twelve houses during this period of revolution. The period of time that our solar system and earth remain in each house is 2,160 years. This is an age or generation in itself. The solar system is at the present time passing out of the house of Pisces and entering the house of Aries (astrological terms). The birth of a nation would be considered the beginning of the cycle of time for any particular nation, and the death of the nation is at the end of the cycle of time for the age.

When the period of time is one solar cycle or one year of 360 degrees, the lesser cycle of 30 degrees is used in describing details; that is for describing individuals, families or cities. The same rule applies to the time of the moon's cycle. To obtain details of time, use the moon's period of time for one revolution, which will show the time of the months, weeks, and days.

It has been shown what the cycle of time is, and what it represents. We will now show how it affects each nation. This is best illustrated by the use of the watch or clock. The watch would represent the nation in question and the different periods of the time from one o'clock to twelve o'clock represent the different parts of the country. Hold the watch with the twelve o'clock figure to the south and you have a map of the nation with the twelve houses pictured before you at twelve o'clock that day. The movement of the hands of the watch is like the movement of the sun and moon in a complete circle. The movement of the sun is represented by each hour of 60 minutes to each of the twelve hours, making 720 minutes for a complete cycle or 1440 minutes in 24 hours. The moon's action is like the single hour hand of 60 seconds to each cycle of 60 minutes, making 3600 seconds. This shows that time was figured to the second by the ancient students before a watch or clock was thought of.

It will be observed that the Bible does not mention the sun and moon in connection with the planets, except for time and space. Time is also figured from the periods when the planet Uranus passes through the houses and is called the ages of the patriarchs. The twelve hours of the clock represent the same influence as the twelve houses of the heavens, that is, they represent the nation or country in question. It is the map of the heaven which has been applied to a certain part of the earth. This is exactly what the ancient writers used in Bible history time.

We now have explained a certain map or place from which to calculate time; the locations of north, east, south and west; the measuring of time, space and localities; and we see the nation or country as a picture in our mind. This gives only the location of the land and the people in question, and so far we have shown only the time and the place for consideration and not what is the cause for certain natural events which take place within this cycle or nation. We will show that the movements of the planets in the heaven affect the elements and produce the condition as described on the earth.

SIDERAL TIME.

The years, as calculated in the Bible, are not figured by the same system as we figure years in the present age. All years and dates, as given in the Bible, are figured in cycles of

360-degree ages, that is, the age is calculated in 360-degree cycles and called generations. The first great cycle is from Adam to the beginning of the Christian age. This is a period of time of 3960 years divided into cycles of 360-degree ages. The Christian age began at 40 B. C. and ends 2000 A. D. The method used is to divide the numbers of years as given by 360, and the figures left over are the number of degrees west from the dividing degree. We can illustrate this by taking 6000 years and divide them by 360 and the result is 16 generations and 240 left over. This leaves us at 240 degrees west or 120 degrees east at the end of Bible history time, which is at the end of the Apostle Paul's time. We next take 3960 years as the period for the old testament up to the beginning of the Roman age and divide it by 360, which leaves us at eleven generations to the very degree.

The cycle for the Christian age began at 40 B. C. and consists of 2040 years. We divide the 2040 by 360 and we get five generations with 240 degrees left over; which is 240 degrees west. The Christian age includes the first 40 years of the Roman age, which must be added to the Christian age, and this leaves us at 240 west or 120 degrees east at the end of Bible time calculated from 40 degrees east.

The life of the Christian age ends at Greenwich in 1920. The spiritual life of Christianity is illustrated in the Apostle Paul and is for the new age, beginning in 1921 as the American age. This age extends over into Japan at 200 degrees west and terminates at the year 2000 A. D. of the calendar years.

This is a very simple system and is the method used in all of the books of the Bible. The location of events, as described, can be calculated to the very degree of longitude within the area of 360 degrees around the earth.

The Jewish calendar-year for 1920 is 5680 and if we add 80 years we get 5760, which is the end of the cycle for the Jewish race. The Jewish year of 5760 corresponds to the year 2000 of the Julian calendar time and is the end of Bible history. If we divide the Jewish time of 5760 by the cycle of 360 degrees we get sixteen circuits around the earth, which is the time of the history of the Jews. The Jewish age records sixteen generations and corresponds to the Christian age of sixteen generations. From this can be seen that the Jewish and the Christian cycles of time originated from the same age and used the same method of calculating time.

CHAPTER 8.

THE HOUSES OF HEAVEN.

We will now explain what is meant by such Bible expressions as "She was barren," "Was a fruitful bow," "A pit of burning fire," 'In the lion's den," etc. These expressions show that the question or topic considered was of the nature of the house spoken of. The houses of the heavens have been divided and arranged so that every element and condition in heaven and on earth is expressed in a systematic and scientific manner. The names of the houses have been changed from one generation to another, as will be shown by the names of the children of Adam, which were the names of the houses of the heavens. The names of the children of Noah, Abraham; even to the disciples of Christ, were the names of the houses of the heavens. In other chapters will be found the names of some of the generations which are self explanatory. The last time the names were changed was at the beginning of the present cycle, known as the Christian generation or age, when the names of the disciples of Christ were used. We will now give the names of the houses of the heavens which are used at the present time by all nations. The names are used today in the same order as in the Bible. The names are: Aries, Taurus, Gemini, Cancer, Leo, Virgo, Libra, Scorpio, Sagitarius, Capricorn, Aquarius and Pisces. The first six houses are the northern houses the last six, from Libra to Pisces, are the southern houses.

The following houses are of a masculine nature: Aries, Gemini, Leo, Libra, Sagitarius, and Aquarius. The feminine houses are: Taurus, Cancer, Virgo, Scorpio, Capricorn and Pisces.

The houses of a fiery nature are: Aries, Leo, Sagitarius. The houses of earthy nature are: Taurus, Virgo, Capricorn. The houses of airy nature are: Gimini, Libra, Aquarius, The houses of watery nature are: Cancer, Scorpio, Pisces. The Cardinal houses are the movable places representing the north, east, south and west, and are named Aries, Cancer, Libra, Capricorn.

Because of the earths peculiar revolution on its axis, which causes the distance or period of time to be longer in one house than in another, there are houses of shorter and longer ascensions. In some of the Bible stories are illustrated the action of the houses and represented as human beings. Some of the people die earlier than others or in other instances some were killed before others. This early death is caused by the variation of longer or shorter ascension. The short ascension houses are: Capricorn, Aquarius, Pisces, Aries, Taurus and Gemini. The houses of the long ascension are: Cancer, Leo, Virgo, Libra, Scorpio and Sagitarius. The fruitful houses are: Cancer, Scorpio and Pisces. The barren houses are: Gemini, Leo and Virgo. The double-bodied houses are: Gemini, Cancer, Libra, Aquarius, Pisces and the first half of Sagitarius. The equinoctial houses are the houses on the equator: Cancer, and Capricorn. The tropical houses are the houses which strike the north and south cardinal points. They are Aries and Libra.

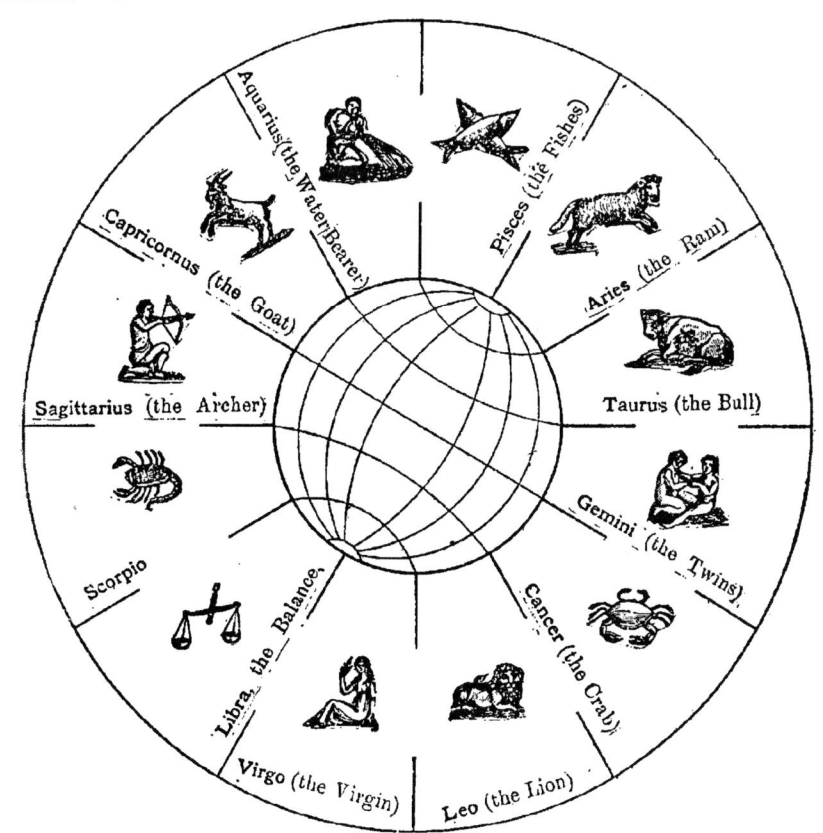

HOUSES IN THE HEAVENS.

We have spoken elsewhere of the different sections of the heaven being illustrated to show the four elements of nature.

There are four distinct elements spoken of and they consist of the basic principle for all material life. Through these four elements God maintains the universe. They are the tools God uses in expressing his will in heaven as well as on earth. The Bible says, "as it is in heaven so is it on earth." The four elements are fire, earth, air and water. The houses of heaven have been divided to represent the four elements which can readily be seen from illustration.

ANGELS AND ANGLES.

It is not generally understood what the angels of heaven are. They are supposed to be living beings, flying from one end of the universe to another, carrying messages. They are the servants of God, as his message bearers, always bringing the message given them. There are good angels and there are bad angels, depending upon those who send the message and where it is to be delivered. In order to be brief, we will say that the angels as spoken of in the Bible are really the different distances of the heavens measured in angles of degrees. Angel is the root word for angle. An angle may be a distance of 60 degrees (two houses) or it may be 90 degrees (three houses) or 120 degrees (four houses) or 180 degrees (six houses) apart.

We will now show the nature of the message which the angles or aspects of heaven carry. A good angel or angle is the one which is in a good location or aspect and this carries a good message, and the bad angels represent the bad angles. If a message is carried from the Savior or Lord of heaven, it is good, but if from Satan, a bad angle, it is an evil angel. A conjunction or association with the Savior is good, but a conjunction with Satan is bad.

A parallel aspect is an aspect in a line with either a good or a bad planet or place. The aspect called the triangle, or trine, has always been a powerful aspect. It occurs when the heavens are divided into three parts of 120 degrees each. The triangle represents the trinity of nature, which is completeness. It obtains power from three parts of the universe and is a good angle. Sextile (60-degree angle, half of a triangle) has power in the nature of the triangle but its importance is not so great. Opposition represents a contrary nature, as two or more planets placed opposite each other. If the Savior and Satan are opposed to each other, there will be conflict or war, which is detrimental to both. Square is 90 degrees or three houses apart, and is half the distance of the angle of opposition. It is a bad messenger. There are many other messengers, or angles to consider, but these are the principal ones.

There are houses of fire, earth, air and water, that is, the nature of the house represents the element spoken of. So when it is said that a certain party is in a hot place, or in a furnace of fire, he is in a fiery house. The same explanation is to be applied to the watery houses, as in the expressions of walking or traveling on the water, speaking of drinking feasts and floods. When reference is made to the airy houses, such expressions as the following are used: "they went up into the mountains," "a mountainous country," or a "high elevation." When earthy houses were considered the Bible speaks of peoples or nations having a material turn of mind, seeking earthly pleasures as opposed to spiritual desires. The same rule is used when the term barren or fruitful is spoken of. It means a barren place or person.

This method of expressing the nature of the house, and the time and location of the event, is best illustrated by the story in the Bible about Jesus, when he was in the wilderness for forty days and tempted by Satan. Jesus was Uranus; Satan was Saturn, and the forty days represent the forty degree cycle. These planets were in bad aspect at the time, as Jesus was fasting, showing that he was in a barren house. These planets finally separated in the mountains; the mountains represent an airy house. Saturn passed Uranus for Saturn is quicker in motion than Uranus.

The Bible mentions the grouping of the houses of the heavens into four groups of three houses to a group. These divisions are very interesting and are also important. First, Aries represents the head, and Pisces the feet of man, and the rest of the houses represent his body. This is shown in illustrations elsewhere.

Besides the grouping of the houses to represent the four principles of man, the houses also represent time, or an age. A complete generation or age is represented by man from his head to his feet; or by the twelve houses of the heavens from Aries to Pisces. The beginning of the age or generation is at the head and the ending of the cycle or generation is at Pisces, the feet.

The method of calculating time has been shown elsewhere and it should be remembered that time and space are measured by the same method. A good illustration of this system, as shown in the Bible, is the well-known story of Nebuchadnezar's dream. He had a dream of a great image of a man who had a head of gold, breasts and arms of silver, belly and thighs of brass, legs of iron, and feet of iron and clay. The Seventh Day Adventist Church has solved the problem of figuring time according to the Bible method of measuring an age. The Bible says that the image from head to feet represents a period of time of 2300 years; the beginning of the period being represented by the head of the image and the ending of the period being represented by the feet of the image. Each of the four parts of the man, as the dream illustrates, is a group of three houses, or 90 degrees. It says it is a period of 2300 years, which is more than a cycle of four groups. We find the fifth division included in the age of iron with the feet of iron and clay. The dream simply means this: that there are four full groups of

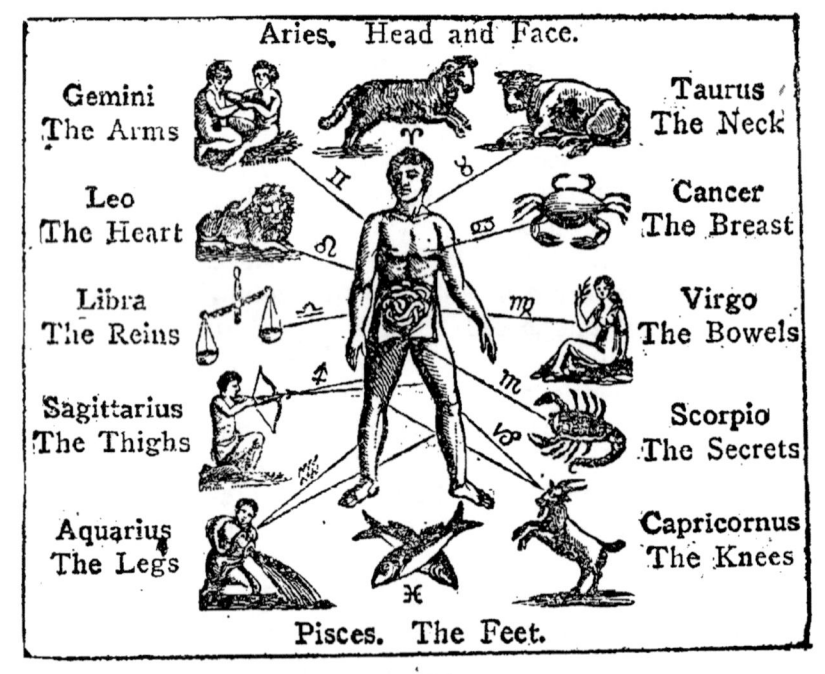

MAN AS A UNIVERSE.

years, each consisting of three houses of 180 years, making 540 years to each of the four groups; gold, silver, brass and iron. This gives 2160 years but as the feet and toes of clay were added to the age of iron, we will add two degrees of 144 years to the four main elements making it 2304 years in all to the end of this age.

The chapters of Daniel and Revelations have been explained correctly by the modern Bible students and the books published by them will be of great help in studying the period of time. The reason why their period of time is correct is that they believe in an individual Savior who is to come to this earth at the end of the present age. It has been proved that the Seventh Day Adventists were right when they figured that the "Lord of Heaven," or as is termed, a "Son of God," would "enter into," or be in "his home" at the end of this age.

February 1st, 1912, the "Lord of Heaven" and "Savior" entered his own house, which is the house of Aquarius. He remains in this house for seven years, which is from 1912 to 1920. If the Seventh Day Adventists would change their belief from an individual God and come to realize that the Son of God they have been looking for is the planet Uranus, they need not fear or worry about the earths being destroyed.

The end of time, or the age, or cycle, whether it be the end of a 30 degree, 360 degree or the end of the great cycle of 6000 years, is represented by the death of the inhabitants of a certain house, cycle or age. It is spoken of in many ways, such as being killed by fire or water, but it is always according to the house Saturn is in. The strong terms used to show the end of the age was: "The temple would be utterly destroyed and not one remain of the old generations." It is stated that at the end of the present age that heaven and earth would be destroyed and, "a new heaven and a new earth created." It is also written in the Bible how many people would enter the new kingdom, that 144,000 in all would be allowed to enter into the new dispensation and live with God. The 144,000 who enter the new age, are the population of the twelve houses. This 144,000 people represent the smaller and greater cycles in the cycles of heaven and earth. In the year 1921, the new heaven and earth begin as a new age or cycle, with two degrees of 72 years each making 144 years; representing the tribes as the population of the United States. This illustrates that the new generation will consist of 144,000.

As the cycle of time has to die before the new generation can begin, and as death causes pain and suffering, as does also the process of being born again or made new; so does the earth and its population suffer from the terrible condition produced at the end of the cycle.

The Bible writers knew of this law for they wrote that at the end of the present generation great tribulation and suffering would take place. It is written in several places in the Bible that extremely troublesome times would take place. The world's war is the expression of the suffering which was to take place. It is the manifestation of a dying generation. It is the crucifying of Christianity. It is the execution of Mohammedanism and Buddhism, including materialism, monarchism and inherited governmental power. Much could be said regarding the dying of the old age, and also the beginning of the new age, but as the Bible explains it in detail, it will not be necessary.

Christ said that he had to be crucified and die but that he would raise from the dead in three days, that is, Christ as an age is crucified in 1918 and on the third day (year) he will raise which represents the beginning of a new era of peace in 1921.

CHAPTER 9.

THE NATURE OF THE HOUSES.

When figuring space or time of the heavens, it should be remembered that an age, or cycle, is complete in itself, whether the period is 30 degrees or any division of the cycle of 360 degrees; or if it be part of the great heavenly cycle.

An age consists of a period of time from birth to death; whatever length of time the cycle may be. When an age, or house dies, it means that time has passed through the degrees of the house, when the house is killed, or dies, as the case may be.

The Bible divides the cycle in all instances into four main divisions, which correspond to the four cardinal points in the heavens as north, east, south and west. The houses that occupy these positions for that special age, now being considered, are the ruling houses, that is, they represent the government, people, or the man, who would rule that particular age.

The houses of the cardinal points east, and west, begin and end at the same time, and those north and south at the same time. These houses that occupy the east quarters rule first, the western last.

The southern house represents the man, who takes his orders from God and issues them to the rest of the children of the tribe and is the leader, called Tetrarchs.

The houses of the heaven have had their names changed with each generation. Each house has been illustrated as animals or other symbolic signs, corresponding to the nature of the houses. It is a very singular incident that some of these illustrations should have maintained the same form during all the ages of the past; as the Sheep, the Bull, the Goat, the Lion, the Scorpion, the Fishes and the Virgin. The Bible uses these names from beginning to end and it is one of the best systems to use, in order to know what house or people is referred to. A very important point to consider is that when the old house dies the next takes its place, as when the house of Pisces ends Aries begins, for it is said, "the first should be last and the last first."

It is written in very plain language in the Bible that at the time when the change takes place from one house or generation to another that it is time for great events. The old Bible writers figured out the time of the end and explained what would take place. They said that the date of the time of the end would not be known, but when the great destruction took place it would be a sign of the time of the end. A detailed description is given of what houses would occupy the four cardinal points, and where the planets would be at this time.

The four corners of the earth were represented as a Man, Eagle, Lion and Bull. It is easy to look up the old charts and see what these illustrations stand for. The "Man" is the house of "Aquirius," the water-carrier; the "Eagle" represented formerly by the Scorpion is the house of "Scorpio;" the "Lion" is the house of "Leo;" and the "Bull" is the house of "Taurus."

The new generation begins with the first degrees of these houses at the four corners. It is said that the Man shall occupy the position of the heavens in the south; the Eagle in the east; the Lion and the Bull in positions opposite to these, or, as it is said in his proper place.

Realizing the position of the houses of heaven and knowing the generations or houses which are dying, and seeing the new houses and being familiar with the nature of them, it becomes easy to explain what the new generation or age will be.

Animals of all descriptions have been used to illustrate certain ages or periods of time. The book of Daniel describes the different forms of government by four beasts each of a different nature according to the time they represent. Each animal represents the four quarters of 90 degrees each.

CUSPS.

When the writers of the Bible have used symbolic illustrations to show the houses at the four corners of the earth, at the same time they explained that the animal had either one or more wings, horns, claws, or had some marks beside the illustration in general. It is usually written that two angels, olive trees, or candlesticks stood on either side of the symbol, many times called a gate. These symbolic signs or marks are the two degrees of the house spoken of. When a lion is spoken of as having two wings on either side, the event spoken of would last for four degrees. In the "Book of the Dead," four lines are running parallel which means that there are two degrees in the old house and two degrees in the new house. These illustrations refer to only the period when time changed from one house to another in what is known as the cusps of the houses. It is to be understood that the marks or signs as placed beside the animals described, mean degrees; one, two, or more, for either side. There are seventy-two years to each degree in the great cycle; 36 years to half degree and 144 years for the two degrees. It is very important to know what the degrees and years indicate, as will be seen by the history of the United States. The two degrees, as illustrated as standing on either side of the cusps, have been figured in the Bible to consist of 72 years each.

It is a surprising fact that all cycles consist of the same explanation, and that Bible students have refused to recognize it. What is meant by all cycles is that each age or cycle repeats itself, in Adam's generation as well as Abraham's and David's. The same years are used, the same story, the same three characters, as the trinity of Uranus, Neptune and Saturn.

From Adam's birth to his death, 4004 to 3074, is 930 years. Jared was born 3544, and lived to 2582. Noah was born 2948 and lived to 1998. The ark was built in 2469. The flood took place 2348. Abraham was born 1996 and died 1846. Moses was born in 1571 and died in 1450. Solomon was born in 1033 and died 975. David was born in 1085 and died in 1014. Nebuchadnezzar was born in 607 and died in 562.

From this it will be found that all the leading events took place at every 500 years. At every 1000 years the greater ruler had control, that is Adam, Noah, Abraham, Solomon, and Jesus.

The above dates are taken from the Bible and this shows that the Bible is correct.

The Bible gives us a very clear idea of the movement of the earth eastward, in fact the history as pictured in the Bible is the movement with the degrees westward. The capturing, slaying and utterly destroying of the entire population, when the chosen people moved to the west represent the destroying and killing of the degrees. It is written in the Bible that God had ordered the population to be destroyed in a certain section of the earth and so when our earth revolves to the corresponding degrees the population as degrees is killed.

The tribes or classes of people spoken of in the Bible who lived on the earth, are degrees of the different divisions of the earth as illustrated in the twelve houses of the Zodiac.

The principal points to be considered are that the age of the cycle is degrees and years, and that the degrees are used to figure time.

CHAPTER 10.

HOUSES AND TRIBES.

The Bible describes the twelve houses as the twelve children of the patriarchs when a reference is made to earth conditions, but when the Bible refers to a condition in the heavens, the houses are called mansions or heavenly homes. These houses of the heavens and the tribes on earth illustrate the nature, character, disposition and temperament which these twelve divisions of heaven represent. Each tribe or house represents a given trait of character and from this character a certain influence or condition is produced. The ancients indicated the nature of the twelve divisions of the heavens by illustrating them as a lion, sheep, bull, or goat, etc. The principle or nature of the illustration represents the nature of that part of the heaven and also of earth. There are forty-eight constellations or solar systems in the heavens; the nature of the different constellations correspond to the nature of the houses in the heavens where the constellation is located. From this it will be seen that there is a creative principle involved extending throughout the entire universe. This creative principle or influence, described as the nature of the house, can be demonstrated by the house of the lion. This animal produces an environment of fear and anxiety, for the nature of the beast is wild, brutish, cruel and destructive toward others.

We have copied the illustration of the twelve houses as used by the ancients and given the nature of the houses according to the description of pre-historic time.

The dividing of the continents and nations marks the placing of God's children. A description is given of the surface of the earth and the condition the planets produce on that given locality for the time described. The earth is described as globular and divided into spaces by a cycle of 360 degrees; the different subdivisions of this cycle are divided into twelve parts and are called the twelve tribes of Israel and are the twelve houses of the Zodiac.

It should be remembered that the Christian Bible is copied from the Hebrew Talmud, and that the Jewish names as used in the Bible only prove that the Talmud was transcribed by and for the Jews. The Egyptians who built the Pyramids used the names and illustrations for the twelve houses and the three planets, which appealed to them. The book of Mormon describes the twelve houses and gives entirely different names than those given in the Bible. From this will be seen that the names as given and the illustrations as spoken of in the Bible represent the descriptive characters given of the twelve tribes of Israel.

The nature and character of the tribes as used in the Bible is shown when a certain person speaks to his own or to other tribes, expressing an opinion or describing others. The children of the patriarchs and the disciples of Jesus correspond to the twelve tribes of Israel and are usually given in the regular order, the same as today we place the twelve months of the year.

At the time of the end of the world the children of Israel are described as the European Nations; the twelve nations of Europe being described as the twelve tribes of Israel. These same nations, as tribes, are again described in other books of the Bible as the disciples of Jesus. From this comparative illustration can be seen, that the dividing of the cycle of 360 degrees into twelve parts is the describing of the country, nation, or people for that particular time and place. The description and calculation of time and space for this cycle of 360 degrees are termed the Laws of Moses and are the contents of the books of Moses.

The nature of the illustrations as given in the houses of heaven is applied literally to the earth, nations, races or sections of the country and also to man as an individual.

When we say that the character of the land or nation and the nature of the country is described as a tribe, nations and as man, it means that the formation of the country must correspond to the illustration as given in the Bible, and when the same illustration is applied to a human being his nature and traits of character must also correspond to the description as given of the tribe. In the first place all nations have a national trait of character which the individual represents. The formation of the land and the country can readily be illustrated by Scandinavia, which is described as the twins of the house of Gemini; an airy, double house. The country (Norway-Sweden) is dual in nature and divided by mountains which represent the air. Not only have the people a dual nature, but also their government and religion. Holland, Belgium, and Denmark are illustrated as a crab and are given the nature of the breast of woman, and is the house of Cancer, a watery, double house. The formation of these countries are low and swampy, drained by canals and irrigation ditches; the nature of the crab is double and his habitation is in a low country by the ocean. From this comparative illustration can be seen the method used by the Bible writers to describe a nation or a given location as well as the people.

The earth has been described in the same manner as the nations; for the distance around the earth has been calculated in cycles of time and called the life of the patriarchs. The beginning of the cycle of time of the earth is at Greenwich going westward, the first 120 degrees represents the house of Aries, the ram, and is illustrated as the head of man. The second cycle is from 120 degrees west to 120 degrees east and corresponds to Taurus the Bull. The third cycle ends at Greenwich and is represented by the Twins, Gemini, and is from 120 degrees east and includes Asia and Europe, as twins. The fourth cycle is from Greenwich to 120 degrees west and is represented by Cancer. A complete cycle is measured by the distance of the twelve houses around the earth four times, each revolution consisting of three divisions of 120 degrees.

Thus the earth is divided into houses beginning with Greenwich and ending with Pisces, illustrated as the feet of man and is the last house and cycle.

In the New World as described in Revelations 21: 18 to 20; the names of gems or precious stones are used instead of the names of the twelve tribes of Israel, and represent the United States.

The comparative descriptive chart called "God's Twelve" illustrates the nature and meaning of the twelve divisions as given in the Bible. It names the generations of Adam, the disciples of Christ, the tribes of Israel, the nations of Europe, the signs of the Zodiac, parts of man as a universe, the houses of heaven, the months of the year, and the gems or precious stones.

The Ecliptic circle of the sun is represented in the circuit of Uranus on earth and located at 36 degrees North latitude. The Bible described a given region or locality from which the north and south is divided and we find that the 36th degree north corresponds to the division as described. It is a peculiar fact, but nature has made this degree a feature of demarcation for Asia, Europe and the United States.

The first story of dividing north from south described in the Bible is that of Cain and Abel in the United States. The next age is the dividing of Asia and Europe between Jacob and Esau representing the twin brothers. The north is illustrated in Jacob and the south in Esau, who later were called Edom and Ishmael.

The 24 degrees from 30 degrees to 54 degrees latitude north are referred to in many places in the Bible as the twenty-four elders. In Revelations 4:4 "and round about the throne were four and twenty seats; and upon the seats I saw four and twenty elders sitting, clothed in white raiment; and they had on their heads crowns of gold.

CHAPTER 11.

THE FINISHED MYSTERY.

It is a fact that the Bible was written by astrologers and that the entire history as described there is the study of astrology. We will continue to prove by the Bible that the Laws of Moses are the laws of the universe, as applied in the study called astrology.

The new age which begins in 1921, is caused by the earth's passing out of the old cycle, the house of Pisces, into the house of Aries, thereby beginning a new cycle. The cycles of the planets and of the earth begin with Aries at Greenwich time going westward at the rate of 72 years to the degrees for the great cycle, and one year for each degree for the earth cycle.

The sun and moon cause an effect upon the earth which causes the seasons of the year. The constellations in their turn affect the earth to a greater extent and produce the conditions on the sun, which the sun and moon produce on the earth. The planets Uranus, Neptune and Saturn reflect this influence and affect our earth the most, in fact control the earth. The position these three planets hold to the sun and to the earth affect the physical condition of the earth itself.

The circuit of Uranus around the sun corresponds to the circuit of our earth around the sun. A belt of 24 degrees latitude around the earth corresponds to the circuit of Uranus. The movement of the planets in the heavens corresponds to this very narrow space on the earth. The location of the planets in the heavens at the present time is the best proof of what effect the planets have on the earth. Uranus was in opposition to Saturn in Aquarius, the house opposite Leo. Neptune is also in the house of Leo, and the location in the heavens corresponds to the location of the present war. As Uranus and Saturn reach the point of perfect opposition and parallel, October 1st, 1918, the war reaches its climax at that time.

The earth's position in 1918 is nearly 3 degrees east longitude. The earth's motion will cause it to progress one degree per year and reach the dividing line in 1921. This is the beginning of the new age at 121 degrees west.

The belt of 24 degrees width going around the earth is the zone of Uranus and is the center of the earth's population and civilization and is the temperate zone of the globe. As the earth revolves eastward and the degrees of longitude calculated westward, so also do both population and civilization go westward.

The cycle of Uranus consists of 1000 years in the great cycle and a space in heaven and on the earth is calculated for each 1000 years. Uranus makes twelve revolutions of 84 years in 1008 years. This is one of God's days.

The Uranian age of 84 years can easily be compared to Bible time, as figured for the time of Alexander the Great at 336 B. C. when he went out of Europe into Asia and began to lay waste the Persian Empire. Take 336 years and divide by 84, this gives four, which represents the four trips that Uranus makes in 336 years. This is one-third of the cycle of 1008 years.

Take the forty-year period. The first book of Maccabees counts forty years. From 176 B. C. when Antiochus Epiphanes ruled as king in Syria, to 136 B. C. when Ptolemeus murdered

Simeon, the high priest, is 40 years, or a cycle of the Persian Empire of 40 degrees.

The 70-year period can be found from 130 B. C. when John Hircanus took Shecham and demolished the temple, to 60 B. C. when Jerusalem was taken by Pompey and the Jews became subject to the Romans.

The last 40-year period as demonstrated in the B. C. time of the Bible is at 40 B. C. Here begins the Empire of the Romans when Julius Cæsar won over Pompey at the battle of Pharsalia and became dictator.

It will be found that the period which corresponds to Nebuchadnezzar's time also corresponds to Buddha's age. The history of the Asiatic races is the same as that of the European. We can go back 6000 years in their age and find a similar history. The beginning of the Mohammedan religion was in the sixth century and it will be found that the 84-year period will divide the reformation of Mohammedanism into the correct cycles.

The cycle of time for the Christian age and all others, is the 84-year cycle, for a reformation has taken place every 500 years. However, the life of Christ is so complete that a general outline is unnecessary. In figuring time for Bible ages use a day for a year and a year for a century.

The three divisions of the earth of 120 degrees each represent the three continents of Europe, Asia and America. A horoscope is set up for each division as a whole, and for each nation as a lesser cycle within the greater. This can be illustrated in the cycle as written for Asia-Europe of 120 degrees. First the country is illustrated as twin brothers, or double period, and divided at 60 degrees east. The children of the twin brothers are the nations of Asia and Europe. The length of life for the different ages depends on the size of the country as a nation.

The distance of Asia is from 120 degrees east to 60 degrees and 30 degrees east. This distance was divided into five ages and called the five races. The distance of Europe was calculated after the age of Asia and was divided into seven races. These two divisions of five and seven races later become the twelve nations of Europe and represent the twelve tribes of Israel.

Each age, or part of the earth, is calculated to rule a given length of time and has been termed a lifetime of a given man, or a period of years for an empire. The length of the age is 72 years for each degree as represented by the nation.

The time as an age for Europe has been divided into 30 and 40-degree ages; which also represents the 70 degrees across the Atlantic Ocean. Previous to the time for Europe the dividing degrees between 30 and 60 degrees east, ruled. This age was a dividing cycle of time between Asia and Europe and was last called the Pompey Age, at 63 B. C. This distance represents the house of Aquarius.

At the end of each cycle a final destruction of the nations and age takes place. The western and younger nations become the power of the age and rule according to the size of the country east and west. This can be illustrated from the Bible in the ages as given in the Romans, Maccabeans, Syrians, Egyptians and Macedonians to the Persians, in the time of Alexander the Great.

A given distance of the earth was illustrated as a horoscope, which means, that this part of the earth is named according to the houses in the heaven and calculated accordingly. The influence, as described, which the planets produce when passing in the twelve houses is applied to the nature of the country and nation. The law explaining this influence is called the "Laws of Moses."

We will describe the system used in giving the nature of the country as a house. This can best be illustrated by the house of Aquarius, as a water-carrier and as a man having a writer's ink-horn by his side. This house represents Switzerland, who carries water to the other nations in the rivers which run from the Alps. He is described as a man clothed in linen with a writer's ink-horn by his side, which is the snow on the mountains and the ink-horn is the water in the rivers.

The house of Aquarius is the home of the two planets Uranus and Neptune, and described in the Bible as a holy mountain or temple. The twelve houses are arranged for each age according to the nature of the country and is described as the nativity of the age. We will call attention to a peculiar fact in connection with the study of the house of Aquarus. This house is described as a double, in the sense of an upper and a lower region. It also represents a philosophy of life demonstrating a spiritual and material existence, illustraing a heavenly condition in the mountains and a hell or destructive condition in the lower plains.

Part II—Chapter 11.

There are three holy mountains, one for each of the three great cycles of 120 degrees. The formation of the country at the three mountains of the ages is by nature made to represent this upper and lower principle. In the United States Mt. Whitney is the holy mountain and Death Valley with the desert of Arizona, located within one-half degree of the mountain, represents the lower region or hell. In the cycle for Europe the Alps represent the holy mountain and Belgium and Alsace-Lorraine represent the lower or hell region, also called the burying ground of Golgatha. In Asia the Himalaya Mountains correspond to the holy mountain and the Plains of Thibet forming a pocket or hole in the mountains, represent the lower region. (The plains of Thibet were first described by Noah and called the plains of Shinar.) This principle of a heaven and hell condition on earth is described in all books of the Bible and given as the word of God, illustrating the philosophy of life.

Each of the twelve houses represents a universal principle and is demonstrated in the nature of the characters described in the Bible. The principle of creation is illustrated in the house of Virgo as a mother of nations and is Turkey. Germany is the heart of Europe and this nation represents the heart of man. Spain and Portugal are described as the thigh of man, and are of a double nature. It is written in Gen. 49:3 that Spain spoiled the map of Europe. Russia represents the knees and is illustrated as a goat in Capricorn. Greece is described as a good-looking woman, but barren. The reason for this is that there is no nation next to Greece west. Greece is Libra; a cardinal house. Austria-Hungary represents Scorpio, a double-sexed house of a destructive-creative nature. Belgium and Holland are described as a Crab with Denmark as the claw of the Crab. These nations are represented as a female principle and illustrated as the breasts of woman in the house of Cancer. Scandinavia is the house of Gemini and represents the arms of man. France and England represent the head and neck of man, as Aries and Taurus; illustrated as a sheep and a bull. As England and France are on the dividing line at Greenwich, so are these nations to be partly destroyed, as represented in the degrees east and west of Greenwich. Italy represents the feet of man and the end of the age, illustrated in the house of Pisces. As Italy represents the end of the age, so will this nation be the last of all the nations of Europe to be destroyed.

"GOD'S TWELVE"

Generations	Disciples	Tribes	Nations	Signs	Man	Houses	Months	Gems	Hours
Adam	Simon-Peter	Ephraim	France	Ram	Head	Aries	Mar. 21	Jasper	1
Eve	Andrew	Manasseh	England	Bull	Neck	Taurus	Apr. 20	Sapphire	2
Abel-Cain	James-Zebedee	Zebulun	Scandinavia	Twins	Arms	Gemini	May 20	Chalcedony	3
Seth	John	Issachar	Holland-Belgium	Crab	Breast	Cancer	June 21	Emerald	4
Enos	Philip	Judah	Germany	Lion	Heart	Leo	July 22	Sardonyx	5
Cainan	Bartholomew	Naphtali	Turkey	Virgin	Bowels	Virgo	Aug. 23	Sardius	6
Mahalaleel	Matthew	Asher	Greece	Scales	Reins	Libra	Sept. 23	Chrysolite	7
Jared	Thomas	Dan	Austria-Hungary	Scorpion Eagle	Secrets	Scorpio	Oct. 23	Beryl	8
Enoch	James-Alpheus	Reuben	Spain-Portugal	Bowman	Thighs	Sagitarius	Nov. 22	Topaz	9
Methusalah	Thaddeus-Judas	Gad	Russia	Goat	Knees	Capricorn	Dec. 21	Chrysophrase	10
Lamech	Simon-Zelotes	Simeon-Levi	Switzerland-A-L	Waterman	Legs	Aquarius	Jan. 20	Jacint	11
Noah	Judas-Iscariot	Benjamin	Italy	Fishes	Feet	Pisces	Feb. 19	Amethyst	12

Part III.

RECORDED HISTORY FOR 6000 YEARS.

Chapter 12.

BEGINNING OF HISTORY.

The Bible description of the creation of the earth is really the description of the erection of a horoscope. It says: "in the beginning God created the earth," and it describes the universe which was created. The description of creation as given in the Bible describes exactly the same process as used by astrologers, when setting up a horoscope to illustrate the principles of creation. The study of creation as illustrated in the Bible is applied to the earth as a whole; and the description of various parts of the earth forms the details of the study. The astrologers spoken of in the Bible were those who applied the same principles to the human race as they applied to the earth. From this it will be seen that the ancient Bible writers were astrologers and set up horoscopes for the different parts of the earth, according to the law which is described as the Laws of Moses.

The Bible demonstrates the fact that the system which is used today in dividing the earth's surface into degrees of longitude and latitude, with Greenwich and the equator as centers, was used in pre-historic time. We take it for granted that the science of calculating in degrees is of ancient origin, and that the present generation is copying the old methods. In other chapters are given a detailed explanation of what the study of the heaven is and what the meanings of the different locations of the degrees are.

The first three chapters of Genesis describe the creation of a universe in general; using the most common terms possible, so that anyone knowing how to set up a figure will know what is meant by the terms used. The principle as illustrated in Adam and Eve is the earth as a whole and is the male and female complete universe. Adam, is the first born and represents 180 degrees west of Greenwich, to the International Date Line. This includes the United States. Eve represents the other half of the earth, from Greenwich east, (Europe and

Asia). The next description given is of Noah as an age, showing the location of the Pacific Ocean. Noah crossed the Pacific Ocean in the ark, illustrating that there was an ocean there and that the ark was a horoscope. The horoscope contained a representation of everything on the earth. The water period was 150 days on the earth, which means that Noah's cycle of time was 150 degrees. Noah's time began on the Pacific Coast at 120 degrees, and adding 150 degrees gives 270 degrees, which brings us to 90 degrees east, and is in the Himalaya Mountains in Thibet.

Noah had three sons, Shem, Ham and Japheth. The description of these sons is the first that is described as a division after the description given of the Garden of Eden. We find that the three sons of Noah correspond to the three central continents of Asia, Europe and America. Ham corresponds to America; Japheth to Europe and Shem to Asia. From this it will be seen that the dividing of the earth into continents, nations and races represents the children of each part of the earth.

The period of Adam and Eve is in the beginning of time; from this we figure that Adam's age was from the beginning at Greenwich going west, including what is now the United States, and part of the "Garden of Eden," where the first description is given of the earth as inhabited at the time of the beginning of the Bible history.

The Bible does not describe the earth as a whole nor does it give a description of the population of the earth, but the description of the country is for a very small space in width in each cycle of time. Instead of describing the entire earth as a globe, a belt is described going around the earth from the 24th to the 54th degree latitude north. This very narrow belt is located in the center of the most populated area of the earth and is the Temperate zone of the life regions of the world. Instead of using the equator as a center the principle of the equator is applied to the ecliptic belt of 18 degrees in width. To the best of our judgment the center which was used to divide north from south was at the 36th degree north latitude. The "Mason and Dixon Line" in the United States is at 36 degrees and the Holy Mountains of California are in the same latitude, so we take it for granted that the 36th degree is the natural dividing line. The ancient Bible writers set up horoscopes for a given space within this belt for each cycle of time

Part III—Chapter 12. 63

for 6000 years. They began with Adam and figured from Greenwich time and space westward around the earth. The space around the earth was again divided into three divisions of 120 degrees each, making three ages of time for a complete cycle. The different cycles of time, as given in the Bible, represent the setting up of horoscopes in rotation going westward around the earth for the different locations within the belt of 24 degrees. From this it will be seen that the Bible writers illustrate a place on the earth to calculate distance in

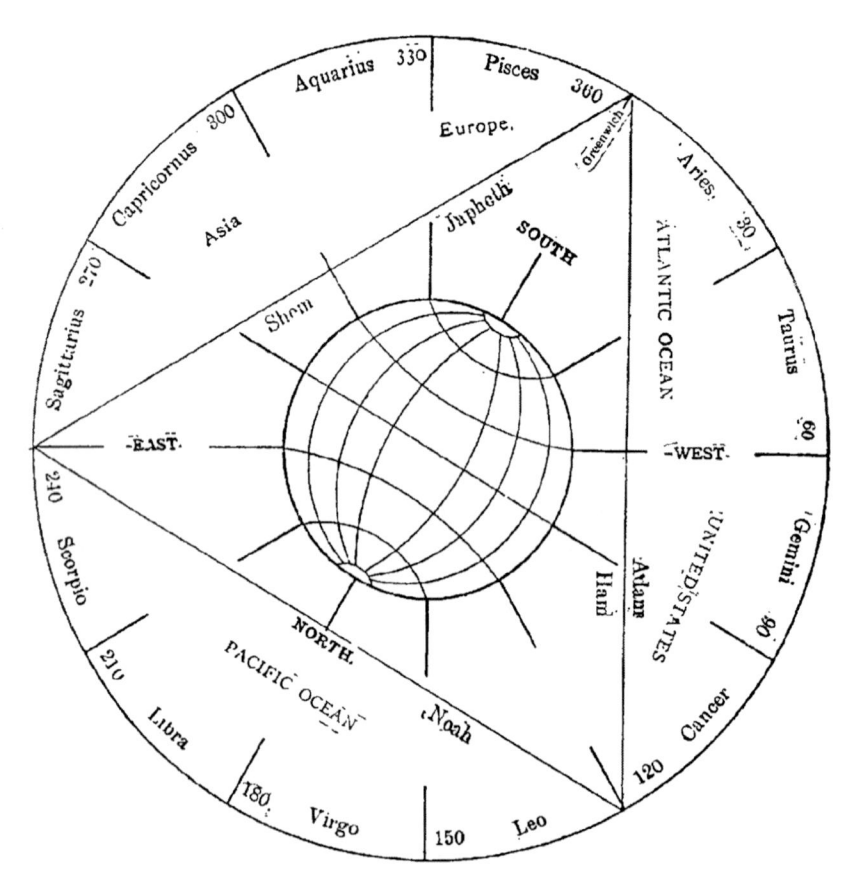

PLATE 5—THE THREE CYCLES.

degrees in cycles of time. We now know what is meant by time, space and the place on the earth and the Bible says that: "as it is in the heavens so is it on earth." From this we can reason that a similar belt is figured in the heavens, and we know that the ancients illustrated the heavens in charts and applied the identical method of figuring space in the heaven as was done on the earth.

The Bible describes the movements and influence of the three planets of Uranus, Neptune, and Saturn in their locality in the heavens and applies the conditions which existed in the heavens to the corresponding place on the earth.

The heavens can be illustrated as a big wheel; and that each solar system is a wheel within wheels; the planets and the earth are smaller wheels attached to the sun and each planet revolves on its axis in harmony with the larger wheels. When the big wheel is run in the heavens a condition is produced and this is reproduced on the smaller wheels, and is called the influence of the planets.

The suns and planetary systems revolve on fixed axis within a given space, so also with our earth. The revolution of the earth on its axis corresponds to a wheel running on cog-wheels and fits in the cogs of the larger wheels, and thereby is a part of a greater machine run from a given center. As there is no vacant space in the universe, each wheel is affected by the conditions of the other wheels, so is this influence reproduced to all parts of creation. From this it will be seen that the movements of the planets in the heaven can be calculated and the locations of the planets applied to the same location on the earth.

The Bible describes what the influence of the three planets is, but it does not say where this information is obtained, except from the influence of the heavens.

The fundamental principle as described in the Bible and illustrated in cycles of time, called the ages, is illustrated as follows: The first principle is the unit of one and is the earth; the second is Adam and Eve, as the male and female, illustrated as the two halves of the earth. The third is the trinity, illustrated by the three planets and the three divisions of the earth into 120 degrees each, making 360 degrees in all. The fourth principle is the dividing of the earth into four quarters, using Greenwich and the equator as centers and containing 90 degrees each. These are the leading divisions of the earth, but it is subdivided into several smaller cycles.

The different distances around the earth, as figured from Greenwich west, are calculated and called angles. It depends on the nature of the earth at the place calculated whether the angle is called good or bad, and we will describe the system as

Part III—Chapter 12.

used. We will take the greatest division first. It is an angle of 180 degrees, half of the earth from Greenwich. We find that 180 degrees strikes the center of the Pacific Ocean; as this is a bad place, it is called a very bad angle. We next take half of 180 degrees, which is 90 degrees; as 180 degrees is very bad, so are the smaller divisions of this angle bad. The 90th degree is at the Mississippi river points in the United States, and in China it is at Thibet. These places are called bad angles; strife, and disagreement, dividing of people and country takes place at these angles. The 90-degree angle also represents the north and south poles. The angle of 120 degrees will be found to be on the Pacific Coast in the United States and on the east coast of China. These are the best places on the face of the earth and are the good angles. The 60 degrees and 30 degrees, as smaller divisions of 120-degree angle, are also good angles and lend a good influence to the country. The 60th degree east divides Europe from Asia, and the 30th degree divides Turkey in Europe and Asia. The 45th degree divides Arabia, Persia and Turkey and is a bad place. From this illustration can be seen what is meant by good or bad angles of the heavens, as described in the Bible.

We have now given a general outline of what the study of the Bible is and we will now go into more details and describe the different places according to the system as used in the Bible. The Bible describes the first period or distance of space and called it the "Garden of Eden." It extends from the Atlantic Coast to the Cascade Mountains and the Sierra Nevada on the Pacific Coast, and from Mexico at 30 degrees to Canada at 54 degrees. This is the place as first described in the Bible. The Bible writers were human beings and described the country as it was and as it is today. It is apparent that the Bible writers lived on the Pacific Coast as this part of the earth is described in detail more than any other. In Europe each nation is described but in the Pacific Coast States, sections and county lines are followed.

It must be distinctly understood that the use of terms as the "Garden of Eden" "Jerusalem," "The Ark," "Solomon's Empire," or "The Roman Empire," all mean the same and represent an age or cycle of time. The space which these cycles represent was degrees longitude. The story as written in the Bible corresponds to the description of the earth and the people described represent the nature of the land and the number of people represent the number of degrees longitude and latitude.

The Bible illustrates a principle of individual characters in Adam and Eve, and the Snake. This principle represents the influence of the planets Uranus, Neptune and Saturn. Adam represents Uranus; Eve represents Neptune and the Snake represents Saturn. When one spoke to the other it is the influence as produced which is expressed in words at the location described.

The second chapter of Genesis begins with the description of the "Garden of Eden." The space of the garden was from 70 degrees to the 110 degrees west, making 40 degrees in all. The Tree of Life spoken of is the 90th degree in the center of the garden and the Tree of Knowledge was the 36th degree latitude. This garden was divided into four divisions or four quarters, that is, it was divided at the Mississippi River points at 90 degrees, and that the north and south was divided by the 36 degrees. This division is better illustrated by the Mason and Dixon Line, and east and west of the Mississippi.

God warned Adam not to eat of the forbidden fruits of the garden but as the tree of life is the 90th degree longitude, it came to pass that both Adam and Eve had to eat of the fruit of the 90th degree and they were put out of the garden and migrated west.

Eve was made of the rib or side of Adam; that is, the garden period is the Adam from Greenwich to 120 degrees west. So is the Eve period taken from the rib of Adam constituting the country west of the 120 degrees and is the Eve as illustrating an age. It is the beginning of another age, and is the mother of the Asiatic nations. From this can be seen that Eve represents the Pacific Coast States as a cycle or space.

After Adam and Eve left the garden of Eden on their journey west, they settled on the Pacific Coast and here is where the story of the Bible happenings takes place.

The Pacific Coast is the "Promised Land." Bible students should know where paradise was located and find out where, in California, Eve obtained her fig leaves. It has been assumed that the Holy Land was in Palestine, and that the Lord Jesus walked on the ground there, was born, lived and died there. It is also taken for granted that all the old patriarchs lived and died in the country from the Euphrates River to Rome. All

Part III—Chapter 12.

history and all hapenings, as recorded in the Bible have been applied to this very spot on the earth. This is the foundation for all error in the Christian age, for the location of the history of Bible events follows the degrees of longitude west around the earth. The United States has been populated and governed as a nation in the same way as it is now, and had the same boundary lines north and south, east and west. It had also the same number of states, namely 48. The people of the Pacific Coast at the time when the Bible was written, were the leaders of the world. In the Bible, the description of the Pacific Coast is perfect. Every section is described in detail. We will only mention here that Moses died and was buried on the Pacific Coast. Joshua captured the country at 120 degrees west longitude and led the children of Israel into the promised land. They traveled in a direct line and went to California, Oregon, and then to Washington. The city of Jericho corresponds to San Francisco of today and Jerusalem corresponds to Southern California. Portland, Oregon, is the second Antioch and Seattle answers to Ephesus. Victoria and Vancouver, British Columbia, were described as Phenecia. The River Jordan is the 120th degree west longitude and represents the mountain range from Washington to Mexico.. We will follow the Bible study and explain in due time in what part of the Bible this description is given. In the book of Joshua is given the description of the Pacific Coast, and anyone familiar with the Coast will recognize it.

In the beginning of Bible history, the country spoken of was the United States, and when reference is made to children being born, it is the dividing of the country. History repeats itself and we can see another "Garden of Eden," period in the history of the United States.

In Genesis 4; is described the dividing of the country north and south by the birth of Cain and Abel. Cain represents the north, and Abel the south. In due time Cain slew Abel when he passed over Abel's territory, or degrees. After Cain slew Abel he was cursed and he settled outside the garden and went into the land of Nod, in the east. This is on the Atlantic Coast, east of the 70th or 72nd degree (Massachusetts). Cain settled there and had a child by the name of Enoch, and he called the city Enoch. Here is where the generation of the United States began. Read Genesis 4:16; for information concerning the first children of the world, and follow as in the Bible time the same repetition or creation for the present age. It must not be forgotten that the world moves in cycles and that the same thing, or happening takes place over and over again in each age, and every age is 1000 years. Now as each 1000-year period extends around the earth there will be the change of the events as it affects each part of the world. The ages of the world proper are divided into three parts of 120 degrees each. The first division or age is from 40 degrees east to 80 degrees west, the second division begins at 80 degrees west and extends to 200 degrees west longitude, and the third division is from 200 degrees west to 320 degrees west or 40 degrees east.

The ages, however, were calculated from Greenwich degree in three cycles of 120 degrees each.

Genesis 5 describes the generation of Adam. It says that Seth was born when Adam was 130 years old. Seth was born at 130 degrees from Greenwich time, which is 130 degrees west longitude and is on the Pacific Coast. Therefore, Seth is the father of the children west of the United States; Cain is the father of the children from the Atlantic Coast west. Adam lived 800 years after Seth was born, and he had sons and daughters. Add 800 degrees west going around the earth twice, beginning with 130 degrees west longitude and we have 150 degrees east longitude, which is the beginning of the degrees for the children of Asia. Adam lived 930 years. Figure from Greenwich west 930 years (degrees), which is 150 degrees east longitude. This is east of Japan. Each child of Adam is to be figured on the same principle. Adam's children are the continents, but the children of Cain are the American continent proper and Seth's sons and daughters are Asia and Europe. Adam died in 3074 B. C.

CHAPTER 13.

ADAM AND EVE.

The first, second and third chapters of Genesis describe the creation and operation of the earth. It is unnecessary to repeat here the meaning of these chapters because it is the description of the law which operates the entire universe, and this has been previously described. It will, however, be found to consist of the four principles of creation, namely: first, the globular formation of the heavens and earth; second, the dividing of the earth by the equator, to form day and night;

Part III—Chapter 13.

third, the dividing of the earth by longitude into west and east; and fourth, the describing by the three principles mentioned above, of the four elements and the four cardinal points.

The Bible does not say that the earth was made at that particular time and at a stipulated spot in the heavens. It says in the beginning God created heavens and the earth. It was in the beginning of the age, and the description of heaven and earth was as God had made it in the previous cycles, or years. There is a distinction between created and made.

We are positive that this earth was not made as a globe in the age of Adam. We are also positive and know that this good country of the United States has existed and was a nation before the time of Adam, and the so-called personal creation of the earth is fiction. We state that we can prove this and more. It is said that anything outside of the Bible can be proved by the Bible, but it is for us to prove by the Bible that the writings in it are correct. We will also compare the Bible with the law of nature and give positive proof, by the scientific facts of astronomy.

The earth is divided by longitude into two halves from 1 degree to 180 degrees, and from 180 degrees to 360 degrees. That part of the earth west of Greenwich longitude is called male and includes the American continent, and the two oceans. The female division begins at 180 degrees going west and includes Asia and Europe. This is the division spoken of in the Bible as the tree of life. Let it be distinctly understood that the dividing degrees of longitude are the tree of life. The principle, as pictured in Adam and Eve, is the male and female part of the earth. Adam is the male principle, as represented by the western hemisphere of America, and Eve the eastern or negative side of earth. Adam represents the earth in character, distance, and an age; as it is said in the Bible, the generations of Adam which are Adam's children, or nations. Adam's age began at 70 degrees on the Atlantic Coast of the United States and if we add his age of 930 years to the 70 degrees, we obtain the 1000 years as his cycle.

The Bible states that the generations of heaven and earth are the dividing of space in heaven and on earth, and that it is not the generations of the human race as taught by the churches. It is described in Genesis 2:4 and 5, "These are the generations of the heavens and of the earth when they were created, in the day that the Lord God made the earth and the heavens, and every plant of the field before it was in the earth, and every herb of the field before it grew: for the Lord God had not caused it to rain upon the earth, and there was not a man to till the ground." It is the heavens and the earth which is spoken of and not man; as the earth is the mother of all generations.

CHAPTER 14.

THE FIRST BOOK OF MOSES.

The book of Genesis describes the meaning of a world similar to the system as used in astrology. The meaning of the different illustrations are described in detail. We will give an outline of the first chapters and show the system used.

The first chapter of Genesis says that "in the beginning God created the heavens and the earth. And the earth was without form, and void." This means that the earth is globular or, comparing it with a figure of the heaven, the representation would be that of a circle. "And God said, Let there be light; and there was light." This is illustrated by dividing the globe in halves, one side of the globe, or half of the circle, representing light, the other darkness. The line of demarcation between these two halves is called the equator. And God said, "Let there be a firmament in the midst of the waters; and let it divide the waters from the waters." This can be illustrated as the Greenwich degree of longitude. The two divisions spoken of are the tree of knowledge and the tree of life. "Let the waters under the heaven be gathered together unto one place, and let the dry land appear." This is the distinction between earth and water. So far there is light, darkness, water and earth; the sun and moon is represented as light and fire. Next is illustrated the air, as, "fowl that may fly above the earth in the open firmament of heaven." Man is next spoken of, with the power to rule over the entire creation.

The principles as illustrated in the first three chapters of Genesis are very simple when making an astrological comparison, everything on the globe must be represented within a circle. It is divided into halves, quarters and into twelfths; one-twelfth for each sign of the Zodiac. Each is so arranged that fire, earth, air and water are illustrated according to the Laws of Moses.

The second chapter of Genesis describes the state in which man is to exist; he is to be both a material and spiritual entity;

he is to have dominion over the entire globe. The six days of creation are the 6,000 years which the earth passes through, and are the creative cycles of the globe. The seventh day is the seven thousandth year of the cycle; and during the seventh period the manifestation of a spiritual nature takes place.

Genesis 2: "And the heavens and the earth were finished." It shows in Genesis 1:27 that God made man on the sixth day, that is, God made a name in the earth for man, and other creeping things, but in Genesis 2:7, "And Lord God formed man of the dust of the ground, and breathed into his nostrils the breath of life; and man became a living soul." Remember that it is on the seventh day that God gives man a living soul.

Genesis 2:8, "And Lord God planted a garden eastward, in Eden;" and there he put the man whom he had formed, which means that man's home is in the eastern part of the garden. The tree of life and the tree of knowledge was in the midst of the garden, and a river went out from Eden which parted the garden in four heads. The tree of life spoken of in the midst of the garden is illustrated by the line drawn from north to south and is the degree of longitude. The tree of knowledge is illustrated in the line from east to west and is the degree of latitude. These two lines mark the cardinal points of the globe. It is very important to know the difference between the tree of life and the tree of knowledge, and to know that the tree of knowledge is crossing the tree of life horizontally. The tree of life represents as the name indicates: life, illustrated as heaven (south) and hell (north). The tree of knowledge means experience or learning; as birth (east) and death (west).

And a river went out of Eden to water the four quarters; which means that an influence emanates in Eden going to the four quarters. "The name of the first is Pison: the land of Havilah, where there is gold, and the gold of that land is good: there is bdellium and onyx stone. And the name of the second river is Gihon: which compassed the land of Ethiopia (Cush). And the name of the third river is Hiddekel: and the fourth river is Euphrates." These represent the cardinal points for a figure of the heaven. The four quarters also represent the four quarters of the earth and describe a given place, which is the United States, divided into the four quarters. Genesis 10:6.

"Of every tree of the garden you may eat freely, but not of the tree of knowledge, which is good and evil; for in the day that you eat thereof you shall die." This passage can be explained the same as the tree of life, for both have the same meaning. We will say that the man in the Garden of Eden dies when he partakes of this tree of knowledge, that is, when the country as a nation has a revolution and the north fights against the south, meaning death to the nation.

God makes Adam a wife of the same material as himself, that is, out of the earth. This means that the wife of Adam is a representation of another part of the earth and of an earthly nature. When we come to the study of the ages we will find that Adam and Eve as described, are part of the earth.

As far as we have studied we can see that the first three chapters of Genesis deals with the symbols of the zodiac. Namely, that the shape of the earth is globular. That the tree of life and the tree of knowledge form a cross in the garden, making four corners of the earth, so arranged as to represent earth, water, air and fire. The cardinal points are distinctly named and described, showing what part of the garden each cardinal house occupied.

In Bible study the cardinal quarters, or as the Bible terms it, "the four rivers," are used to explain the operations of the laws of the universe.

Chapter 4 describes the generation of Adam and Eve. We will not take space to describe them in detail, but will say that they represent the twelve names giving the twelve houses of the zodiac. In the United States Abel represents the Southern division, Cain represents the tiller of the ground, raising stocks; the North. The names of the generation of Adam and Eve and the houses that they represent can be found in another chapter and there described as God's twelve.

The different ages as a new figure constitute a new period of time for another part of the earth. The names of the houses and planets change at each age. The ages of Adam, Abraham, Moses, constitute new periods.

It must be remembered, as stated before that the book of Genesis deals with the erecting of a figure and explains briefly the movements of the planets.

The second book of Moses, or Exodus, shows the movements and the action of the planets westward as they pass with the degrees through the houses. Remember that this is Exodus, which means to move from one place to another. It is written that the children of Israel did move.

Part III—Chapter 14.

The third book of Moses, or Leviticus, deals with offerings. The offerings represent the influence of the houses and the planets' aspects. Moses and Aaron in a given house are making offerings; God speaking to Moses is a representation of the influence of the planet Uranus; God spoke to Moses which again shows the nature of the aspect.

The fourth book of Moses, or Numbers, speaks for itself. It describes the degrees, years, or ages, as the first principles. It will be found upon figuring, which are the houses of long and short ascensions; for the Bible shows clearly the numbers of degrees in each house and how long the house lasts. It also shows how long the planets stay in the various houses.

The fifth book of Moses, or Deuteronomy, which is the actual reading of a figure, explains the activity of the planets. It will be found that Jehovah speaks to Moses and explains what he wants; which is the influence God produced on Moses as the planet Uranus, when Jehovah gives Moses the law. The houses are described in Chapter 33 and given as the blessings of the twelve tribes.

The rest of the books in the Bible deal with each generation. It is the repetition of the planets' travel through the houses; and the description of the end of the cycles by the symbolic death of the planet as a patriarch.

The story of Moses is the same as the story of Jesus. They were both trying to save the people at the end of their life. They had wars at the conclusion of each cycle, similar to our own days, when many were killed. It will be seen that at the end of each cycle there is a new Savior, or leader born, who takes the place of the old. They die that the new age may live; which is illustrated in all ages from Adam up to the cycle of Jesus. The list of the names and ages of the patriarchs will be found in another chapter, and will be useful in the study of the cycles.

For those who are interested, it may be of benefit to study the question of the tribes of Israel. It will be found that the nations of today are the tribes described in olden times. A number of books have been published on the subject, but as the authors have tried to find the tribes as based on a religious principle, they have failed. The nations of Europe represent the disciples of Jesus, and also the twelve tribes of Israel.

NOAH.

The cycle of time described as the generations of Adam and Eve with Cain and Abel are very brief, however, it contains a complete cycle from the birth of Adam in 4004 to Noah in 2948. This covers a period of 1056 degrees (years).

The second thousand year cycle begins with Noah in 2948 but the flood did not take place until 2348 in the 600th year of Noah's age. Noah's cycle begins at 120 degrees west, and the cycles from Greenwich westward around the earth constitute Noah's age. Noah represents the watery house of Cancer, which is called the flood and is from 120 degrees west from the Pacific Coast to 240 degrees west in Asia. Noah's age begins at 60 degrees east at the dividing of Europe and Asia, but his history is not counted from his birth, but from the period of the flood to the death of Noah in 1998, covering a period of 950 degrees (years).

In Genesis 6:3 is described how long in degrees a cycle of time is, without qualifications. "And the Lord said, My spirit shall not always strive with man, for that he also is flesh; yet his days shall be an hundred and twenty years." This is not described as the age of Noah, but the age of man as a cycle. Noah's age as a cycle of time was 950 years (degrees). In verse 4 is shown where the 120th degree is calculated from, for it says, "There were giants in the earth in those days." The mountains are the giants and this describes that the 120 degree is located in the mountains. The 120th degree is located near the Sierra Nevada and Cascade Mountains and has been figured as the place from which the age is calculated. The illustrations describing the flood were given to show that the cycle of time had to pass over the ocean, which was described as the flood.

The building of the Ark is the same description as the setting up of a horoscope. It is described that the Ark contained a complete universe of all living beings, which again means that Noah had in the Ark a complete horoscope of the earth.

Chapter 7:6 gives the degree when Noah reached the International Date Line. "And Noah was six hundred years old when the flood of waters was upon the earth." The six hundred years equals 180 degrees and is in the middle of the Pacific Ocean. The next important degree is described in verse 12. "And the rain was upon the earth forty days and forty nights." Verse 13, "In the self same day entered Noah, and Shem, and Ham, and Japheth, the sons of Noah and Noah's wife, and the three wives of his sons with him, into the Ark." This shows that there was a 40-degree space before getting to the 180 degrees represented in the 40 days and nights of rain.

It is shown in verse 12 that it rained 40 days and nights, which brings Noah to 180 degrees. In verse 17, "and the flood was forty days upon the earth; and the waters increased, and bare up the ark, and it was left up above the earth," which means that the ark had reached another 40 degrees and was on land; this takes Noah at this time to the 140th degree east of Greenwich in Japan.

In verse 20 is described how high the water was. "Fifteen cubits upward did the waters prevail; and the mountains were covered." Which means that the place as described in cubits were 15 degrees north from a calculated center at Noah's 600th year of 180 degrees. The tree of knowledge represents the ecliptic and is located at 36 degrees north latitude. We add 15 degrees north to 36 degrees and we have 51 degrees, which is at the Aleutian Islands in the middle of the Pacific Ocean. It says that the mountains were covered, which describes that it is the islands spoken of. The 51st degree corresponds to the location of the present war in Europe, for the northern boundary of Belgium is at 51st degree.

The place, as described in chapter 7, covers the space across the ocean and when Noah was at the 180th degree at the International Date Line, he describes the location and illustrates this to be the end of a cycle or age, for all life was destroyed. Verse 21, "And all flesh died that moved upon the earth." In verse 23 "Noah only remained alive, and they that were with him in the ark." This shows that Noah represents a new cycle of time as illustrated in the 180 degrees from east to west, which is half of the degrees of the surface of the earth.

Verse 24, "And the waters prevailed upon the earth an hundred and fifty days." The beginning of Noah was in the mountains at 120 degrees west and the water period was on the earth 150 degrees; so we add 150 degrees to 120 degrees which equals 270 degrees and corresponds to the position of Thibet in the Himalaya Mountains at 90 degrees east.

God ordered Noah to build the Ark 120 years before the flood; which means, the 120 degrees from Greenwich to the Pacific Coast at the 120th degree.

Chapter 8:4 describes where the ark landed. "And the ark rested in the seventh month, on the seventeenth day of the month, upon the mountains of Ararat." It will be found that the Himalaya Mountains is the place where the ark landed and from which all calculations were made for Asia. The ark represents a principle similar to the laws of Moses and the giving of this law has been illustrated being given from a mountain, as being above the earth, as the home of the Lord of Heaven.

Chapter 9 describes Asia and Europe as the two brothers of Shem and Japheth. The third brother, who was cursed, is Ham, who represents the United States and he was to be a servant of Asia and Europe. The life and age of Noah is given in verses 28 and 29, "And Noah lived after the flood 350 years. And all the days of Noah were nine hundred and fifty years." The 350 years are figured from 120 degrees east as the place after the flood, and is at 130 degrees east of Greenwich (using the 360-degree cycle), which is at Korea in China. The 950-degree period is from the 120 degrees west at the beginning of Noah's cycle and extends around the earth twice, leaving 230 degrees westward from Greenwich, which is at 130 degrees east at the location of Korea.

Chapter 11:1 describes the beginning of the race and the generations of Noah in Asia. "And the whole earth was of one language, and of one speech." Verse 2, "And it came to pass, as they journeyed from the east, that they found a plain in the land of Shinar; and they dwelt there." Verse 4, "And they said, Go to, let us build us a city, and tower, whose top may reach into heaven; and let us make a name, lest we be scattered abroad upon the face of the whole earth." Verse 5, "And the Lord came down to see the city and the tower, which the children of men builded." Verse 9, "Therefore is the name of it called Babel; because the Lord did there confound the language of all earth; and from thence did the Lord scatter them abroad upon the face of all the earth." The interpretation for Chapter 11 is that the sons of Noah traveled together until they reached the Himalaya Mountains which represent the "Tower of Babel," and are holy mountains for Asia (Babylonia). In this mountain God spoke to the people and scattered them westward into the different nations and races. The reason why there was only one language before reaching the 90 degrees, is that China is one nation up to this place. The scattering of the people means the dividing of the earth into nations, as India, Afghanistan and Persia, and all the nations west have different languages. In verse 10 is described where Shem's generation begins. "These are the generations of Shem; Shem was an hundred years old, and begat Arphaxad two years after the flood." From this it will be seen that Shem is the name for Asia, beginning at 118 degrees east. It will be found in other chapters that this is the beginning of many of the calculations for the different cycles, up to the time of the Romans.

The cycle of time as described by Noah, according to the Bible, takes place from 2948. The flood comes at 2348, and Noah dies in 1998, when Abram's cycle begins.

ABRAM-ABRAHAM.

The cycle of time for Abram begins at Greenwich and is described in Genesis 12; in the year 1921 B. C. The description of the age of Abram is the continuation of the time after Noah and is the begining of a new cycle and a new generation, with Abram as the father of his cycle of time.

Verse 4: "So Abram departed, as the Lord had spoken unto him; and Lot went with him; and Abram was seventy and five years old when he departed out of Haran." Which means that Abram left Europe and went to the United States and reached the Atlantic Coast at the 75 degree longitude, as indicated by his age of 75 years. The description, as given in verse 10, that he is going to Egypt, means that he is going south to begin the cycle, which will be verified later, for at the beginning of all cycles a trip is made south. Abram represents the period for the eastern division of the United States.

The north and south are divided at the 36 degrees, and Abram is the north and Lot represents the south, which is also described as Egypt. The story of Abram's wife Sarai, who was represented as his sister, also represents a fixed law, for at the beginning and ending of all the different cycles the same story is repeated.

The life of Abram is the life of the United States in a former cycle, and since each cycle repeats itself, it can easily be followed. The period that Abram went to Egypt corresponds to the Mexican war in 1846 as described in Genesis 13. After Abram came back from Egypt (Mexico) he settled and was prosperous. His herdsmen and Lot's herdsmen had trouble about the feeding ground and there was strife. They finally divided the land; speaking comparatively, Lot had the south and Abram the north. This story corresponds to the civil war from 1861, and is described in verse 5. Every good American citizen should read the 13th chapter of Genesis in full and see what a great country the United States is, as the Lord said it was when he spoke to Abraham and described it in verses 14 to 18.

Chapter 14: Abram's country is described to be from the 75 degrees to the 115 degrees west. The end of Abram's territory is the Sodom and Gomorrah section, and is in the desert of Utah-Arizona. It will be found that at the end of the cycles a destruction takes place, when the inhabitants are slaughtered. This destruction is divided into two periods and corresponds to the nature of the country. The period of Abram told about in chapter 14 describes what took place at the Sodom or Arizona, when Lot was taken prisoner. The Mamre spoken of is the holy mountains, and is Mount Whitney in California. This event takes place in 1913 B. C.

In the 15th chapter of Genesis, God promised Abram a son, who should come out of his own bowels, and the population of Abram's son should be as many as the stars of heaven. From verse 9 to 18 is a prediction for the country of Abram as a horoscope, which is explained from verse 13: "And he said unto Abram, Know of a surety that thy seed shall be a stranger in a land that is not theirs, and shall serve them; and they shall afflict them four hundred years; And also that nation whom they shall serve, will I judge: and afterward shall they come out with great substance." Verse 16: "But in the fourth generation they shall come hither again; for the iniquity of the Amorites is not yet full." Verse 18: "In that same day the Lord made a covenant with Abram, saying "unto thy seed have I given this land, from the river of Egypt unto the great river Euphrates." The meaning of the 15th chapter is, that the country of the United States, after Abram's time, should be forgotten 4,000 years, but in the fourth or last cycle it would again be populated as in Abram's time. The two rivers which are translated as the Euphrates, is the Pacific Ocean; and the river of Egypt is the Atlantic Ocean; for Europe is described as Egypt, in all ages. That is, Abram's land is from the Atlantic to the Pacific.

The 16th chapter deals with what is now Mexico. This

Part III—Chapter 14.

country is represented as a handmaid, whose name was Hagar. This Hagar had a child by Abram and became despised.

Verse 7 describes that Hagar was found by an angel (angle), at a fountain of water in the wilderness. This fountain corresponds to the Gulf of California, and Hagar's son represents lower California as the son Ishmael "A wild man." This takes place (Abram's age) at the 86 degrees west, as described in verse 16, and corresponds to the Mexican trouble in 1913. The year, as a cycle, is 1913 B. C.

Chapter 17 describes the time when Abram became 99 years (degrees) of age. He had a talk with the Almighty God at this time and he was promised children as a reward. This is the time he crossed the 99 degrees longitude in the middle of what is now the United States. The name of Abram was changed to Abraham and the name of Sarai was changed to Sarah. At the time when Abraham is 99 years (degrees) old, Ishmael is 13 years (degrees) old and this degree corresponds to the location of Mexico in degrees longitude, up to the Gulf of California. When Abraham was 100 years (degrees) old, Isaac was to be born, illustrating a new age. Isaac represents the Pacific Coast cycle and when he becomes 20 years of age he will rule. The circumcision spoken of in this chapter is the change to the Asiatic race.

The 18th chapter describes that Abraham entertains three angels (angles) and that he was near the mountains of Mamre. The three angels represent the three divisions of 120 degrees each, and the place is described as being where there was water. The angle of 115 degrees strikes the Gulf of California and the story as written is described from there. The length of an age is 120 degrees and at this time the angel described that Sodom, which is the desert in Arizona, is to be destroyed, as being east of the 120th degree. The pleading of Abraham to save the people, if there were only a few left, is of no avail, for there were not 10 left who were pure in heart. This illustrates that the cycle of time for Abraham was at an end and that there was not 10 degrees longitude left of Abraham's time. This takes place in 1898 B. C.

Chapter 19 illustrates the end of the age in the destruction of Sodom and Gomorrah. The end of the cycle is in the west and the two western houses, illustrated as daughters, the houses of Virgo and Libra, are described in verse 8. These houses as daughters are located as Utah and Arizona; one daughter is north, the other south of the 36th degree latitude and that is the reason why Lot's wife, who is Utah, had to be destroyed. The pillar of salt as described in verse 26 is Salt Lake of Utah, which illustrates that Salt Lake was at this place in the age of Abraham and Lot. The location of Moab and Ammon is described as the children born to Lot by his two daughters east of the 120 degrees and south of the 36th degree. This place is called Zoar and is the desert east of the Sierra Nevada Mountains.

The 20th chapter describes the relation between Abraham and his wife. Abraham again describes his wife as a sister, and God informed Abimelech that she was Abraham's wife. This chapter illustrates a principle represented in Abraham's wife and is the planet Neptune.

Chapter 21 describes the birth of Isaac, representing the Pacific Coast cycle north of 36th degree. In the same chapter is described the son of Hagar (Mexico) which is lower California. Hagar is sent south on her way to the wilderness of Beer-sheba. In verse 19 "And God opened her eyes and she saw a well of water; and she went and filled the bottle with water, and gave the lad a drink." The bottle of water represents the gulf of California.

Verse 20, "And God was with the lad: and he grew and dwelt in the wilderness, and became an archer." The name of lower California as an archer is given to show it is a descendant of Spain. The place called Beer-sheba is at the Gulf of California. at 115 degrees longitude, illustrating the dividing degree and spoken of as, "From Dan to Beer-sheba." Verse 33: "And Abraham planted a grove in Beer-sheba and called there on the name of the Lord, the everlasting God." This grove spoken of is also described by Moses.

Chapter 22: In this chapter is described that Abraham is tempted to offer Isaac for a burnt offering, which means that at the end of the cycle, offerings or sacrificing takes place. The description given, that he saw a ram which he used for a burnt offering, is that the ram is the first house in the new cycle, represented as Aries. The angel which called to Abraham at this time is the 120 degree angle, who blessed Abraham, showing it was a good angle.

Chapter 23 describes the death of Sarah the wife of Abraham, and Abraham's buying a burying place for future generations. The lifetime cycle of Sarah was 127 years (degrees) beginning in the holy mountains of Europe, the Alps, at 7 degrees east and ending at 120 degrees west, making 127 degrees (years).

The burying place which Abraham bought from the children of Heth is located at Mount Whitney in the Sequoia National Park in California. This mountain is called Mamre and the cave of Machpelah means Death Valley. This mountain is located near the 36th degree latitude and illustrates the principle of a holy place. There are three places on earth described as holy places; they are the Himalaya Mountains, the Alps and Mount Whitney in California. There is a principle described in the placing of a burying ground at the 120 degrees longitude. It is described as the burying ground for the generations, and it will also be found to be the burying ground for the Christian age at the present time.

Chapter 24: "Abraham was old and well stricken in age; and the Lord had blessed Abraham in all things." This shows that the end of Abraham is near. This chapter, illustrated in the selection of a wife for Isaac, that his country is not entirely in the United States, for he has to go to the place where Abraham's family lived to get a wife. The well described, where Abraham's servants met Rebekah, is the Pacific Ocean. Abraham's brother Nahor represents Asia and Rebekah is the house of Virgo, the virgin, as figured for the cycle of Isaac and is in the middle of the Pacific Ocean. The reason Rebekah had to travel to Isaac is that his time begins in the United States and the age of Rebekah and her children's age is in Asia. The Camel spoken of is Camela Pardalis.

Chapter 25 describes that Abraham again takes a wife and has six children which simply describes another horoscope with a new generation and represents the Pacific Northwest. Verse 7, "And these are the days of the years of Abraham's life which he lived, an hundred three score and fifteen years." Abraham was born at 55 degrees east and died at 120 degrees west in the year 1822 B. C. He was buried in Mamre in the family cemetery by his two sons, Isaac and Ishmael.

ISAAC AND JACOB.

Isaac's cycle is from the Pacific Coast in the United States to the 120th degree east longitude in China. This age is described in chapter 25 of Genesis, and is in the year 1822 B. C.

The beginning of the description of Isaac is written in verse 11. "And it came to pass after the death of Abraham that God blessed his son Isaac; and Isaac dwelt by the well, Lahai-rai." Which means that Isaac lived near the Pacific Ocean. The illustration is given in verse 21 that Rebekah was barren, but had two sons as twins. Verse 23 gives a perfect description of the two children as nations. "And two manners of people shall be separated from thy bowels; and the one people shall be stronger than the other people; and the elder shall serve the younger." The meaning of the two children to be born are, that Asia and Europe are born as twins; and "the elder to serve the younger," means that Europe will be the leader. The two children born are Esau and Jacob. Esau was born first and represents Asia and Jacob, Europe. Esau was later, also, called Edom and lived in the south. Esau sold his birthright to Jacob, who also obtained the blessing of his father. This shows that Jacob is blessed and is represented as a double generation of Asia and Europe, north.

Chapter 26 describes the same story, that a famine was in the land and a trip to the south was planned, but the Lord told Isaac not to go south. It is described in verse 7 that Isaac implied that his wife Rebekah was his sister, because she was fair to look upon. This is the same story as described in chapter 20; about Abraham. Abimelech is again spoken of as a disturbing element. Chapter 26 describes the many places which Isaac speaks of as wells, instead of land, as in former ages, showing that his age was at the location of the many wells, which are the ocean and rivers.

Chapter 27 is a description of two animals, with two kinds of hair, when Jacob obtains the blessing of his father. In verse 11: "Esau my brother is a hairy man and I am a smooth man." The goat's skin, which Jacob put on to deceive his father, represents the house of Capricorn, always illustrated as a goat, and the smooth man represents Sagitarius as a horse. The condition is described in the nature of the continents, for Jacob is blessed because his country is in the temperate zone of the life region of the earth.

Chapter 28 describes that Jacob begins his trip to the country of his mother's people, and is charged to take a wife over there. Esau is of the south, as Edom, and takes a wife from the family of Ishmael. The travels of Jacob are to the holy mountains where he had the dream of the ladder reaching up to heaven. In verse 17: "And he was afraid, and said, How dreadful is this place! this is none other but the house of God, and this is the gate of heaven." This is the Himalaya Mountains where the tower of Babel was built. It is a dreadful place and the house of God, which is a good description of the Himalaya Mountains.

Chapter 29 describes that Jacob is at the place of a well where he meets Rachel. As Haran is the place from which Abraham came and as his days were 55 degrees (years) east, we find this place to be 36 degrees latitude, at the Caspian Sea. The 60 degrees longitude divide Europe and Asia, and here is where the two houses of Libra and Virgo meet, and at this place is the home of Rachel and Leah. So from this calculation the well of Haran must be the Caspian Sea. The story about Rachel and Leah as the wives, whom Jacob had to work for, is simple. Jacob is the representation of Uranus passing through the period for Asia and Europe. Uranus stays seven years in each house and had to pass both houses as represented in Virgo and Libra, going from east to west. The youngest is Rachel who was barren and is Virgo, and the oldest is Libra and represents Leah east from Greenwich. From this it will be seen the reason why Jacob had to pass both houses in his cycle.

Chapter 30 describes the generations for Europe in the birth of the children by Rachel, Leah and the maids, Bilhah and Zilpah. The names, described and given as children at this time, are the names of the twelve tribes of Israel and correspond to the nations of Europe, as illustrated in the chapter on Tribes. Verse 14 is a description of Reuben, finding mandrakes at the time of wheat harvesting. Reuben represents Arabia in Asia, and Spain in Europe. Reuben and his mandrakes represent a saving principle, which will be described in the next generation when Reuben aims to save his brother Joseph. In order to illustrate the correctness of the birth of the nations read chapter 30:16 where it describes the result of Reuben's mandrakes and the birth of a new nation. The son born was Issachar, which again is Holland-Belgium. As all cycles repeat themselves we find that the mandrakes of Reuben correspond to the Spanish Influenza in the present cycle, and that the child born is Holland-Belgium, which demonstrates the saving influence of Reuben. The children born now will be the new nation of the present Holland-Belgium. The time described in all chapters in the Bible is for the ending and beginning of the cycles only, and since we at the present time are living in a similar age, the happenings are now being repeated.

In verse 25 begins the description of the dividing of Asia and Europe when Joseph was born. "Send me away that I may go unto mine own place, and to my country." The dividing of the goats, cattle and sheep as described, is the dividing of the races. The ring-streaked, speckled and grizzled cattle, mean the white, black and yellow races and is the division of the Asiatic and European races. The reason why Joseph continued to feed Laban's flocks, was, that the southern part of Europe does not begin until Turkey is reached, and that is where the dispute takes place.

Chapter 31 tells us that Jacob, with his two wives are going to Canaan and that they get to the Caucasus Mountains, which divide Europe and Asia in Turkey, when Laban overtakes them. The description that Rachel took Laban's image and put it in the furniture of the camel, is the representation of some value, as oil in the earth, in the place of the camel; which is at the Caspian Sea. The distance of Asia is described in verse 41. "Thus have I been twenty years in thy house; I served thee fourteen years for thy two daughters, and six years for thy cattle; and thou hast changed my wages ten times." These periods added together are 50 degrees as years and are calculated from the 90th degree longitude to the 40th degree east, which is from Thibet to Turkey. The heap of stones described in verse 51 are the Caucassus Mountains, which was to be a witness that Laban and Jacob had made an agreement in dividing territory. Chapter 32 describes that Jacob and Esau are still represented as twin brothers, Jacob north and Esau south of the 36th degree. They meet going from the 60th degree to the 45th degree longitude. As this is the beginning of another cycle, Jacob goes south and he meets his brother there.

Verse 24: "And Jacob was left alone; and there wrestled a man with him, until the breaking of the day." The wrestling means a bad angle as 45 degrees; the break of day is the beginning of a new cycle. The 45th degree strikes the Euphrates river in Turkey and is an ancient landmark and dividing line, for the beginning of a new age. Verse 25: "And when he saw that he prevailed not against him, he touched the hollow of his thigh; and the hollow of Jacob's thigh was out of joint, and he wrestled with him." Verse 28: "And he said, thy name shall be called no more Jacob, but Israel; for as a prince hast thou power with God." Verse 30: "And Jacob called the name of the place Peniel for I have seen God face to face and my life is preserved." Verse 32: "Therefore the children of Israel eat not of the sinew which shrank, which is upon the hollow of the thigh, unto this day; because he touched the hollow of Jacob's thigh in the sinew that shrank." This takes place in Arabia at the 45th degree, which strikes in the middle of the Arabian desert. The thigh on man is illustrated as the house of Sagitarius, which again represents Reuben. From this will be seen that Arabia is the thigh which shrank and became out of joint as the location of Arabia indicated. The reason why the children of Israel do not eat of this sinew is that it is desert country. The changing of name from Jacob to Israel simply illustrates the change from Asia to Europe. The end of the cycle for Asia is in Aquarius and when Uranus is in this house he creates new nations.

Chapter 33 illustrates that Jacob and Esau meet and travel together in Turkey until they reach the 30th degree east.

Chapter 34 describes Turkey as the daughter of Jacob and gives the first mention that Turkey acts as a harlot, and the location is at the gate. Turkey divides Europe and Asia and here is where Asia, as an age, had to be destroyed, as described from the 25th verse.

Chapter 35 repeats the same method as used in describing Abraham's cycle. It concludes with the description of Turkey and the travels to the land of Canaan (United States) and the Chapter closes at Mamre in the holy mountains of California, where Isaac dies. This chapter is a review of the previous chapters and gives the names of the nations of Europe, and the birth of Joseph as described in verse 17.

Chapter 36 describes the generations of Esau, but as his life is not described in detail the names of his generation are only given.

Chapter 37 begins with the description of the period in Europe as illustrated in Jacob's son Joseph.

JOSEPH.

Joseph's cycle, the next after Jacob's cycle, is in Europe and begins at 40 degrees east. It is described in chapter 37:3: "Now Israel loved Joseph more than all his children, because he was the son of his old age; and he made him a coat of many colors." Jacob's time ends at Greenwich, and Joseph represents the last of the age. The coat of many colors is Europe, representing the different nations, and is Joseph as an age. The dream of Joseph described from verse 5, is a prophecy of what would take place in Europe during his period. We can see the print of the events then as we see it now; in that Joseph represents the twelfth son of the age and corresponds to the Roman Empire in our age. The rest of the children of Israel become subject to the rule of Joseph. Verse 14 describes that Jacob sent him out from Hebron, which is at the beginning of Europe. Verse 23: "And it came to pass, where Joseph was come unto his brethren, that they stript Joseph out of his coat of many colors that was on him." Verse 24: "And they took him, and cast him into a pit; and the pit was empty, there was no water in it.' The place spoken of as a dry pit is the Arabian desert, from which Reuben tried to save his brother; this is the same saving trait of character which is represented in Reuben's mandrakes, spoken of in a previous chapter and corresponds to the Spanish Influenza at the present time. It is a dry well and compares favorably with the Spanish Influenza as a disease, and is one of the saving influences to stop the world's war on Joseph, as Europe now. They took Joseph's coat away from him showing he was not in Europe for Arabia is in Asia. Verse 28 describes that Joseph was sold for twenty pieces of silver and they brought Joseph to Egypt. The twenty pieces of silver is twenty degrees and as the cycle of Egypt (Europe) is 30 degrees east, we add the 20 degrees and we get 50 degrees east in the Arabian desert and this corresponds to the dry well. Joseph was sold to Pharaoh, who ruled in Egypt and corresponds to the European age which ruled at 1729 B. C. The country included in the age of the Egyptian extended as far east as India to the 70th degree east.

Chapter 38 describes the period of Turkey, included in the Egyptian age. The chapter illustrates a principle of creation, which is described in Turkey as a harlot. Turkey is called a "harlot sitting in the gate," which means that Turkey is the gateway between Asia and Europe and as the 36th degree dividing line is also at Turkey, this country is in the true sense of the word a mother of Europe. The term harlot means that Turkey is a virgin, who is also the mother of all countries, both north and south of the 36th degree latitude.

Part III—Chapter 14.

Chapter 39 describes the planetary condition at the end of the cycle. Joseph represents Uranus, Pharaoh, Saturn, and Pharaoh's wife is Neptune. The contention of Joseph means that he represents Uranus and is in aspect to Neptune who at this time is in conjunction with Saturn. Verse 20 tells us that Joseph was put into prison which means that Joseph, as Uranus became in bad aspect to Saturn, because at this time at the end of the cycle he is in prison.

Chapter 40 describes the butler and the baker of Pharaoh being in prison which means bad aspect and war. The butler and baker are Holland and Belgium as characters. This chapter describes the aspect of the planet Uranus in the house of Aquarius, in opposition to Saturn in Leo. The life of Joseph as an age is from 60 degrees east and extends as a power from 40 degrees to the Atlantic Ocean and terminates at 70 degrees west. The Bible in all cycles describes this distance as the space of Europe.

Joseph's dreams are descriptive of a condition in Europe and what would take place during his cycle. The dreams are written in chapter 37:9 and means that Joseph was the leader of the children of the age. The life of Joseph at this time was about 1718 B. C.

Before going farther we will explain that the beginning of this generation was the family of Jacob. His name was changed to Israel when his cycle entered Europe and Joseph represents Israel. The twelve children of Jacob are the nations of Europe, named for the first time in the book of Genesis. This shows that Asia and Europe always have been divided at the 60 degrees longitude east. A complete cycle consists of 120 degrees and as Europe and Asia are divided at 60 degrees east, nature divided the twin brothers to the very degree. The house of Jacob is therefore a double house, represented by the double cycle of Jacob and Joseph. The time of Joseph is therefore the age of his father, but Joseph did not come into existence until Europe was entered at 60 degrees east, when his mother, Rachael, as Asia, died. The influence of Joseph's period began to be felt in Europe when Joseph reached Turkey, and Pharaoh; which is the real beginning of Joseph's age. From this it will be seen that Jacob represents Asia, and Joseph, Europe.

After all the children of Israel, as the nations of Europe, have been born and named as Joseph's brothers (Genesis 41);

Joseph interprets Pharaoh's dreams which again are nothing but the explanation of the coming of a great disaster over Europe. This disaster is to last seven years, and during this period Joseph is to be reconciled with his brothers who have wronged him. The dream of Pharaoh and the interpretation of the dream illustrates the ending of the cycle in Europe and corresponds to the present age and war of seven years.

Joseph's power began at 40 degrees east and he was 30 degrees (years) old when he was made ruler by Pharaoh in Egypt. It should be understood that Egypt means Europe and is the nation called Egypt as a power. It is a singular coincident that Alexandria in Egypt and St. Petersburg in Russia are both on the 30 degrees east longitude.

The cycle of Europe represents Benjamin as Joseph and is the double house of Pisces. Greece represents the eastern half as an Empire and is called the age of Egypt; and Rome as the Roman Empire the western half. In the present age this same power or empire is illustrated in the Roman and Greek Catholic Churches.

Chapter 41 describes what the conditions in Europe were at this time and is very interesting reading, for history is repeated in the present age. It will be found that when the world's war is over, that the condition which is described in the chapters of Genesis 42, 43 and 44, will be the condition of Europe.

In chapter 41:50 the birth of Joseph's two sons are described: "And unto Joseph were born two sons before the years of famine came; which Asenath the daughter of Poti-pherah priest of On, bare unto him." Verse 51: "And Joseph called the name of the first born Manasseh: For God, said he, hath made me forget all my toil, and all my father's house. Verse 52: "And the name of the second called he Ephraim: "For God hath caused me to be fruitful in the land of my affliction." The two sons of Joseph represent the United States; at this time Manasseh is described as first and represents the eastern division, and Ephraim, the Pacific Coast States. The description of the mother of these two sons as Poti-pherah's daughter is similar to the description of Moses and Pharaoh's daughter, and also as given in Revelation 12: for the present cycle as a woman clothed with the sun, which was the mother of the United States in 1776. It is the planet Neptune referred to in all cycles.

Part III—Chapter 14.

It must be understood that France and England represent Ephraim and Manasseh for the cycle of Europe and that Joseph's two sons are the new age of the United States, both sons as one and not one. The blessing of the Pacific Coast as the first born is interesting as described in Genesis 48:13-22.

The story pictured in the famine of seven years when Joseph ruled in Europe is a representation of the world's war of the present time. The story shows that Jacob's and Joseph's cycle of time were nearly over and that the regular seven years of hardship took place. .The food they got when Joseph's brothers went to Egypt are the conditions of famine and war. Jacob in the third year of the famine in 1706 B. C. sends his family to Egypt to take part in the war; which is getting food, the same as the United States did in the third year of the present war. In the end Joseph gets all the money, land, and a mortgage on the future production of the country. As this is a counterpart of the present war, we can see the handwriting on the wall, who gets the money. It is Joseph's family. Anyone can follow the history of the present war and apply it to these chapters of Genesis. The children of Egypt (Europe) had to pay one-fifth of their income to clear their indebtedness for food obtained during the famine. From this we may know who is going to pay for the present war.

Jacob does not want to be buried in Europe. He makes his son Joseph promise he will bury him in Canaan in the field of Mamre and Joseph swore he would do so. The end of Jacob's life is concluded in chapter 47. We are now around the earth, having made the trip with Abraham, Isaac and Jacob. There are still 3 degrees left of Joseph's age and we see in chapter 48 that another short period is in the near future. Jacob now prophesies what is to take place and what Joseph is to do with the children.

The cycle as represented in Isaac and Jacob are figured in degrees. Isaac was born at 100 degrees west and died at 180 degrees (years) or 80 degrees east. Jacob was born at 160 degrees west and died at 147 degrees, or 53 degrees east. Joseph began to rule at 40 degrees east and ruled to 70 degrees west, making his age 110 degrees (years).

The children of Israel described in chapter 49:1-47, have been explained in detail in another chapter.

Chapter 50 records the burying of Jacob in the family cemetery beyond the Jordan where Abraham and Isaac were buried before him.

A description is given of the last periods recorded in Genesis 50:1-3, when Jacob had his father embalmed, "And forty days were fulfilled for him; for so are fulfilled the days of those which are embalmed; and the Egyptians mourned for him three score and ten days." The 40 days represent the space of 40 degrees east as being the space for those who are to be embalmed (dead) and the 70 days are the 70 degrees across the Atlantic Ocean. This ends the first book of Moses as Genesis in 1635 B. C. The second book of Moses begins in 1706 B. C. and describes the new cycle of time. Joseph's age ends in 1635 and the next age begins after the 70 degrees for the Atlantic Ocean is added, making it 1706 B. C.

CHAPTER 15.

THE SECOND BOOK OF MOSES.

The book of Exodus describes the continuation of the period in Europe, which begins at 3 degrees east, Greenwich time; it begins at the end of Jacob's cycle. Attention is called to the fact that the 3 degrees or days which are spoken of in the first 12 chapters of Exodus, correspond to the 3 degrees east in Belgium where the present war is taking place, and is the same 3 days or degrees before the passover, or Greenwich time is crossed. It will be found that at the end of every cycle, there is war and destruction which lasts for seven years, prior to entering the new cycle. By comparison Pharaoh (Saturn) rules Egypt (Europe) and Pharaoh's time is a cycle of 30 degrees in space to Greenwich. The time when the Egyptian cycle was figured in years was about 1700 B. C. The beginning of time for the cycle of Moses was 1571 B. C.

Moses was found by Pharaoh's daughter, floating in an ark, which is the place for the beginning of the cycle for Moses. The beginning of the cycle proper is at Greenwich, and since all the cycles have had their beginning at England, so does the time of Moses begin at England. From this it will be seen that England is the ark in which Moses was found. The North Sea is referred to as the "Bullrushes."

The time of seven years which it took Moses to plead with Pharaoh to bring the children of Israel out of Egypt is the same period of time as our own, that is, the end of the cycle. Chapter 2 describes that Moses was hid by Pharaoh's daughter for three months which corresponds to the 3 degrees east;

because the children born east of Greenwich had to be destroyed with the old generation, and as time passes on Pharaoh orders all children under two years (degrees) of age to be killed.

In Exodus from chapter 4 to 12 is found a very interesting description of the war which took place then, and proves positively that all cycles repeat themselves. Each of the seven plagues which Pharaoh put on the children of Israel corresponds to a year. At the end of each cycle there is always seven years of strife; we can find many illustrations of this in the Bible; for instance, at the end of Joseph's age, when seven years of famine took place, and now in the present day, Kaiser William, has produced seven years of war. Note the fact that the plagues are on the water, on land and in the air and also by fire. The story in the Bible is a duplicate of the present war, year by year, and the nature of the plague is the nature of our war. The place where Moses talks with God was in the Alps, which is the house of the Lord. The Alps must have been in eruption at the time, for God spoke to Moses from a burning bush. It is apparent that both the Alps and Mount Whitney in California were in eruption at the age of Moses.

It is unnecessary for us to copy the ten chapters of Exodus which described the life of Moses, but it will be advisable to read them in order to get the benefit of this study.

The 12th chapter begins with the first degree of the New Age, west of Greenwich. The children of Israel are now on their way westward. The Red Sea, which is spoken of in chapter 14, is the Atlantic Ocean. Moses and his Israelites get over dry, but the Egyptians, who live east of Greenwich, are all drowned. This means that the age east of Greenwich was killed, when the new cycle west of Greenwich began. The water of the Atlantic Ocean called Marah, described in chapter 15:23, was bitter, that is, salty, so they could not drink it.

Next they come to Elim. "Where were twelve wells of water and three score and ten palm trees, and they encamped there by the water." Chapter 15:27: the twelve wells of water mean that they were at the place of twelve tribes, or the United States and the 70 palm trees are the 70 degrees west to the east coast of the United States.

Chapter 16 explains that they are at the 90th degree west or at the Mississipi river, where Moses gave them quails to eat. The manna given them is the fruits of the 40 degrees in the space of the old garden of Eden. In chapter 16:35 it says the children had manna 40 years, until they came to the borders of the land of Canaan. These forty years are the space from 70 degrees to 110 degrees west, at the borders of Canaan.

Chapter 17:15 is a testimony to the Lord; for it shows that the old Indians have left a name behind them. The name Jehovah-nissie is written very plainly in the Bible and is the Mississippi. We are now at 90 degrees west in our travels and at the Mississippi river where the children of Israel were begging Moses for water. It is apparent that the name of Jehovah-nissie is the original name for Mississippi as used by the Indians. The word "nissie" is not common in the Bible and being added to the word Jehovah, which is self-sustaining, it is evident that the river marked the 90th degree and was the stopping place. Read verses 5-6. "And thou shalt smite the rock and there shall come water out of it, that the people may drink. And Moses did so in the sight of the elders of Israel;" this shows that there was a river at this very important place. The reason why Moses described the Mississippi river country, and had so much trouble there, is that the 90th degree is the place where the earth is divided into quarters, and is called a bad angle.

Chapter 18: In this chapter is described a new form of government when at 100 degrees west. Moses let the people handle the law and assist in governing themselves. This age corresponds to the year 1920 of our time, when the law is changed.

Chapter 19 is also very interesting; it is now nearing the time of the end of the cycle, and we are now at 110 degrees or 115 degrees west. Moses remains at this place for some time, and speaks to God face to face, in Mount Sinai.

We believe that Mount Whitney in California is the location of Mount Sinai, from the description given in the Bible. It is one of the high and peculiar mountains in Southern California and corresponds to the mountains called Mamre.

Moses' period begins at 70 degrees and ends at 120 degrees west; from this we can figure that Mount Whitney was the mountain described as Mount Sinai. The Sodom and Gomorrah district in the borders of Utah and Arizona was the place where the Israelites stopped when Moses was in the mountains. The highest and most prominent places have always marked the degrees in dividing the cycles. The Grand Canyon of the Colorado, or possibly Casa Grande, was the headquarters for the Israelites when Moses was in the mountains. The section from Mount Whitney to Salt Lake, including the Navajo Indian Reservation and the Grand Canyon of the Colorado is the location of the country for the time of Moses. This is the location of the Mormon Church in Utah, and as near to the holy mountains of Mount Sinai as the Mormons could locate. Moses went up into the mountains, which were in eruption; at the time, as God did not let the children come near the mountains for they would be destroyed.

We will advise every citizen interested in the welfare of Colorado, Arizona or Utah to locate the place where the children of Israel worshipped the "Golden Calf," when Moses passed through on his way west. In chapters 19 to 40 is described what took place between God and Moses at the time. The Laws of Moses were delivered here and the Golden Calf destroyed, being at the end of the age.

The teachings of Joseph Smith are the teachings of nature. The Laws of the Mormon Church were found by Joseph Smith and described in the Book of Mormon and as taught by them, are the same as the Laws of Moses. We have been informed that Joseph Smith was directed by spirits to locate at Salt Lake as the natural place for their teachings, and he located at the very degree which represents the end of the cycle. Note that the Mormons call themselves the "Latter Day Saints."

Chapters 20 to 40 inclusive describe the Laws of Moses as given from Mount Sinai; the population was 3 degrees east of the mountains, which brings the time to 115 degrees west. This is the same place as described as Sodom and Gomorrah and is in the desert in Arizona, illustrating a desolate, barren and volcanic country, where the race is killed.

The Tabernacle which is spoken of in chapter 26, is the representation of a figure or horoscope. The dimensions and plans in general are the calculations of space and time, as given in other chapters. The "Tablet of Stone" which was made on Mount Sinai for Moses, is the astrological teaching or the method used to read the Laws of Moses. The first two slates were destroyed, illustrating the end of the cycle, but new slates were made for the new cycle.

The slates or tablets of Moses, given on Mount Sinai, are the Laws of God. We have studied some of this law and we are now trying to show others what this law is and the method used in reading it. The Laws of Moses, given to him by God, are the laws of the universe and not the law which man originated with a personal God.

In the books of Moses there are three characters which represent the age. Moses, Aaron and Pharaoh. Moses is Uranus, Aaron is Neptune and Pharaoh is Saturn. The in-influence of Saturn is felt only at the ending of the cycles or ages, when Saturn rules and kills Uranus.

Chapter 16.

THE THIRD BOOK OF MOSES.

The Book of Leviticus is simply the description of the different aspects and their influence; these are called the offerings of the tribes. The "burnt offerings" are the destroying, or bad, aspects; the "peace offerings" are the good aspects; the "sin offerings of ignorance" are Neptune's neutral aspects; the "trespass offerings" are the passage through a house. Moses consecrating Aaron by washing his feet is the description of the influence represented by Moses and Aaron, being in conjunction in the watery house of Pisces, the feet. The nature of the aspect is indicated by the nature of the offering, as a "burnt offering of the herd or of fowl," means the nature of the house; a burnt offering of the herd indicates a fiery house of the nature of the animal described.

The Mount of Sinai is the holy mountains for the time of Moses and is the house of Aquarius. The wilderness of Sinai spoken of is the fiery, barren house of Leo and is in the borders of Arizona and Utah. The house of Virgo corresponds to the state of Utah as the western house, and the end of the age. The Laws of the priests, as given, are the laws of the aspect of Neptune for the different houses. The laws are always given when Uranus is in Aquarius, called the holy mountains. Uranus is at the present time in this house and is now making laws for the nations of Europe; and the Alps are the holy mountains there.

The entire Book of Leviticus is the description of the laws. The offerings at the tabernacle are the horoscope; and the congregation is the degrees of the houses. The book tells us what the nature of the tribes or houses represent and gives the explanation of the aspects when the planets are in the different houses.

CHAPTER 17.

THE FOURTH BOOK OF MOSES.

The Book of Numbers begins when the children of Israel were 20 years and over (90 degrees west). Each tribe and the place they are to occupy are described in chapter 2: It is the building of a house in heaven and we can use no better expression than the terms of setting up a horoscope. It describes how the figure is to be set up; what tribes are to be at the four corners; north, east, south, and west, and gives detailed instructions of what the aspects mean.

Chapter 12 describes the beginning of the westward movement from the 110 degrees in Utah, when spies are sent out by the south-western routes. They came to Colorado river and there obtained one cluster of grapes which was carried on a staff back to Moses by two men.

In chapter 13:29 is described where the tribes are located. "In the south the Amalekites, then the Hittites, Jebusites; in the mountains, the Amorites and the Canaanites dwell by the sea and the coast of Jordan."

The period spoken of in chapters 12: to 36: is the time of the approach to the coast, where is described the Pacific Coast country; which is the promised land. The degrees are the children of Israel who had to be killed before they could cross over the mountains; they have to wait until Moses becomes 120 degrees (years) of age.

Moses sent men to the coast in order to describe the land before he sent the children of Israel. This is the beginning of Joshua's age and he was one of those sent. He came back and said that the Pacific Coast country was the land of milk and honey; read chapter 14:6.

God told Moses that it was too early to go west but if they wanted to go and get killed, to take the road by the way of Arizona, and the south, which is described in chapter 14:. They finally did go, and many of them were killed. Chapter 16:46 to 50 describes where many more were killed and the glory of God proclaimed. The third time was by the way of Mount Hor when they tried to get to the coast but failed. Chapter 20:14. The three times they attempted to cross into the new age corresponds to the 3 degrees at the end of all cycles. After this follows the description of the killing of Aaron. They take him up on Mount Hor and stripped him before he is killed and leave him in the mountains. This is the last of Aaron. Mount Hor is one of the mountains near Mount Whitney in California and is at 118 degrees west; and denotes the end of the cycle of Aaron.

The description of the land and the people as fierce and giants, means the nature of the mountains and forests of the country. The land of Og and Canaan are the Pacific Coast country proper, on the west side of the mountains. A special description is given in a chapter devoted to the locations of the tribes. The country west of the 115 degrees was included with the coast tribes. The division is made from Colorado river in the south, following the 115 degrees north, as the eastern border of the tribes. Moses made the Colorado river when he passed by. Chapter 20:2 describes the need of water for they were in the desert of Zin at the time. In chapter 27 Moses is told to name Joshua as his successor for he is going to die, and also to name Eleazar as the successor to Aaron. This takes place east of the mountains for Moses could not cross the Sierra Nevada Mountains, for they are at 120 degrees; and Moses can go no farther west than 120 degrees.

CHAPTER 18.

THE FIFTH BOOK OF MOSES.

The book of Deuteronomy describes the actual entering into the promised land. It took eleven days as described in chapter 1:2 to go from Utah at 110 degrees to the 121st degree. In verse 2 the 110th degree is described as the end of the 40-degree period.

The first chapter deals with the trip in the "great and terrible wilderness" before the Israelites entered the country of the Amorites. Moses told them to go, for the way was prepared. The places are named in chapter 1:7; that they are to go by the way of the Amorites and then to the Canaanites and to Lebanon and to the Pacific Ocean, described as the Euphrates. In chapter 2:9 they are told not to settle in the south as Lot's children are to have that land, but to go westward and then north. The chapters from 3: to 38: describe where they are to settle and how to worship God. In all of these chapters Moses is giving advice, how to act and what land to possess and to avoid. It is the nature of the country, in the different houses as tribes which is described. It is written distinctly that the children of Israel are not human beings, but that they represent the land. In chapter 29:5-6 it says "And I have led you forty years in the wilderness; your clothes are not waxen old upon you, and thy shoe is not waxen old upon thy feet. Ye have not eaten bread, neither have ye drunk wine or strong drink; that ye might know that I am the Lord your God." This is self-evident that reference is made to the 40 degrees, for they do not use clothing or food.

The land of Heshbon and Bashan constitute the territory of Reuben, Gad and Manasseh and is east of the 120th degree, from the mouth of the Colorado river north and west of the 115th degree. Reuben is in the south and Manasseh in the north, described in chapter 29:8.

The chapter 31:2 describes Moses' age to a degree. "I am an hundred and twenty years old this day, I can no more go out and come in: also the Lord had said unto me, Thou shalt not go over this Jordan." If this is not plain, nothing is. The Jordan is the 120th degree and is the mountain and not a river; which explains why Moses can not go over. The life of Moses is the period of time up to the 120th degree and here he dies. This is the same Jordan which Joshua passes over without getting his feet wet.

Chapter 33 gives a full description of the tribes; it goes so far as to say that Benjamin shall dwell between the shoulders. The tribes are described whether they are on the coast or in the mountains; read 33:24, it says that Asher is to be where there is oil, iron and brass. Anyone who can read, can see at a glance what is meant by the children of Israel. It is the land as the location of the tribes which is described. In chapter 32:48-50: "And the Lord spake unto Moses that self same day, saying, "Get thee up into this Mountain Abarim, unto Mount Nebo, which is in the land of Moab, that is over against Jericho; and behold the land of Canaan, which I give unto the children of Israel for a possession: And die in the mount whither thou goest up, and be gathered unto thy people; as Aaron thy brother died in mount Hor, and was gathered unto his people." Moses was east of the mountain in the plains of Moab and mount Nebo is in a direct line west from there. The great mountain which Moses went up to that he might die there, is the holy mountains for the age and is in the house of Aquarius. Mount Hor and Mount Nebo are Kaweah Peak and Mount Whitney in California.

Chapter 34 describes the entire coast from Naphtali, to Judah, which is from British Columbia to Mexico. Moses looked over "Dan, Naphtali, Ephraim, Manasseh, Judah and to the Sea." In other words he stood at Mount Whitney, Tulare County, California, and looked over the entire six coast states, which was the last thing Moses did before he died. Moses was buried east of the mountains but "no man knoweth of his sepulchre unto this day."

The history of Moses is the giving of the law. The explanations of the aspects and the position of the planets are described in such detail that it is tiresome to study it. The description of a horoscope for the different tribes is so long and continuous that a study of it becomes misleading. It illustrates a system of worship instead of the laws of nature.

The actual travels of Moses described in the Bible are the same as those of Abraham, when he travels from England to the 120 degrees west.

Moses' journeys represent the principal angles of the degrees as, at the Atlantic coast 70th degree; the 90th degree in the Mississippi river district; the 100th degree when a permanent government was established, and 110th degree in Arizona-Utah where Moses stopped until he died. From this it will be seen, that the actual life of Moses in action is not important, but it is the Laws of Moses which makes his history so important.

The life of Moses is to be applied to the nation of the United States for it really is the history of the United States. The travels of Moses represent the time it requires for the emigrants to go from Europe and to settle in the west. It can be compared in time to the past 142 years of the present cycle. The travels of Moses correspond to the time the United States has been organized and the laws made; the death of Moses corresponds to the end of the present form of government in 1920 of 144 years, at the end of the first cycle.

The life history of Moses begins in Egypt (Europe) by bringing the Israelites out, representing the freedom of this country and the birth of a new nation. The story of Moses also corresponds to Abraham's cycle and the events of the Mexican war, the Rebellion, the Spanish war, and the present war. The cycle of Moses ends in 1452 B. C. and includes the life of Joshua, ending at 12 degrees in the new cycle.

CHAPTER 19.

THE BOOK OF JOSHUA.

The book of Joshua describes the beginning of the Pacific Coast cycle in the west from the 120th degree to 120 degrees east longitude, including Japan and the coast of China.

Chapter 1 describes the beginning in regard to the 3 degrees in the same way as the other books; verse 11 "within three days ye shall pass over this Jordan," representing the 120th degree and corresponds to the mountains. The first four chapters deal with the capture of Jericho and the country thereabouts, as the promised land. Chapter 2: describes the entry into the country west and the trip over the mountain. The twelve men who were selected to pick up the stones is simply the mentioning of the twelve tribes. It is written that the stones were carried and put east of Jericho. The place called Gilgal where Joshua stopped is that part of California east of Oakland; the stones spoken of were dropped here and from this place the twelve tribes of Israel were formed. The entire book of Joshua is very interesting as it deals with California and describes the country in the capturing and slaying of an imaginary enemy, just forget the people and remember that it is the degrees which are being murdered. What is spoken of as the Red Sea is the Atlantic Ocean.

Chapter 6 describes the capture of Jericho, which is San Francisco, and corresponds to the emigration in 1848. It is evident that San Francisco was a great city at that time, as it is now. The woman Rahab is still living there; she was saved by Joshua then and was saved during the earthquake and fire of 1906. Chapter 7:22 deals with the tribe of Judah and the place Achor. It is shown that in this place can be found gold, silver, and oil. The Achor as spoken of is in the tribe of Judah which is the Los Angeles part of the country where the gold and oil are located. In chapter 8:29 is mentioned the Golden Gate and the coast range north of San Francisco which was called Ai. It was taken by strategy and is described as being taken in two divisions, one on each side of the coast range.

The country east of the mountains and west of the 115 degrees was captured during the age of Moses; and is part of the country of the twelve tribes described in chapter 9. Joshua captured everything around the central part of the state before going north, which contains the capture of the Shasta and Siskiyou Mountains. Chapter 9:3-6: "And when the inhabitants of Gibeon heard what Joshua had done unto Jericho and to Ai, they did work wilily, and went and made as if they had been ambassadors, and took old sacks upon their asses, and wine bottles, old, and rent, and bound up; And old shoes and clouted upon their feet, and old garments upon them; and all the bread of their provision was dry and mouldy. And they went to Joshua unto the camp at Gilgal, and said unto him, and to the men of Israel ,"We be come from a far country; now therefore make ye a league with us." Be sure and read chapter 9, it means that the people of the country north of San Francisco heard that Joshua had captured the territory east of the mountains and the bay district up to Humboldt County and that he was coming north to take their country and they were afraid. When the inhabitants of Gibeon heard about Joshua and his work, they played a trick on poor Joshua. An agreement was made whereby the inhabitants of this part of the state should be the servants of the country to the south; they should be the "hewers of wood and the drawers of water unto the congregation." This describes that there is woods in Northern California and that the Sacramento river runs out from this section of the coast. The location of the tribe spoken of is described in verse 16 as being three days' journey north (3 degrees), which is the Shasta district and the home of Gibeon.

Joshua next goes south and slays all in the country south and slays five kings in all. That is, he slew and captured everybody from San Francisco to San Diego, which is from Jericho to Gaza.

We aim only to give a reference to the chapters in the Bible for topic and location and to show that it is California and not Palestine, which is spoken of. We expect all Bible students, when they read this book, to refer to the Bible for every chapter. The description of the country is fairly good, as for instance the Bible says: "Lachish is two days journey south;" and it corresponds to Lake Tulare, which is 2 degrees south of San Francisco. Chapter 10:32.

Southern California is divided into five sections and is described in Joshua 10:5. It is the five kings of the Amorites: Jerusalem, Hebron, Jarmuth, Lachish and Eglan.

In chapters 11 to 19 are the descriptions of the capture of the land north of the Shasta mountains, which are the states of Oregon and Washington.

Part III—Chapter 19.

After the three coast states had been captured, Joshua divided the country into the twelve tribes and gave their location, described in another chapter.

The twelve tribes, as described by Joshua, are located from the 30th degree to the 49th degree north latitude, that is, from the Gulf of California in Mexico to British Columbia. The Philistines and Phœnicia are north of the United States.

The seven tribes are on the west side of the mountains and the three tribes of Reuben, Gad and the half tribe of Manasseh on the east side. For the description of the seven tribes read Joshua 10:19 and try to discern the reference made in the description. From San Francisco up to the Columbia river in Oregon is a good guide for Ephraim and Manasseh. The Puget Sound for Naphtali, Asher and Zebulun; Southern California corresponds to Judah and Simeon.

The entire book of Joshua describes the entering and capturing of the Pacific Coast and the dividing up of the country into the twelve tribes.

There is neither religion nor philosophy in this book; it consists of description of land and boundaries of the divisions of the tribes. Joshua's period of time is 110 years (degrees), beginning at the 120th degree west and extends to the 130th degree east, which takes us across the Pacific Ocean to Japan.

During Joshua's time he made the sun stand still for one day. Chapter 10:12. The change of time corresponds to the daylight saving of one hour during 1918-1919.

Joshua was not a prophet, he was a leader and held the same territory as Isaac in the age previous. Joshua died in 1443 B. C. in the Siskiyou Mountains, which is Mount Ephraim and was buried on the north side of the hill, as described in chapter 24:29-30. It must be remembered that the age of Joshua extended across the ocean and that the tribes on the coast are part of the tribes in Japan and China up to the 120 degrees.

The last two chapters, 23 and 24, refer to the oceans in specific terms. In chapter 23:4 it says "even unto the great sea westward." In chapter 24:3, "And I took your father Abraham from the other side of the flood, and led him throughout all the land of Canaan." This reference is made to prove that the Bible writers knew that there were two oceans and that the earth was globular.

Joshua represents Uranus in all and every act in the dealings with the tribes.

The next age is the description of the period north of San Francisco with Siskiyou Mountains as a center; which is the period of the Judges. This period in the north is also described in other books of the Bible as the "Ten Tribes" and "Samaria," which is later included with "Galilee." It takes in the states of Oregon and Washington.

The Shasta Springs in northern California are described in Judges 1:13-15, showing that the springs were there in the time of the Judges. They were called "the upper and nether springs."

The five books of Moses represent the period in degrees from the beginning of the Bible history in 4004 B. C. to 2552 B. C., as degrees. The book of Joshua contains a life history of 110 years (degrees), but Joshua's time represents only nine degrees on the Pacific Coast. His time in years, as calculated in the Bible was from the time Moses died in 1452 B. C. (120 degrees west) to Joshua's time. Joshua's period began at 1452 and ends in 1443; making 9 degrees in latitude. Calculations can be made of these years according to the 360-degree cycle and the location of Joshua will be found to be at the beginning of the 8th circuit around the earth. Divide 2552 by 360, which equals seven cycles and corresponds to the Pacific Coast period. The age of 1443 can be calculated the same way, as four times 360 are 1440 and the 3 degrees extra are for the 3 degrees at the end of all cycles.

CHAPTER 20.

REPETITIONS OF CYCLES.

The book of Judges contains a description of the tribes on the Pacific Coast and is a continuation of the age of Joshua. The age of the Judges is for the country north of San Francisco and rules the seven tribes of Israel. It should be remembered that Moses and Joshua divided the country west from Salt Lake and Colorado river, from Mexico to British Columbia and to the Pacific Ocean.

The five tribes of Judah and the seven tribes of Israel as the opposing element spoken of elsewhere can be compared from description. The twelve tribes, representing the cycle for Europe today, are the same division of the five and seven at war now. Germany with her allies are the five tribes of Judah and the other seven are Israel.

We will state here that the original five tribes are the children of Shem, which is Asia and the seven represent the children of Japhet which again is Europe. These two factions are the twelve tribes of Israel.

The age which began with Moses at Greenwich includes Joshua, Judges, Ruth, Samuel, Saul and with David covers the cycle from Greenwich to Greenwich.

The Judges represent the country north of San Francisco with the Siskiyou Mountains as the center and holy mountains called Mt. Ephraim. This is the section also named "Canaan" and the "Ten Tribes."

The sons of Zebedee represent Zebulun the twins, an airy house of a double nature. The two mountains of Mt. Baker and Glacier Peak represent this tribe.

The tribe of Asher is on the coast from California to Puget Sound. The Olympic mountains are located in this tribe and were called Tyre and Tyrus, representing one of the holy mountains for Asher. The tribe of Asher represents Greece in the cycle for Europe and misled the translators to place all events of the tribe of Asher in Greece.

The tribe of Isacher included the mountains of St. Helens, Mt. Adams and up to Mt. Rainer. The original place described as the burying ground for the cycles of time is in Cancer, as the tribe of Issacher. This tribe is located in the southern part of the state of Washington and is described as the original Magiddo and the plains of Esdraelon. This tribe and place in the cycle for Europe correspond to Belgium as the Armageddon for the age of Europe. It is the place where the age is killed and the location of the tribe corresponds in all cycles.

The twelve tribes on the Pacific Coast are called the Israelites proper and their home is in Canaan and Judah is in Jerusalem.

The twelve tribes of Asia are in Babylon with Ur in Chaldeah to represent the temple of Judah.

Europe was called Egypt and the temple of Zion is the Alps as the holy mountain for Judah and the five tribes of Judah were called Jews for short instead of Judah.

For the benefit of Bible students not familiar with astrology, we will explain the reason why the same names are given to places in America and also in Europe and Asia. Horoscopes are set up for a 30-degree or 40-degree distance and the names of the places within this figure are the same for all cycles. This can best be explained by the formation of the twelve tribes; as the names of the tribes are the same in Europe as in America. The nature of the tribes are also the same and are given in the same order as a horoscope, regardless of the country and distance it is set up for. This can best be illustrated by the name of Moab, which is located as Arabia in Asia and in the United States it is located as Arizona. The distance as described from "Dan to Beer-Sheba" in Europe is from Austria-Hungary to Spain and in the United States it is from Colorado river on the 115 degrees to British Columbia. The best way of locating the places as described, is in the method used in writing of the names, as a slight difference is made in spelling the same names in the different cycles. From this it will be seen that there is Ephraim, Manasseh, etc., in all cycles around the earth but the location corresponds in all cycles.

It should be remembered that after Joshua's time a cycle consists of fifty years. This corresponds to 60 degrees in space beginning at the 120th degree west.

The space calculated for the Judges consists of 60 degrees and is the last of the cycles terminating at 120 degrees east.

Without going into detail in describing the cycle from the Judges to David, a general outline only will be given.

The book of Judges is a continuation of the story of Joshua's age, beginning in 1452 B. C. The life and activity of the Judges is extended from America to Asia. The actual work of the Judges is the dividing of and judging between the tribes; giving judgment and explaining aspects. This can best be explained by Samson. His father was of the tribe of Dan (Scorpio) and his mother was of Manasseh (Taurus), and the son was the tribe Judah as Leo (Lion). The incident of Samson and his wives represents the time of age in the Pacific Northwest and in crossing the Pacific Ocean. Samson is the illustration of the house of Lion. The strength of Samson shows the character of the house; the power of Judah, which the house represents. Samson's two wives are Virgo and Libra in the Ocean.

The time of the change across the Pacific Ocean is described in the Book of Ruth. This book is for the south and represents Mexico as south of 36 degrees in going across the Ocean.

Part III—Chapter 20.

The time for the change from the American side to Asia is described as Deborah and Barak. Judges 5. The Book of the Judges covers the period up to the 120th degree in Asia.

The two Books of Samuel represent the age of Asia and Europe. It is the cycle of Samuel, Saul and David which repeats the cycle of Jacob, Israel and Joseph. The age of King David corresponds to the age of Moses and also to the story of Jesus, covering the distance of Europe.

The beginning of the new age, as described in Solomon, is for the age of the American cycle and written in the Books of the Kings. The age of Solomon is from the end of David's rule in Europe to Nebuchadnezzar's age, ruling in Babylon as Asia from 600 B. C.; which is from the 180th degree east of Greenwich. Second Kings, 24:

Solomon is the son of David and his age is the most important, for it takes place at 120 degrees west at the Pacific Coast division. It will be noted, when the Bible describes events on the Pacific Coast, these events always have the greatest leaders, men with prophetic power and wisdom, and is the beginning of the cycles.

Solomon became a leader of Israel 480 years after the time Moses led the Israelites out of Egypt. First Kings, 6:1. In order to prove that Solomon's time was at 120 degrees west, we will repeat the four ages of 120 degrees each, making the 480 years spoken of; Moses, Joshua, Judges, Samuel, Saul and David ruled the time from Greenwich to Greenwich, which is 360 degrees. David began to rule in Europe and extends to 120 degrees west, making 480 degrees in all.

Solomon's age is from 1012 B. C. to the time of Nebuchadnezzar at 600 or 606 B. C., including all the rulers from the Pacific Coast in the United States to China. In this period of time the Israelites had been killed and destroyed again and Nebuchadnezzar became ruler supreme.

The Bible students of modern time have figured back to Nebuchadnezzar's time and find him to be the ruler of Persia in the sixth century B. C. They do not figure farther back and here is where the present day Bible students begin.

The age of Solomon extends over into China at 120 degrees east. Nebuchadnezzar's age is figured from 120 degrees east, at the east coast of China and his cycle precedes the cycle of Alexander the Great at 336 B. C. and also that of Cæsar's at 40 B. C. to the Christian age. From this is will be seen that Nebuchadnezzar did rule east of Persia and had charge of the Asiatic period before what is known as the Christian age.

Alexander and Cæsar are the last of the old cycle and deal strictly with Asia-Europe as the age governing the country from Asia to Europe, and to the end of the age.

The Christian, or Christ period, is the European division of the age which began with Nebuchadnezzar as the Asiatic age. The Christian earth life age ends at Greenwich in 1920. The spiritual life of the Christian age is the Apostle Paul's history which ends in 2000, in the Pacific division.

We have taken each period and age consecutively and have shown what an age is and who and what the age represents. We have shown the westward movements of these periods and ages around the earth for four times. Each period consists of three cycles or rulers. We explained in detail the first six ages, to show the method used in finding the location of the age. Much could be written and explained but there are too many chapters in the Bible to explain. Some of these explanations will not be understood unless the students are familiar with the study of the heaven, as well as the Bible, because the names and expressions used will be as much of a mystery as the Bible. But to students of nature history it will be simple.

The main points to be considered are that the history, as recorded in the Bible, is not confined to Palestine and the south of Europe, but that it extends around the earth. When years are spoken of in the Bible they represent the degrees of longitude. An age is a cycle of 1000 years as degrees. There are two periods to the cycle. It takes six ages to make the six days of the creative period of the earth. The seventh age as days is the age corresponding to the "Garden of Eden" story. The Bible contains history for seven ages only.

The recorded history of the Bible begins at 4004 B. C. and the present age ends at 1920 and 2000. From this we figure that the age just closing is the last of the great cycles of 6000 years. We can depend on the actual year to year method of figuring ages as applied in the Bible, for it is correct. We believe that we have passed a period of time of 6000 years since Adam's recorded history and we know we are not far off. The beginning of time is 4004 and 1920 makes 5924 and if we add one cycle for the spiritual life of Jesus of eighty years (which is the time of Uranus) we get 6004 years in 2004 A. D. We have given the ages as calculated by the degrees and feel confident the Bible figures are correct.

It will be found that the age beginning at 4004 B. C. and ending at 1920 is not the complete age of 6000 years. There are 3960 years in the periods from Adam to the beginning of the Christian age at 40 B. C. The Christian age consists of 2000 years and 1920 leaves us at 5920, lacking 80 years to complete the age. This 80 years is the circuit of Uranus in the Pacific Coast period and illustrates the end of the cycle for the American age. The end of Bible history is not fulfilled as Nero in 2000 A. D. will destroy the United States. This period is described in the Acts, Chapters 27 and 28; as the life of the Apostle Paul.

When Jesus ascended to heaven it is written that two men stood by him. These two men are two degrees, which are counted from the time of 1920 when Jesus as an age will begin in his spiritual Kingdom. This period of two degrees of 144 years ends in 2064 when the space representing this age is killed, and is for the distance to 264 degrees west, or 96 east in Thibet.

The six ages from Adam in 4004 are divided into the different cycles from Greenwich to Greenwich in the following order.

The first cycle consists of Adam, Eve and Abel-Cain.

The second cycle is called Noah, with his three sons, Ham, Shem and Japeth, from 2948 to 1998.

The third cycle represents Abraham, Isaac, Jacob, with Joseph and part of Moses, to 1571.

The fourth cycle represents Moses, Joshua, Judges, Samuel-Saul and part of David, to 1015.

The fifth cycle consists of David, Solomon, Nebuchadnezzar, Alexander and up to the Romans, 1012 to 40 B. C.

The sixth cycle represents the Roman power and is the Christian age, from 40 B. C. to 1920.

The age described as 4 B. C. corresponds to 1776 and represents 4 degrees of 72 years each consisting of 288 years. The four degrees of 288 years are added to 1776 and we get 2064 which is the end of the cycle.

The ages from Adam to the Apostle Paul's time describes the condition on this earth for six cycles as the six days of creation.

The seventh cycle as a day is after the time Jesus ascended to heaven when the disciples are teaching the spiritual life of Christ, which begins in 1921 as the life of the Apostle Paul.

There is no reason given in the Bible why God's children had to be born and destroyed as illustrated in the cycles. The only information given is, that as it is in heaven, so is it on the earth; which is the best and clearest description that it is the laws of the heavens which are meant. The Bible has been so carefully written that it has been impossible until now to read and explain the system used.

We do not care to make a guess for the beginning of time as given in the Bible and when the Bible was last understood. It is, however, apparent that the Greeks, Egyptians and those in Palestine and in the Euphrates valley did not understand the entire system used in the Bible. This fact could not be known at those ages when the Pacific Coast country was not known and populated. The last age describing America is for Solomon's time, previous to Nebuchadnezzar, and we believe that the Bible has been a secret ever since, except for what Mohammed obtained out of the Bible as described in the Koran.

The final and closing description of history as described in the Bible is in the story illustrating the life of the Apostle Saul-Paul.

The spiritual age as represented by the Apostle Paul takes place after the cycle of Europe and is for the Pacific Coast cycle. Paul travels across the Pacific Ocean and is shipwrecked at the International Date Line. (180 degrees). Paul was stung by the sign Scorpio at this age. The last part of Paul's story describes Japan and China up to the final and closing period of Bible history, when at the end of Nero's rule, Paul is killed.

CHAPTER 21.

SOLOMON'S EMPIRE.

Solomon's Empire age is a well-known topic and interesting as a study. Solomon's age is from 1033, he ruled from 1012 and is supposed to have died in 975 B. C. His empire consisted of the territory on the Pacific Coast both in America and Asia, his father, David was the founder of the Empire and constitute the American cycle. After Solomon's time the Empire was divided into five kingdoms.

Part III—Chapter 21.

The Kingdom of Syria was on the north coast and westward from the Rocky Mountains to the Ocean; it included the entire circuit of Washington and the Puget Sound country. (In describing the Pacific Ocean, the name Euphrates is used).

The next is the kingdom south of Syria and is the Kingdom of Israel of Ten Tribes, founded by Jeroboam, 975 B. C., at the death of Solomon. At the time this kingdom was a large territory; it took in at one time the country from San Francisco to British Columbia. This kingdom ruled the country east of the mountains and was called "east of the Jordan." This Empire of Israel is Oregon and California north of San Francisco. It had nineteen kings representing several dynasties. The capitals were changed to several cities; it was first located at Shechem, then at Omri; the last place was Samaria, which soon became to Israel a center, as Jerusalem was to Judah. Later the name of Samaria was applied to the entire division. This is northern California and Oregon on both sides of the mountains. They had two sanctuaries within the province, one in the territory of the tribe of Dan at the northeast and Bethel on the south, where the national calculations were made. At that time the calf or bull, as the age of Manasseh was used. The country as divided north and south was figured from the Siskiyou Mountains south to San Francisco and the temple north was the border of Syria or Washington.

The kingdom of Judah included the tribe of Judah, Benjamin and Simeon. Their country extended from the Bay of San Francisco and west of the mountains to the south into the desert east of San Diego. The low hills on the coast were called the Shefelah Mountains, and is the Coast Range, which was mentioned as important. The kingdom was ruled by twenty-nine kings all of one family. It was destroyed by Nebuchadnezzar 587 B. C. The fourth division is the Moab; this section was not called a kingdom for it used to be a dependency of the Kingdom of Israel, which ruled or controlled all the territory east of the mountains.

Moab, a desert country, extends from Arizona and Colorado River as western boundaries including Utah and Arizona, but how far east and south is not given.

The fifth division is Edom, which is also a dependency and was subject to Solomon's territory. It is the country west of Moab between Arizona and Colorado River as the eastern boundaries and the mountains west.

These five provinces, or kingdoms, are represented as the age of Solomon to the time of Nebuchadnezzar. The life and death struggle of these kingdoms extended over a period of time from 975 B. C. to 884, during which time the three kingdoms, Syria, Israel and Judah, were fighting for supremacy. This extends from the reign of Jeroboam to Jehu in the north, and from Rehoboam to Joash in Judah.

The next age mentioned is from 884 B. C. to 840; which is the beginning of the end; there were revolutions and trouble in all three of the coast Empires; Damascus, Samaria and Jerusalem when Hazael mounted the throne of Syria. Jehu of Israel and Athaliah the queen-mother ruled in Judah. This is a description of the tribes extending from the American side to the Asiatic side and is the Pacific States. It should be noted that passing the 180-degree longitude the queens ruled and the country to the east of their territory will now be captured as all of the territory east of Jordan was reduced to a vassalage. Israel was conquered; they took Judah and let Jerusalem stay after paying a heavy tribute.

The next topic is in 840 B. C. to 780; it is the time when the ten tribes rule in the northwest; it takes place when Jeroboam second ruled; both Judah and Syria were in due time made tributary to Samaria, which then became the leading power of Solomon's Empire. This period was marked as the era of two great prophets, Jonah and Joel. The short time of this age was called the "Indian Summer of Israel."

We will call attention to the fact that in this age, Jonah travelled across the Pacific Ocean in a whale.

The real fall of Israel took place in 780 B. C. to 721, for the decline of the nation was very rapid. It was through anarchy and uprising that the country was lost and practically melted away. The country on the other side in Asia was prosperous because their kings were warlike. Samaria was finally taken by Sargon and the ten tribes carried into captivity to Halah and Habor. This period is part of what is termed the Assyrian age, as it extended over into China.

The fall of Judah, as a power, took place from 721 B. C. to 587 and extended 100 years after the fall of Israel, but was subject to the laws of the "great king" of Assyria, which is in Asia. This is the final history of the Great Solomon's Empire, which is the same cycle as that of Joshua and the Judges.

CHAPTER 22.

NEBUCHADNEZZAR'S DREAM.

Book of Daniel, chapter 2, describes that: "There is a God in heaven that revealeth secrets, and maketh known to the king Nebuchadnezzar what shall be in the latter days." In a dream by night the Lord gave to Nebuchadnezzar, king of Babylon, a clear historical outline of the course of world empire to the end of time and the coming of the eternal kingdom. "Thou, O king, sawest, and behold a great image. This great image, whose brightness was excellent, stood before thee; and the form thereof was terrible." "This image's head was of fine gold, his breast and his arms of silver, his belly and his thighs of brass, his legs of iron, his feet part of iron and part of clay." "Thou sawest till that a stone was cut out without hands, which smote the image upon his feet that were of iron and clay, and brake them to pieces. Then was the iron, the clay, the brass, the silver, and the gold, broken to pieces together, and became like the chaff of the summer, threshing floors; and the wind carried them away, that no place was found for them; and the stone that smote the image became a great mountain, and filled the whole earth."

The prophet next declared the interpretation. And now follows the history of the world. The parts of the image, then, of various metals, from head to feet, represented successive empires, beginning with the Chinese Empire as the kingdom of Babylon, represented by Nebuchadnezzar, was the head of gold. The breast and arms of silver in the great image represented India-Afghanistan, which followed the Babylonian, "inferior" to it in brilliancy and grandeur, as silver is inferior to gold.

"And another third kingfidom of brass, which shall bear rule over all the earth." The third kingdom" after Babylon was Persia which overthrew the empire of India-Afghanistan. And Persia's dominion fulfilled the specifications of the prophecy, which indicated a yet wider expansion of empire. Its sway was to be over "all the earth," said Daniel, the prophet, foretelling itsh istory.

While Persia's supremacy under Alexander was disputed by none, there was a power rising in the west that was soon to enter the lists for the prize of world dominion. Some of the ancint writers say that at the time of his death Alexander had in mind to push westward to strike down the growing power of the city of Rome, of which he had heard. Plutarch says that this man, Alexander, "who shot like a star, with incredible swiftness, from the rising to the setting sun, was meditating to bring the luster of his arms into Italy. * * * He had heard of the Roman power in Italy." Sure it is that after Persia there followed the Roman Empire, the strongest and mightiest and most crushing of them all. This fourth universal empire the prophet proceeded to describe, as represented by the legs of iron in Nebuchadnezzar's dream of the great image.

"The fourth kingdom shall be strong as iron; forasmuch as iron breaketh in pieces and subdueth all things: and as iron that breaketh all these, shall it break in pieces and bruise." Next is described the Kingdoms of Modern Europe.

"Whereas thou sawest the feet and toes, part of potters' clay, and part of iron, the kingdom shall be divided; but there shall be in it the strength of the iron, forasmuch as thou sawest the iron mixed with miry clay. "And as the toes of the feet were part of iron, and part of clay, so the kingdom shall be partly strong and partly broken. And whereas thou sawest iron mixed with miry clay, they shall mingle themselves with the seed of men: but they shall not cleave one to another, even as iron is not mixed with clay." The fifth part, or clay, is the nations of Europe not controlled by the Roman power. As the stone cut out of the mountain "without hands," smote the image in such a manner that all its parts, representative of national dominion, were ground to dust and blown away, so the coming kingdom, set up "without hands," by no human power, but by the power of the eternal God, will rule the nations of the earth.

The stone which smote the image on its feet is a representation of the present world's war. The feet of the image represent the feet or end of the age in Europe, as a cycle of time. The image ground to dust means that the present form of governments for the nations east of Greenwich will be destroyed and a powerful combination of nations will form a new government, as illustrated in the great mountains, which filled the whole earth. This is the God's kingdom or Universal Republic, which is to have power over the entire world.

CHAPTER 23.

ALEXANDER THE GREAT'S EMPIRE.

This age can be divided into different nations; the Persian, the Macedonian, the Egyptian, the Syrian, the Maccabean, down to the Roman. Each had part of the country and ruled their given time. The Empire began in the east in 536 or 538 B. C. as the Persian Empire and extended to the beginning of the Roman Empire.

The beginning of a real independent nation in Palestine did not take place until the Maccabean age in 166 B. C. Palestine, as a nation, only existed 125 years. The rest of the time Palestine was a dependency of other nations. After Palestine comes Greece as a dividing line. The recorded history of Greece is the same story over again, it is a horoscope for that part of country for that time.

Rome as a power over the eastern nations began in 63 B. C. when Pompey captured Jerusalem, after which time the Romans had control over the entire country. The Maccabean as Greece ruled during the Roman age until 40 B. C.

The beginning of the Roman Empire was the birth of the Christian or European age, set at 40 B. C,. which is 40 degrees east longitude, and was during the time when Cleopatra was queen of Turkey. It was during Cleopatra's time that this part of the country became subject to Rome. Cleopatra ruled over Egypt and the rest of the nations in Turkey. She was forced by Rome to give birth to the Roman Empire as an age.

Turkey is the house of Naphtali or Virgo as a virgin, and Turkey and Palestine is the birthplace of the age. The great and beautiful queen Cleopatra ruled in Turkey at the time of the birth of the Christian or Roman Empire and she was the virgin, through which the Child was born, as seen from an historical point of view.

The years used in the Bible are the degrees; the Roman Empire and the Greek and Roman Churches represent the Christian religion as the Christian age. The beginning of the age was at 40 degrees B. C. The real beginning of the western or European age was at 63 degrees east. The rulers from 60 degrees to 40 degrees were the Maccabees and are included in the Roman division.

The Bible states that the time of the Roman Empire was from 40 degrees B. C. to 70 A. D., which is 110 years or degrees. 40 degrees east of Greenwich gives the eastern borders of Palestine where the Roman Empire begins. 70 A. D. gives the east coast of the United States at 70 degrees longitude west of Greenwich and here is where the Roman Empire as an age, dies.

CHAPTER 24.

THE SAVIOR.

Jesus, the Christ and Savior, has been described as a man, but is really a representation of a period of time as a cycle. It is the Christian age and is also known as the dominion of the Roman Empire.

The cycle as illustrated by Jesus is the last of the twelve similar periods of which the Bible gives a record, and is for the double house of Pisces. It is the cycle of time for the Greek and Roman Catholic Churches, which began when our solar center was at 36 degrees east and ends at 4 degrees east.

The few years of recorded history of Jesus has been illustrated by the Catholic and Christian Churches to have taken place in Palestine and this mistake we aim to correct.

First, it should be remembered that Jesus the Christ is always a representation of the planet Uranus "The Savior." Jesus as Uranus, was born in Palestine and his life (or cycle) continued until he was within four degrees of Greenwich, or in the Alps Mountains, where his life cycle ended. We must repeat that it is entirely a mistake to think that a philosophy and doctrine of life as complete as Jesus represents, covering the laws of the universe, could have been lived in thirty-two years by any human being. We should follow the laws as laid down by Moses and we will see, that the life principle as illustrated in the life of Jesus and his disciples is greater than any one man's life.

Christ represents a principle, a doctrine of life, the teachings of the Christian spirit of the age. The philosophy as presented in the Christian religions is in the true sense of the word Christianity, but the teachers of this doctrine are misinformed as to what the terms Christ or Savior mean. The Bible illustrates the doctrine of the Christ as a universal law of God. The Christian churches have made it a teaching of ceremony and church worship of a personal God. The Bible describes a universal and eternal life and the churches teach personal opinions regarding conditions in places called heaven and hell.

There have been millions of books published on the life of Christ in Palestine, and not one book about his life of 2000 years, giving the truth of what his life actually was.

The Savior has lived, as an age, in the name of the Greek and Roman Catholic Churches, and has been misrepresented.

His life work was perfect but the human race did not want to accept his teachings, and at the end of his time he was taken by force and crucified. He did not object to being crucified as he knew the scripture had to be fulfilled and he carried his cross and was crucified by the multitude who had listened to his teachings. From this it will be seen that the Christian nations are the crucifiers of Christ.

During the life of Christ a great mistake was made by all; that God needed an authorized assistant on earth, one who God appointed as dictator over his children. God needs no pope, priest or clergyman to represent him in the manifestations of His Laws of the universe, as his doctrines are for an eternal life, regardless of belief or man's opinion. The Bible illustrates that life is eternal and it does not matter where man lives and what his belief or opinions are, because life cannot be destroyed.

The circumcision (or reformation) spoken of in the Bible referred to the different races and in educating them to follow Christ and live according to Nature which is to worship God. To sin is to make error or mistakes and abuse the law, if we realize that life is eternal we should be educated not to make mistakes, which we will be sorry for later in life.

As the Christian age, as a period of time, had a beginning and ending, so has all life a time to manifest in, whether this manifestation be what is considered erroneous or not. The cycle of time for the Christian churches as well as for all other churches is now at an end, when the facts shall be known and the truth shall make all mankind free.

We have spoken of the life of Christ, which comes to an end in 1918 as an age. We will now take up the life of the Apostle Paul as a principle, described in the Book of Acts. The perfect and beautiful teachings as presented in the character of Christ is now illustrated by the Apostle Paul. The ancient Bible writers knew what would take place at the end of time, for they had observed the same conditions in former ages. We know that history has been written ahead of time for a reason. Disregarding the reason why, we will aim to explain that the philosophy of life as presented by Paul is transferred from Europe to the Pacific Coast. There is a reason why the life of Christ should be lived in Europe. After the termination of His age, a spiritual life or a life after death, is to be known, and brought out from the Pacific Coast States. We will give the same reason for this as the Bible does. Abraham, Isaac and Jacob did not want to be buried outside of the Land of Canaan; so the Christian age also is to come to an end in Canaan.

We will say for example that Christ as an age is dead and buried, that the time between 1918 and 1921 has passed. The three years between 1918 and 1921 represent the three days before Christ's resurrection. When the new age begins it will be found that a teaching will come from the Pacific Coast States which will positively prove that Christianity in the flesh is dead, but that a higher life, a life after death is a reality. The Bible gives us this information in the New Testament which is the law for the new age. The life as illustrated by the Apostles is the teaching that Christianity is not to die when Christ dies; but that Christ lives in the spirit. We will find that Christianity will leave the churches as creed organizations but will have the Christ within their hearts. This is the New Age. It is the life which shows that Christ had entered his heavenly home and lives with his father and rules the spiritual kingdom.

The teachings written in the new testament are to begin on the Pacific Coast and will spread over the entire world; this doctrine of eternal life will be the religion of the world for the next one thousand years.

The reason for this law is that there is a God-given law, a power above all, which is the father of all creation. God, the almighty father, and creator of worlds, has given this law. It is the same God who let the sun shine, the rain fall and the wind blow. Those who question the power of God to make this law are the ones who have false Gods, but we are informed that they have eyes to see and ears to hear, but see and hear not. In the new age the spirit will come over them and they will see and hear God. They will see that the death of Christ in the flesh on the battlefield of Europe is comparatively the same as the death of the human body of flesh; but as Christ rises from the dead and lives in the spirit so does the human being live after the torture of death, as life is eternal with the father. The philosophy of the Bible is to teach the principle that to die is to be born again from a lower to a higher form of expression. From this comes the term that "there is no death" for it is only a change.

We happen to live in the age when the Christ principle or doctrines change from the material, or church age, to the new age of the Universal Republic. The Christian spirit will now manifest God, and worship in temples not made with hands.

This is when God has destroyed the old and made all things new.

We have said that the manifestation of the new age will take place on the Pacific Coast and that the doctrine shall spread all over the worlds. We will now mention the places on the Pacific Coast where this teaching is going to originate. The Bible writers have described the place and we will give them according to the Scripture.

The City of Jerusalem corresponds to Los Angeles, and is to be the headquarters for missionary work. The Los Angeles section belongs to the tribe of Judah, as Leo, and is the heart of things on the Coast, spiritually. The people of Los Angeles will be the first to realize that Christ is not dead. Whenever the place of Jerusalem is spoken of in the Apostles' time, the Los Angeles section of California is meant.

The City of Gaza is San Diego, and here will be the establishment of schools and hospitals. San Diego will be the city for right and justice and the citizens there will practice the golden rule. As Los Angeles will be the headquarters for business, so will Gaza, as San Diego, be a place for spiritual unfoldment, a place for training of teachers who understand the Law of God. The Theosophical Society will now find Christ within, and they do not have to come back and reincarnate. San Diego County is in the country of the tribe of Simeon and is the home or house of the Son of God.

The city of San Francisco has been called by many names in Bible history. A new name has been given to this city in nearly every age. The oldest name on record is in Joshua's time when it was known as Jericho. San Francisco has always been illustrated as a bad woman but she was healed and saved in every instance.

It will be found that when San Francisco is spoken of, that the one who saved her was let down in a basket. The name of Ceasarea was used for San Francisco. There are many other names but these are the principal ones. In the later years Ceasarea was used. San Francisco is apparently not going to produce any special spiritual manifestations, but will be one of the headquarters for the reform movement. When the Apostle Paul is spoken of as going to Ceasarea he is going to San Francisco, and each one of his stops made on his various trips is made at this city. San Francisco is in the country of the tribe of Benjamin.

The city of Portland, Oregon, corresponds to Antioch and to Antiochus—Epiphanes of Greece. It is situated by the river Orontes, which corresponds to the Willamette River.

Antioch is situated, the Bible says, near a deep pass in the mountains, this represents the pass between the Taurus Mountains of Washington and the Lebanon Mountain range, which is the Cascade Mountains in Oregon. We will ask Bible students to take notice, that the Columbia River separates the Taurus and the Lebanon Mountains, and that the Willamette River is spoken of as the Orantes River. The city of Antioch corresponds to a great city and covers the territory where Portland is located. It must have been located on its present site because the description is perfect. It is one of the stopping places for the Apostle Paul and one of the places from which the gospel of truth is to come. Joshua sent his army north from Jericho; they came up through what is now the Willamette Valley but did not stop long in any place. They went as far as the Puget Sound and captured the country there. The Siskiyou Mountains are the Carmel Mountains spoken of. Portland is in the country of the tribe of Manesseh.

Ephesus corresponds to the city of Seattle. Speaking comparatively it is situated in Lydia and belongs to Greece. The population are Greeks and not very religious but good business people. This is at best the description given in treatise published in church literature. The cities on the Puget Sound are described in Bible study literature as being located in Greece and part of them in Asia. The travels of the Apostle Paul from Antioch and to the seven churches are very plain; the description is as accurate as though it had been written today.

The Puget Sound is illustrated as the Eagean Sea; Vancouver Island, British Columbia, is shown as Peloponesus, Corinth is Victoria and Athens corresponds to Vancouver City, B. C. The counties of the state of Washington on the Sound correspond to the places in Greece as from Thessalonia to Lycia. The inland country corresponds to Galatia, the situation of Spokane. The city of Tyre is the Olympic Mountains. The great Zidon is the mountain of Rainier; which is the highest mountain in the northwest.

The Bible students have made a great mistake in placing the travels of the Apostle Paul in Greece; but they had no other place to locate them for they did not fit in Palestine. The Bible says it is located west, so the translators made it Greece. It says he traveled from and to certain places and described the places. If the corresponding cities on the Sound were travelled by Paul; he took in Olympia as Tarsus; Tacoma as Patara in Lycia; Seattle as Ephesus in Lydia; Everett as Troas in Mysia; Spokane as Tavium in Galatia; and we believe the city of Iconium is located east of the mountains.

Paul, like Jesus, had a definite circuit to travel and he made his four journeys, including the retrograde action of Uranus, when Paul made a return loop on his trip. We must not forget that Paul is the planet Uranus and when it says he visits the seven churches in the west, he calls at the same time on the seven tribes or houses which are located west of the mountains.

At the time of the beginning of the new age in 1921, the Pacific Coast States will consist of five sections. See chapter on the United States regarding Judeah, Samaria, Galilee as the States of California, Oregon and Washington. East of the mountains Perrea is Nevada and Decapolis is the inland empire.

The next division is that of California, becoming a separate nation and having five tribes within her boundaries. The northwest as Oregon and Washington is to be a nation and has the seven and later the ten tribes. Paul travels the same road as Joshua and the Judges; he first stays in California, then he moves northwest and finally passes north on his way to China, where he is finally killed.

Part IV.

BIBLE PROPHECIES.

CHAPTER 25.

EARTH LIFE COMPARED.

It is our aim to show that the Bible contains the study of the heavens and that the Laws of Moses are the laws of the universe which govern the sun and planets in their respective orbits. Each and every one of the cycles of time which have passed have been illustrated as a human being and the life of each of the individuals, from birth to death, has been the representation of an age. The last of the periods of time is the life of Christ as illustrated in the Christian age, beginning with the Romans and Julius Cæsar and ending with the Romans and Kaiser Wilhelm.

The Christian age comes to an end with the crucifying of Christ in the present war, terminating in 1918.

The next age is the life of the Apostles and the same system is followed out in the new dispensation as in the former. When the patriarchs die there is always an individual who takes the place of the leading spirit. When Christ died the Apostle Saul-Paul became the leader; he will now represent the planet Uranus in the next generation for he is Saul at the beginning of the cycle at 120 degrees west and becomes Paul in the north Pacific Coast divisions. It is the same story over, only the story is now of a spiritual nature.

We will repeat here what we have stated elsewhere that the illustrations as pictured in the Bible are the moving westward with the degrees of the Zodiac and that the planet Uranus is the center from which this calculation is made.

The earth is divided into three great divisions of 120 degrees each constituting an age. The great cycle begins and ends at Greenwich time, but the ages begin at 40 degrees east and terminate at 80 degrees west from each of the three 120-degree cycles. This means that 360 degrees are divided into three 120-degree ages; which is again divided into three 40-degree ages.

In order to illustrate this, we will say that the constellations and the stars constitute a universe. The earth is a universe in itself and so is each part of the earth within certain degrees, a cycle within a cycle. There are several divisions of the earth

Part IV—Chapter 25.

within the zone of Uranus, which according to the Bible, are centers for the patriarchs. The Uranus zone is a belt of 24 degrees width and is between 24 degrees and 54 degrees latitude north, which encircles the globe.

The calculation of ages is for a distance of degrees and the length of the age is according to the number of degrees within a given space. The cycle, or ages, as figured within the zone of Uranus consist of degrees counted from Greenwich, and contain one year for each degree; the different cycles are divided into minor angles or ages according to the nature of the country described. A center is established and degrees calculated west- and east from this center, which constitute a cycle.

The ancient or Bible writers set up a figure of the heavens and called it a life time for their particular section according to the age they lived in. That is, the Greeks set up a figure for their cycle; the Babylonians set up for Asia and the Turks set up a figure for Palestine for their time. This is what is known today as the setting up of a horoscope, called a nativity.

The figure for a nation or age is the building of their temple; that is, if a figure is to be set up for the United States, the 40 degrees east longitude and the 80 degrees west of the 120th degree is used as a center. The twelve houses or signs of the heavens are then arranged according to the law, as laid down by Moses, and calculations made for the time when the planets pass through the twelve houses. The planets Uranus, Neptune and Saturn are the planets which are spoken of in the Bible together with the fixed stars.

The dividing and subdividing of each part of the country is decribed in detail in the books of Moses and Joshua. The twelve children of any of the old patriarchs or the twelve divisions of the heavens are simply the dividing of space into the twelve sections. The division of seven spoken of in the Bible are the seven houses; for instance, the seven churches are the seven tribes of Israel; the five houses are the five tribes of Judah; which are the opposition element in Israel.

The main features to be considered are the travels of the planet as illustrated by the patriarchs or age through the heavens and the aspects of the planets to each other and to the different locations. When it states in the Bible that Jesus travelled from one town or location to another it is a representation of the travels of Uranus through the twelve houses of the figure for Europe. From this will be seen why Jesus did not get outside of a very small space, as the horoscope set for Palestine was for only a few miles.

The horoscope which was set up by the ancient Bible writers for the Apostle Paul, is set up for the Pacific Coast section. The entire coast is laid out and described in the Bible. We will take the space and describe this part of the story in detail, as it is apparent the writers were very well familiar with the country.

The horoscope for the Pacific Coast reaches from Mexico to British Columbia and from Utah to the Pacific Ocean. The coast was laid out in the twelve divisions and called tribes. The same names for the twelve tribes are used here as were described to be in Palestine and represent the character and nature of the country. The names of the cities as described in the age of Palestine were used, but many new names were given. The names of the cities of Jerusalem, Gaza, Bethlehem and many others were used, but in the north, Greek names were given. The Bible students who have illustrated that the Apostle Paul's travels were in Greece have failed utterly, and they say themselves that they do not know where the travels, as recorded, take place.

The Apostle Paul is Uranus and his trips up and down the Pacific Coast are the travels in the twelve houses. Uranus stays seven years in each house and his time can easily be figured. The other Apostles or helpers he had represent the houses he meets and works with in his mission. The Apostle Peter spoken of is the house of Ephraim or Aries and when it says that Paul sent for a certain helper to meet him in a city or place, it means that the helper is the house he is going to, which he has sent for. So instead of going to the place, he sends for the place to meet him. It will be found that the description of Simon-Peter, James and all the disciples of Jesus representing the tribe is written in the New Testament and is a representation of the European Age. The description of the Israelites is found in the Old Testament and represents the nations of Europe called Egypt, and in Asia is called Babylonians.

It should be remembered when studying the Bible that the Israelites and Judeah tribes are the Twelve European Nations of today, and are called the Jews and Israelites in many places in the Bible. The opposition of Israel are the Jews and constitute the five tribes of the Germans, Turks, and their Alps. The records of the Judah tribes are the Mormon Bible and the records of the Israelites as twelve tribes are the Jewish or Christian Bible.

The seven tribes of Israel are the nations of France, England, Scandinavia, Italy, Switzerland, Russia and Spain. The five tribes of Judah are Germany, Austria-Hungary, Greece, Turkey and Holland-Belgium.

The two Bibles with the prophecies for the present time correspond, that is, both Bibles say that the Israelites will win the war and that Judah will lose and be driven out of their country. The coming or new age, however, will be in peace and harmony, for the "lion and the lamb shall lay down together" and one shall not hurt the other. From this we see in the prophecies what the condition in Europe will be, as it will terminate in peace, happiness, and friendship.

CHAPTER 26.

HISTORICAL EVENTS.

It will be necessary to give an outline of history as recorded by historians of Bible study, so we may know that it is a fact that the historical events as recorded are the moving of the tribes westward. It must be remembered that a nation, tribe, a section or an empire, means the same. It is the building of the temple as the building of Jerusalem and means the setting up of a horoscope for a given territory. It is the same as the Roman Empire, which means an age. The temple, or age, for Rome is from 40 degrees east to 70 degrees west. The destruction of the different temples is the capturing and killing of the old cycles or territory when the new and western kingdoms and empires become rulers. This is the slow progress of the moving with the degrees and civilization westward and around the earth which is spoken of elsewhere.

As the history of all ages has been recorded to have taken place in Palestine and nearby countries, so have the names of the cities and places there been given by the translators of the Bible. This is best illustrated by the name of Jerusalem; this city is in Palestine and represents the same to Palestine as Rome does to the Roman Empire. It is not Rome as a city which is meant; it is the Roman power as a nation and church controlling an age. The city of Rome is a Jerusalem, and the Christian religion is now being crucified and the Romans as Catholics and Christians are the crucifiers of the age. The city of Constantinople is described the same way and is another city on "Seven Hills," the same as Rome. Constantinople is the home for the harlot of the Mohammedan Church and represents the cycle of Asia and is the Jerusalem for the degrees between 30 and 60 east. It is very unfortunate that the names of Palestine should be translated and used for places in Asia, Europe, and America, but as all names and places correspond to a given location it is easy to follow.

In reference to the period of time as recorded in the Bible, we find that the beginning of Bible history corresponds to the year 4004 B. C. We will copy a few eventful cycles in order to show that all dates correspond to the cycles we have given.

From Adam's time 4004 to the cycle of Noah 2948 is 1056 years. From Noah to Abraham in 1996 is 952 years. From Abraham to David 1085 is 911 years. From David to the Roman Empire in 40 is 1045 years. The first 40 years of the age of the Romans are added to the old cycle in order to make it correspond to 4004 years in all. The ages as given are copied from the Bible and are correct.

The following years also copied from the Bible for the purpose of giving students of cycles dates to figure from.

From Adam 4004, at Greenwich, to Noah on the Pacific Ocean at the time of the flood in 2348 is 1656 years. From the flood to the beginning of Abraham's cycle at Greenwich in 1921 is 427 years. From the time Abraham enters Canaan in 1921 to Moses' death in 1452 is 469 years. From the death of Moses in 1452 to the time of Solomon in 1012 is 440 years. From the time of Solomon in 1012 to the time of captivity in Babylon in 588 is 424 years. From 588, which is the beginning of the Asiatic age called the captivity, to the Roman Age at 50 B. C. is 538 years. We must add the 50 years of the Roman cycle to make the full 4004 years.

It is interesting to note that the year when Abraham entered Canaan (United States) was 1921 B. C. This is the time of the ending of the cycle at Greenwich and corresponds to our own year of 1921 A. D. Abraham was born in 1996 but he is allowed 75 years to build a temple, which is the 75 degrees across the Atlantic Ocean. We subtract the 75 from 1996 and get 1921. Take the age of Belshazzar's feast in Nebuchadnezzar's time at 538. This age can be figured accurately and the location of the place calculated to the degree. We follow the system, as explained in the chapter of cycles, and use the 360 degrees for years. Deduct first one cycle of 360 degrees from 538 and you

Part IV—Chapter 26.

have 178 degrees. From an atlas of the world can be figured 178 degrees west of Greenwich and we find the place where the cycles begin at the International Date Line.

This is the beginning and place of Modern Bible study, where history was made, as pictured from Nebuchadnezzar to the time at 30 degrees east to the Egyptian age. The Julian Calendar's age begins with the Egyptian period and extends to 1921.

The 2300-year period as spoken of in the Bible is the 32 degrees from Palestine to the Alps. This is the time that the Bible system of figuring 72 years to the degree can be proved, for 32 times 72 is 2304 years. Palestine is 36 degrees east and Belgium 4 degrees east, making the age of Christ 32 years.

Egypt is translated as the center from which all the calculations were figured for Joseph's time.

Egypt is located at 30-degree latitude as well as 30-degree longitude and was a great center up to the time of Greece and Rome. It must be remembered that the time of figuring degrees for Egypt stops with the Roman age. It is, however, interesting to follow Bible history to see what periods each age describes. Nebuchadnezzar began at 600 B. C., which is 62 degrees before Belshazzar, who ruled at the 182nd degree east. The beginning and ending of the empires is figured the same way in degrees. Nebuchadnezzar's period began at the 120th degree east and from this to the 30th degree in Egypt is easy to follow. The 70 years referred to as Jerusalem's fall, is the 70 degrees west of Greenwich as being added to the Roman age.

The degrees to figure from are, Nebuchadnezzar at the 120th degree east and the beginning of the Roman Empire began 40 B. C. (degree) east to 70 degrees west of Greenwich. From this can be figured all the ages within this period in years. Do not confuse the Julian Calendar years with the beginning degree of the Roman Empire, for the Calendar changed time later. We will, however, follow the story of the Bible and make comparison as to the time of events.

It should be understood that both the Mohammedan and Christian Churches are described in the Bible and that it is very difficult at times to know which one is meant, but since both represent the same principle and are described the same, and both are going to their doom at the end of time, it is immaterial which one is meant.

We can go back and figure from the time at the beginning of the cycle at 538 B. C. All Bible students know that this is the beginning of a complete generation. From 538 B. C. to 538 in the Christian Age gives 1076; this is Pope Gregory's time.

Bible students have found that the year 1798 is the end of a certain cycle, but can give no reason for it. It is apparent that this year is the end of the time for church cycle; which is correct. The darkest of all the periods of church time was when Pope Gregory the seventh (Hildebrand) held the power in Rome at 1078. It was at the time of the trouble with King Henry of Germany that the Pope ruled and ruined. The central or controlling power of Christianity reached its height in the year of 1078. The cycle began at 538 degrees to which we have to add the 1260 degrees (years) which brings us to 1798. The 1260 represents the seven houses as the time from 538, which is 7 times 180 and equals 1260. Which again is from Belshazzar's space to Greenwich. The year 1798 subtracted from 1918 leaves 120 years (degrees west).

In 538 at the time of Belshazzar, who is also called the Prophet Daniel. He gives us time to figure, and describes the different periods up to the end. He illustrates the different times with the picture of animals to show the nations and conditions which would be during the next 2300 years. Read in the 10th chapter of Daniel and the entire vision is very clear. It should be remembered that each division consists of 180 years to each house of the heaven and three houses make one division of a quarter cycle of 540 years. When Daniel makes a calculation of time, it is for the houses of heaven, but Gabriel is the planet Uranus and when he is spoken of for time, it is the 84-year period.

We will take 538 B. C. as the beginning and add a cycle 538 A. D. giving 1076 the time of Pope Gregory. The time of Uranus is 84 years and he has made twelve revolutions, 12 times 84 equals 1008. Add the 70 years (for Jerusalem's fall) making 1078. It will be found that 1080 is one-half of 2160 years and in this age all three of the planets were in the same aspect to each other, as they are at the present time.

The following is an extract from a book published by the Seventh Day Advent Church: "Which then is the Church? The one which rose at about the time, and operated 42 prophetic months, or 1260 years, (538-1798) was the papacy. She calls herself the Holy Catholic Church." This is a fact in both ways and we take it for granted the church was established in 538. We will show that God established the church Empires according to his wisdom, and also all other churches. Take the year 538 or 540, figure any way you want, you will not go many years out of the way. The 1260 year, as here spoken of, is the time of the seven houses of the earth, each house is 180 years and seven churches of Israel makes 1260 years. The planet Uranus makes a circuit in 84 years; half of 84 is 42 years or prophetic months.

The 2300 period can also be calculated in a previous cycle from the time of the flood. This is in 2348 B. C. and when we allow for the 49 years to the Roman age, it will be found correct.

We will give one more positive figure that the Bible ages as given in years, are the degrees as figured from Greenwich. The ages, as given by the Prophet Daniel, gives us the correct degrees to figure from. Daniel describes the beginning of the age for Asia-Europe as the Church-Empire from 538 B. C. It is described in the book of Daniel that at the time of the end certain events would take place. The years of 1260, 1290 and 1335 are spoken of as eventful and at the conclusion of these events as described, is the time of the end. The year 538 B. C. together with 1260 brings us to 1798. Which is the year of the beginning of the end of the Roman Church, when the Pope was taken prisoner by France. The next is 538 degrees and 1290 degrees; by adding these we get 1828; this is the end of the Turkish rule as a Mohammedan power when Turkey lost in the war with Russia. The year of 1828 was the beginning of the special cycle of Uranus of his last circuit of the houses. To 1828 add 84, the time of Uranus and this gives 1912, which is the year Uranus entered the house of Aquarius and when the Balkan war started. We next take 538 and add 1335 and we get 1873, the end of the Prussian-Franco wars; which brought on the hateful condition between France and Germany.

In Daniel 12:5 is described a prophecy of a period of years to the end of time. It says "it shall be for a time, times and a half." "A time" is a cycle of 360 degrees, "times" is two cycles or 720 degrees, and "A half time" is 180 degrees. Adding these together we get 1260 degrees, which is the correct age. Bible students have figured this cycle but they did not know how it was calculated by Daniel. The 538 degrees is calculated the same way; 360 degrees from 538 degrees is 178 degrees, which is near the International Date Line. These degrees indicate that the Mohammedans and Romans would rule Asia and

Europe up to the time of the end. The calculations for the events of the two great religions will be found in Daniel 12 and in Revelation 18 and 19.

We find that the calculations of space and time around the earth, as described in the Bible, is correct and that the 360-degree cycle is used entirely for the tribes when time is figured. This is what we have termed the location for events which take place where time and space are measured.

The events figured in degrees from Adam to the present time is in cycles of time of the planet Uranus and is calculated in 84-year cycles. The Uranus cycle of 1008 years has been lost to the church people during the Roman age, but the astrological books give his cycles and the knowledge of Uranus is now known. In mythology the Uranian age was described as Uroanna, which means the Uranus cycle of time.

The 6000 years from Adam to the present time is figured from the cycles of Uranus. From this we figure that the time of the end is now. We also know that Uranus entered Aquarius in 1912 which is the time from which to calculate, together with 1918 when Uranus and Saturn were in opposition.

By adding 4004 to 1912 gives 5916 years; if we add one cycle of 84 years it brings us to 6000 years. If we begin with the Julian calendar year and calculate to the end of the age at 1912, adding 84 years we have 1996 which coresponds to the year Abraham was born. Adding 1920 and 84 years gives 2004 years, the beginning of the Julian age, to the end of the Uranus cycles. The four years of the 4004 in the "Garden of Eden" and also the 4 B. C. is for the 4 degrees east of Greenwich when Uranus is killed at the end of the cycles.

The modern Bible students have proven that the prophecies of Daniel are the prophecies concerning the Persian, Greek and Roman periods. The history as described by Daniel is from 538 B. C. to the present time, and the events as described have actually taken place. Students of Bible prophecies have followed events described in the Bible and traced the leading events of the age, and found that history was actually written beforehand from 540 B. C. time to the present.

There is a singular similarity between the modern Bible students' view on Bible time and the Catholic Church's time, that is, they both stop at the time of their prophecies. The Roman Church stopped at the birth of the Christian age in Palestine and is no further today than it was at the beginning of the age. The present day Bible students have found that the time of the Bible extends to the Roman age and read in the prophecies the history of the Catholic Church and of the period up to Rome and stop there. If they will continue to read the Bible and see what is to take place, they will see their mistake. Modern Bible students are still talking about the Turkish Empire and the Palestine time and age. The Roman doctrine is that the world with Jesus, as a man, lived in Palestine and this doctrine has been forced into their minds until they are all blind. If our good friends will extend their philosophy a few miles west of Rome and on to Greenwich they will find that the end of the age and also the end of the world is there. It is a mistake to think that the age began with Adam and stopped with the birth of Christ in Palestine. It stands to reason that the age has to be lived and that the Christian age does not terminate before the death of Christ. The Christian age is now being crucified on the battlefield of Europe, and the power, which was held by nations and churches east of Greenwich, is now at an end for now is the time of the end.

The cycle for the Christian age constitutes 2000 years which means 200 degrees in distance on the earth. This cycle began at 120 degrees east and extends to 80 degrees west, making the 200 degrees in all. The Bible describes that the philosophy of life, which originated in Babylon (Asia) would continue for 2000 years and be destroyed at the time of the end. From this we can see that the philosophy promulgated by the Roman and Greek Catholic Churches did not originate in Greece or Rome, but followed with civilization westward from Asia to Europe.

We have given a number of comparative illustrations of the method used in the Bible from which to calculate time and space and we feel confident that this system is understood.

Attention is called to the fact that the three great religious organizations of the world are located within the 120-degree cycle east of Greenwich. They are the Buddhist, Mohammedan and Christian. These organizations are spoken of as harlots, robbers and murderers who are to be destroyed at the time of the end of the world.

CHAPTER 27.

THE LIFE OF JESUS.

The life of Jesus, described in the Bible, contains too many topics to be referred to in detail, but we will select a few principles to illustrate the system used by the Bible writers.

The method used in the Bible to locate the degrees within the age is very interesting. We will describe the age of Jesus as an example and show how to locate the different degrees given for his age.

The life of Jesus is described to take place during the time of the Roman Empire and as the Roman Age begins at 40 degrees east, (in Turkey) and lasts to 70 degrees west we must figure within this distance to locate his life. It is written that Jesus was born of a virgin and we find that this house is located at 36 degrees east. The period of time or life of Jesus was 32 years, (degrees) when he is described to have been crucified. As Palestine is 36 degrees east we subtract 32 degrees from the 36 degrees which equals 4 degrees east or 4 B. C. where he was killed. The 4 degrees east strikes in Belgium and France where Jesus, as an age, was crucified, as illustrated in the present war.

The children of Israel and the disciples of Jesus represent the nations of Europe and it is for the period of Europe, as the Christian Church age, that the life of Jesus is described. The first event in the life of Jesus was at 8 days of age, when the circumcision took place. The 8 days means 8 degrees east and represent the location of the holy mountains of the Alps, giving the exact degree. The second event describing location is where he was taken from Bethlehem ot Jerusalem at 40 days of age, which means that he was represented as the entire 40 degrees as from his birthplace to the temple (the Alps) in this Jerusalem. He was here recognized as the Messiah of Israel (Europe). The third event described is when Jesus was taken to Egypt (Europe) in order to escape the jealousy of Herod the Great. This illustrates the end of the age of Asia, when the children under 2 years of age east of the 30 degrees are ordered to be destroyed by Herod. The fourth event of the life of Jesus is described at 12 years of age, when he went to the temple to attend the passover. The 12 years indicates the location of Rome, which is 12 degrees east. He attended the passover, showing the end of a period of time in the Roman age. The fifth event is described at 30 years of age, when he began to teach Christianity to the Israelites. The 30-year age spoken of is the 30 degrees from Egypt to Greenwich as a complete house of 30 degrees. The sixth and last age is at 32 years of age when he was crucified. This constitutes all the actual years as degrees described in the Bible for the events of the life of Jesus.

The other events giving the life work of Jesus are the

description of the nations of Europe showing the travels of Jesus in the different locations. It must be remembered that the life of Jesus is the representation of the planet Uranus and that the philosophy of life as given in the name of Jesus is the influence the planet Uranus gives in the different houses of the heaven. The same condition is produced and illustrated in the name of John the Baptist, who is the representation of the planet Neptune. John the Baptist as a prophet and teacher represented the church as a principle of a spiritual life. Jesus, as the Son of God, represents the doctrine of life for the entire human race. The story describing the beheading of John the Baptist is the same repetition of the death of Neptune a short time before that of Uranus. Neptune was described in all ages as the wife of the patriarchs, or the prophets, who assisted the leaders of Israel and this character as Neptune always died first. It was a virgin (Virgo) who asked for the head of John the Baptist and received it. The meaning of the asking for his head is that Neptune was in bad aspect to Saturn in the house of Virgo, (Turkey); illustrating the death of Neptune being at the end of the age. This event, as illustrated in the death of John the Baptist, is the killing of the power of the church empire or spiritual power of the church. John the Baptist was the prophet of the Christian Age and represented the church power of the Roman Catholic Church; when he was killed the church lost its power. The death of Neptune as John the Baptist took place in 1776, and after this time the Roman Church lost its power.

The Life of Christ at the present age is referred to in the Bible when Jesus partakes of the passover. Read Matthew 26: which corresponds to the year 1912 when the Balkan Nations began to make real trouble. From this period the powers of Europe tried to produce war. (This is the year Uranus entered the house of Aquarius). It must be remembered that the World's war is the crucifying of Christ and the arguments about Jesus before Pilate and other authorities are preparation or excuses for starting the war. In Matthew 26:57 Germany is named as Calaphas. The United States is called Peter who was represented in Germany to see the end.

The actual crucifying of Jesus is the war of the present time, each day as written in the Bible represents a year and the seven days as years count from 1914 to the beginning of 1921. The first 2 days (from 1912 to 1914) represent the events as described in Matthew 26. It says in verse 2: "ye know that after two days is the feast of the passover, and the son of man is betrayed too be crucified." That is, after 2 days, the war was to begin, which it did in 1914. The woman with the alabastar box represents Turkey, and the wasting of the ointment described in verse 8 represents the Balkan nations' first disturbance and war which took place then. The description, as given in verses 14 to 16, shows what the Roman power did to start the war. In chapter 26:17-57 is the description of the time of 2 years from 1912 to 1914 as the period of preparation for the crucifying of Jesus. From verse 57 is described the actual war in the taking of Jesus and bringing him before Calaphas who represents the German power. It is written that Jesus took Peter and the two sons of Zebedee with him; they represent the United States and Scandinavia. He asked them to wait for him, but they went to sleep; which means that they did not take part in the war.

In Matthew 27 is the description of the war from day to day as years. Pontius Pilate represents Saturn. From verses 3 to 10 is described the part the church takes in the war as Judas Iscariot. In verses 11 to 17 is described an imaginary accusation of crime, "Art thou the king of the Jews?" which means: Are you representing the Christian nations of Europe? In verses 19 to 25 is a description of Turkey and the part she took in the war at this time. In verse 19 is shown that Turkey did not want to enter the war. From verses 26 to 28 shows the time Turkey entered the war, when Barabbas was released and when "they stripped him and put on him a scarlet robe," meaning a robe of blood. In verses 29 to 32 is described the main part of the war and the man Simon of Cyrene represents Belgium, whom they compelled to bear his cross. In verses 33 to 34 "And when they were come unto a place called Golgotha, that is, a place of a skull, they gave him vinegar to drink mingled with gall." The place of the skull is the head of man and as France represents the head, it is in the upper part of France as the top of the head or skull, the Golgotha spoken of is located. The vinegar given is the liquid fire which was used by the Germans on this battlefield. From verses 35 to 44 is described the continuation of the war, when the Germans were dividing the country spoken of as the dividing of his garments. In verse 36 it says "And sitting down, they watched him there," which means a period of time. The two thieves crucified with him are the Buddhist and Mohammedan doctrines.

Part IV—Chapter 27.

The time of the actual death of Jesus is described from verses 45 to 50 when he died. This period corresponds to October 1st, 1918, when the Germans recognized their defeat. The condition in Germany and her Allied countries are described from verses 51 to 56. The many women spoken of are the nations named in verse 56, and are named respectively Greece, Turkey, Holland, Denmark and Scandinavia.

The rich man of Arimathæa, as Joseph, represents the United States, spoken of in verses 57 to 60. He asked for the body of Jesus from Pilate and obtained permission to bury him, which he did in his own new tomb, wrapped in clean linen cloth. The body of Jesus represents churchology; the linen cloth is a book and the tomb represents the mysteries of the ages. This means that a book will be published from the United States and in Europe explaining the life of Jesus and the teachings of the Bible. It says, "he rolled a great stone to the door of the sepulchre, and departed." The great stone is the astrological teachings which the new book contains. In verse 62 is described the condition from 1919, when the soldiers are still watching the grave so the war will not come to life again.

Matthew 28 describes the year 1919-20, "as it began to dawn toward the first day of the week." Verse 2, "And behold, there was a great earthquake; for the angel of the Lord descended from heaven, and came and rolled back the stone from the door, and sat on it." The earthquake means revolution, strikes and war all over the earth; the angel is the angle of 120 degrees from the Pacific Coast in the United States. It is this angel who sits on the stone after it has been rolled from the grave. The meaning of the stone being removed is, that the knowledge of what the Bible contains has become known. This knowledge comes from the good angle of 120 degrees and is in the publication of a "Little Book Open" as described in the book of Revelation. Chapter 10.

We will describe the condition during the three years after the death of Jesus in 1918 to 1921. This is the three days referred to when Jesus remains dead and is in the tomb before he raises from the grave. It is during this period the soldiers are stationed at the grave as watchmen. The soldiers are the Allied nations' army, which are maintained in Europe to watch so that the war does not come to life again. It is during this watchful-waiting period of three years that the earthquake is described to take place. The earthquake represents a revolution in Europe and as this has not taken place, we look for this event to take place in 1919-20. This revolution or earthquake is described to be so great that the whole earth is affected. The soldiers stationed at the grave left their post of duty and fled for their lives. From this can be seen that a great disturbance is to come over Europe, which is to spread to all parts of the world. The soldiers, as the Allied army, will, however, remain as guards at the grave until the real revolution takes place and peace restored.

CHAPTER 28.

CRUCIFYING CHRIST.

We have made the statement that Christ, as Christianity, is the Christian age. The following explanations show that the age is being crucified and that we live in the last days of the present cycle.

Isaiah 6: to 12: Read this part of the Bible. It is a prophecy of the present time. It describes the different nations at war, showing the conditions which would exist at this time. Germany and Austria-Hungary with the Turks are now, in the year 1918, dividing the garments of Christ. Remember that the Golgotha, where Christianity is being crucified takes place in Belgium and France.

Read chapter 10:26-34. This part shows that the United States enters the war and that they are "over the pass," and have taken lodging at Geba (in France). This is very clear, for it is the part the United States takes in the war. It shows clearly that the United States will do justice and help the Allies to win the war so completely that there will be nothing left to do. The Kaiser is not forgotten; his name is written in chapter 10:31, it is as "Madmenah, a fugitive," and the inhabitants of the country flee for safety.

It is not the intention to explain the Bible prophecies, but only to show what they mean and how to read them. The best and clearest part of the Bible showing the present time is written in Matthew 26:47. Read to the end of 28: The beginning of verse 47: describes the beginning of the war. In verses 51 and 52 describes the killing of Archduke Ferdinand. as being a servant of the high priest. The individual representing Judas Iscariot is Italy who had authority as a disciple to deliver Christ for a price, and when he saw the result of the war he died.

In Matthew 26:57 they take Christ to Calaphas, another country, and have consultations where the high priest, scribes and elders were gathered together. This takes place in Germany when they decided to make unreasonable demands of Serbia. In verse 58 begins the explanation of the United States. Peter is the United States. "He was standing afar off unto the court of the high priest, and entered in, and sat with the officers to see the end. The chief and the entire council sought false witness against Christ, that they might put him to death and they found it not." That is, Germany tried to get a reason for starting the war and the United States, as Peter, was there at the time, for Ambassador Gerard was there representing this country. In verse 69 is shown that the United States, as Peter, denied Christ or that "he knew Christ," and that he denied Christ three times before "the cock crew twice." This part is very well known to all, so we will only repeat and say that during the first two years of the war is the time the "cock crew three times." (The cock represents France.) The United States refused three times to enter the war and said "he is not one of them." During this period the citizens of the United States had to deny that they were not English. Read verse 73; "of a truth thou also art one of them; for thy speech maketh thee known." This shows that the United States was not to enter the war before the third year. The first two years of the war were the preparation for the final act of destroying Christianity. The Bible counts days as years and in chapter 27 begins the third year of the war, when "the chief priests and the elders of the people took counsel against Christ to put him to death:" This was when unrestricted submarine warfare was declared, in other words, when Germany began killing innocent people of all nations simply for the sake of destroying life and property. This was when Christ was delivered up to Pilate, the governor. Matthew 27:3; "Then Judas, who betrayed him, when he saw that he was condemned repented himself." It shows that Judas was the catholic nations and means that they committed suicide for playing the Judas and repented. The price they received was of no benefit to them as it was used to buy a "potter's field," which is a graveyard. From this it will be seen why Russia is a living graveyard and that Italy will be destroyed.

Matthew 27:6, "And the chief priest took the pieces of silver and said, "It is not lawful to put them into the treasury, since it is the price of blood." From this it will be seen who was the real Judas Iscariot and that the money went into the potter's field. Matthew 26:24, "The Son of man goeth, as it is written of him, but woe unto that man by whom the Son of Man is betrayed; it had been good for that man if he had not been born." From this we see why the church in Russia is suffering destruction for betraying the confidence of other nations.

Matthew 27:11 tells of the beginning of what was done to the Turks. The question was if they should sacrifice Turkey or end the war. The answer was, release Barabbas (Turkey) and prosecute the war. Verse 20. "Now the chief priest and the elders persuaded the multitude that they should ask for Barabbas and destroy Christ." This means that the German government wanted the war to continue, and they had their way about it. In verse 22 is shown clearly that all nations wanted to continue the war, for they said "Let him be crucified." In verse 25, "And all the people answered and said His blood be on us and on our children." As this is the final act of all Nations, it shows clearly that all the people are backing their governments and that they want to prosecute the war to the end. They said that the responsibility or the last part of the war shall fall on them and their children.

In Matthew 27:33 is shown where the battlefield is called Golgotha, the "place of the skull." It shows that Christ suffered on this battlefield, that He was given wine to drink, mingled with gall. This is the liquid fire given to the Christians. Finally at the end of the fight for life on this battlefield the Christ dies.

When the critical period is nearly over, even before Christ dies, the crucifiers began to divide his clothing among themselves; this is the dividing of the country they have captured. In verse 36 is shown that a time has to pass, as it says, "and they sat and watched him there." In verse 37 a notice was put up over Christ's head on the cross: "This is Christ, the King of the Jews." Which means that the Israelites as the nations of Europe are the crucifiers of Christianity.

Verse 38 speaks of a new subject not previously mentioned, two robbers are to be crucified with Christ. As Christ stands for Christianity and the other two who could be crucified with him on this battlefield are the Mohammedans and the Buddhists, and they are there in battle today. The churches have always been called robbers, so we take it for granted that it is these two organizations which are meant as robbers.

Matthew 27:45 begins with the sixth hour and says that from the sixth to the ninth hour there was darkness over the land, that is, war continuous. This takes place in the fourth year as the year begins in March. The time from the sixth to the ninth hour is the third quarter of the year, which makes the sixth hour September, the ninth hour November, according to our time. So we figure that from September to November is the time when Christ actually dies. In this period of time the outcome of the war will be decided.

In verse 46 it says about the ninth hour Christ cried with a loud voice saying "My God, My God, why hast thou forsaken me!" This is to show that between September and November 1918 there will be the greatest battles of the present war In this period Christ gives up the spirit, and what will take place then must be the closing of the war. We look to October 1st, 1918, as the time when the big drive will take place and will be the climax of the war, and the end of Christianity as an age.

Verse 55 describes the many women who were there watching the Christ being crucified. The many women as the "Mary Magdalene and the other Mary," are the Red Cross workers and nurses who are administering to relieve the sufferings of Christianity.

CHAPTER 29.

THE BOOK OF ISAIAH.

Chapter 1 of the Book of Isaiah describes the time of the end; "The vision he saw concerning Judah and Jerusalem." First the four cardinal houses are named showing the time in Judah. From verse 2 to 7 is described the condition of Europe today. In verse 7 "Your country is desolate; your cities are burned with fire; your land, strangers devour it in your presence, and it is described as overthrown by strangers." This chapter speaks of the condition of Judah at the time of the end. In verse 18 Jehovah asks Judah (the tribe of Judah is Germany) to reform and to do right and all will be forgiven, and in verse 20 "but if ye refuse and rebel, ye shall be devoured with the sword, for the mouth of Jehovah hath spoken." Jehovah is Uranus and he speaks to the five nations of Judah to stop burnt offerings of rams, bullocks, lambs, or of he goats; which means that the wars should be stopped on the nations represented by these animals. We will see later what is the meaning of this admonishing and what the threats refer to.

In Isaiah 1:8 is described Alsace-Lorraine, and brings out another question from which we can read the meaning of the chapter. "And the daughter of Zion is left as a booth in a vineyard, as a lodge in a garden of cucumbers, as a besieged city." Verse 9, "Except Jehovah of hosts had left unto us a very small remnant, we should have been as Sodom, we should have been like unto Gomorrah;" which means that Switzerland and Alsace-Lorraine would have been as naked as the desert of Arizona and Mt. Whitney in California.

The two first chapters of Isaiah deal with the house of Zion and as Zion is the same as Sodom and Gomorrah we know what this means. A few is left and Zion is not to be destroyed. Zion as Gomorrah is Alsace-Lorraine and Switzerland. The house of Zion is divided in two, that is, the house is of a dual nature, a double house. It is a mountain and a valley. The mountain is the masculine and the valley is the daughter of Zion. Switzerland is the Holy Mountain and Alsace-Lorraine is the daughter of Zion. These two countries represent the house of Aquarius. Much can be written of what these two countries represent in Bible study, for it teaches a principle of a higher law; than the government made by man. The meaning of the chapter is that if these countries were not saved the entire tribes of Zion and Judah would be destroyed.

From this it will be seen why Switzerland and Alsace-Lorraine are the central countries of the war and not destroyed. Aquarius is the house of the Lord of the heaven, the house of the Prince of Peace. In verse 21 it speaks of what Alsace-Lorraine is today. "How is the faithful city become a harlot; she that was full of Justice! righteousness lodged in her, but now murderers." The rest of the chapter is devoted to both Switzerland and Alsace-Lorraine saying they will both suffer in order to rid them of outside influence.

In verse 27, "Zion shall be redeemed with justice, and her converts with righteousness." But the "destruction of transgressors and sinners shall be together and they that forsake Jehovah shall be consumed."

In Isaiah 2:2, "And it shall come to pass in the last days, that the mountains of Jehovah's house shall be established on the top (or at the head) of the mountains, and shall be exalted above the hills, and all nations shall flow unto it, and many people shall go and say come ye and let us go up to the mountain of Jehovah to the house of the God of Jacob; and he will teach us of his ways, and we will walk in his paths; for out of Zion shall go forth the law, and the word of Jehovah from Jerusalem. And he will judge between the nations, and will decide concerning many peoples; and they shall beat their swords into plowshares and their spears into pruning hooks. Nations shall not lift up sword against nation, neither shall they learn war any more." The meaning of this is very simple, as it shows, at the end of the war the meetings and arrangement of peace will be held in Switzerland. The new form of government to be established in the different countries will be of the pattern of Switzerland. The headquarters of the world peace conference will be held there "for out of Zion shall go for the law and the word of the Lord from Jerusalem" from the Allies. The peace conference will not be held at the Hague, but in the holy mountains. The word spoken of means terms which are to come from the British Allies.

The peace conference will have the power to decide many international questions and in the settling of the war, the dividing of the nations will be settled in justice.

The rest of the second chapter of Isaiah deals with the war as it describes the condition of the present war. In verse 20; "In that day men shall cast away their idols of silver and their idols of gold, which have been made for them to worship, to the moles and to the bats; to go into the caverns of the rocks, and into cliffs of the ragged rocks from the terror of Jehovah, and from the glory of his majesty when he ariseth to shake mightily the earth." There is no doubt about the meaning of this, for it is an every day occurrence; men are living in holes in the mountains and in the ground. Read in full the first two chapters of Isaiah; they deal with Alsace-Lorraine and Switzerland; together with the conditions which exist today in Europe.

In Isaiah 9:14 "Therefore Jehovah will cut off from Israel head and tail, palm branch and rush in one day. The elder and the honorable man, he is the head and the prophet that teacheth lies, he is the tail." This means that the countries referred to are the head and the feet, and are France and Italy. The prophet spoken of represents the church.

Isaiah 9:19, "Through the wrath of Jehovah of hosts is the land burnt up; and the people are as the fuel of fire; no man spareth his brother. And one shall snatch on the right hand, and be hungry; and he shall eat on the left hand, and they shall not be satisfied; they shall eat every man the flesh of his own arm. Manasseh, Ephraim; and Ephraim, Manasseh; and they together shall be against Judah." This is very clear for it refers to the present war and the conditions which exist now. It also shows that France and England should be together as one to fight Germany.

The chapters of Isaiah from the 13th to the 23rd describe the nations in war at the present time. It is a peculiar fact that the events as described in Isaiah have already taken place. Isaiah 19 describes the condition in Europe which is described as Egypt. In verse 2 it says, "And I will stir up the Egyptians against the Egyptians and they shall fight every one against his brother, and every one against his neighbor, city against city and kingdom against kingdom. And the spirit of Egypt shall fall in the middle of it, and I will destroy the council thereof." Verse 4, "And I will give over the Egyptians into the hands of a cruel lord, and a fierce king shall rule over them." "And the waters shall fall from the sea, and the rivers shall be wasted and become dry." Verse 13, "the princes of Zoan are become fools, the princes of Memphis are deceived, they have caused Egypt to go astray, that are the cornerstones of her tribes, Jehovah hath mingled a spirit of perversness in the midst of her and they have caused Egypt to go astray in every work thereof as a drunken man staggering in his vomit. And the land of Judah shall become a terror unto Egypt, every one whom mentions thereof shall be afraid." Verse 18; "In that day there shall be five cities in the land of Egypt, that speak the language of Canaan and swear to Jehovah of hosts, one shall be called the City of Destruction." Verse 20; "and he will send them a Savior and a defender and he will deliver them." This chapter is very interesting as Europe has actually passed through part of what is described in chapter 19. The nations have fought between themselves; their spirit is broken; the cruel lord who rules them is Germany; the waters falling away is the taking of the coast by Germany; the "princes to be fools" means that the government acts as fools and goes astray. The land of Judah is Germany, also known as Assyria, they are afraid of. It says there shall be five cities, that is, they shall be divided into five sections and one of them is to be a traitor (Russia). A savior will be sent to save them, that is, some other nation (the United States) will go to Europe and free them from war and help to establish a government.

Chapter for chapter of Isaiah describes year for year the nations, their location and their activities for the present time. The book of Isaiah does not describe any cycle as a period of time, but for only the time of end.

CHAPTER 30.

THE BOOK OF EZEKIEL.

The Book of Ezekiel represents the present time and it describes the time, place and condition at the time of the end of the age. Ezekiel's book was written from 595 B. C. or 125 degrees east.

Ezekiel 1. "Now it came to pass in the thirtieth year, in the fourth month, in the fifth day of the month." "In the fifth day of the month, which was the fifth year of King Jehoiachin's captivity." This means that the thirtieth year is thirty degrees. The fourth month is June being the fourth from March and the fifth day corresponds to the 25th day of June. In verse 2, it says "the fifth year of the captivity" which is the fifth year of the war, when Uranus is in Aquarius. In other words Ezekiel gives the date of June 25th, 1919.

The first chapter describes the time, place and the location of the signs of the houses in the heavens. In verse 10 is mentioned the face of a man, the face of a lion, the face of an ox, the face of an eagle. This describes the houses of the four principal points of the heavens. The description and the location of these houses (or tribes) are correct.

The wings which are spoken of in this chapter are the four degrees on the cusps, two on each side. The wheels within wheels referred to represent the different nations of Europe being wheels as nations within Europe as the big wheel. This description corresponds to the coat of many colors in Joseph's age and means that the description given is for Europe at the present time.

Ezekiel 2: He is sent to the children of Israel to see their condition which is bad. The children of Israel represent Europe.

142 *Key to Bible and Heaven.*

Ezekiel 3:15. He is sent to the country which corresponds to Turkey to inform the inhabitants that Turkey is the watchman, and to watch for the time. In verse 22 he is sent to the country of Switzerland, where he is to be abused, imprisoned and not allowed to talk. When he is in the different places he describes the conditions which exist there. Of Germany he says: it was written lamentation, mourning and woe." Of

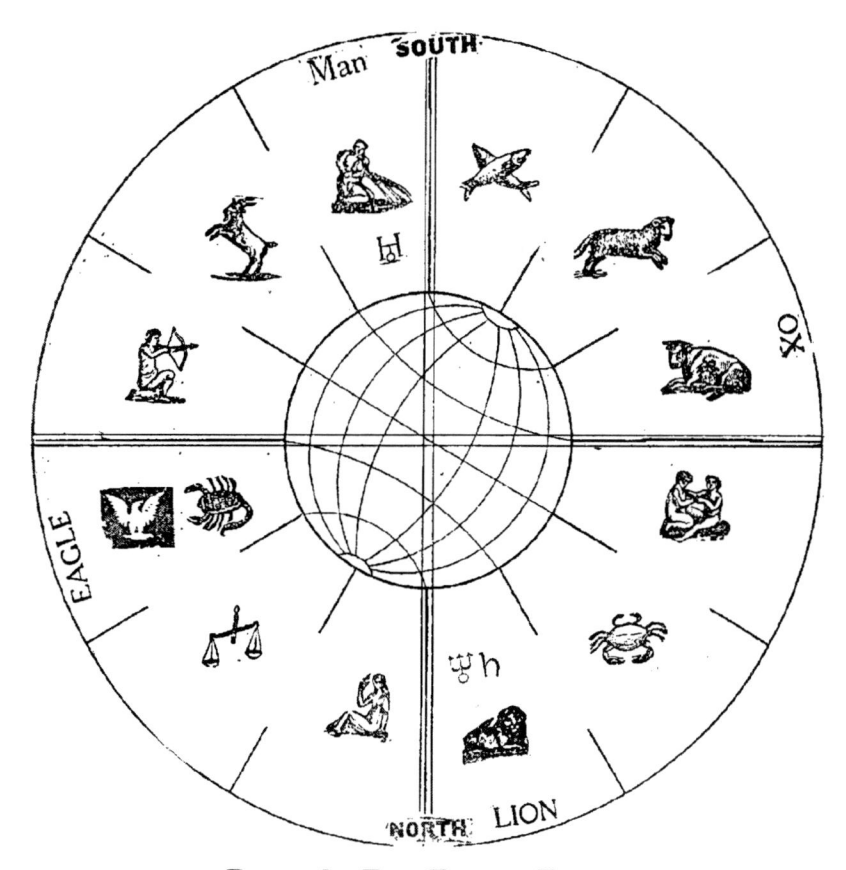

PLATE 6—THE END OF TIME.

Switzerland he says to "Go and shut thyself within thine house," which means that they will be closed in on all sides, and not allowed even to give information or, as it says, to be "a reprover."

Ezekiel 4 says that Israel will be besieged 390 days on one side and 40 days on the other side. The 390 days equal 30 degrees west and the 40 days are 40 degrees east. The thirty degrees mean that the war extends to the place at 30 degrees in the Atlantic Ocean and the 40 degrees east is in Turkey. Verses 9 to 17 describe the condition of Germany at the present time.

Ezekiel 5 deals with France and describes the location and condition of the battlefield. "At the top of the head and to the beard." France represents the head or Aries and this part is to be shaved as with a sharp razor. A third part of France is to be taken, when a sword is to stop the conquest. In verse 3 it says a few Germans are to be taken prisoners. In verse 4, "Then take of them again and cast them into the midst of the fire, and burn them in the fire, for thereof shall a fire come forth into all the house of Israel," which means that the Germans are to be driven back into Germany, represented by the fiery house of Leo, and a fire or war is to start from within Germany. The rest of the chapter speaks for itself and shows what is to take place in Germany, as disease and famine. A third part of France will be destroyed and laid waste.

Ezekiel 6: The topic is now changed to the mountains. These are Switzerland, showing that all nations (tribes) shall be destroyed and suffer for they have not followed after the word of God.

Ezekiel 7: Deals with the condition which will exist within Germany in the year 1919, at the end of the age. Verse 14: "They have blown the trumpet, even to make all ready; but none goeth forth to the battle: for my wrath is upon all the multitude thereof. The sword is without and famine within, he that is in the field shall die with the sword; and he that is in the city, famine and pestilence shall devour him."

Ezekiel 8: Describes exactly the time of Germany's downfall. It is in the sixth year, the sixth month, and the fifth day of the month. Uranus stays seven years in Aquarius, which is from 1912 to 1920. The sixth year is 1918, and the time as described is September 26th, 1918. Verse 5 speaks of trouble being close to the borders of Switzerland, and Alsace-Lorraine. The door of the court is Alsace-Lorraine and the condition there is described in verse 7. The American army will pass through there and with the help of God will overcome the Germans. The woman weeping for Tammus is Alsace-Lorraine, as described in verse 24; she is weeping at the destruction of Belgium. In verse 16 he says "between the porch and the altar were about twenty-five men with their backs toward the temple of the Lord, and their faces toward the east, and they worshipped the sun toward the east." This is the twenty-five degrees of Aquarius the planet Uranus was in at October 1st, 1918. Uranus is to retrograde and goes backward in his house when he is in opposition to Saturn. The place of the porch and altar is at Alsace-Lorraine, where the United States army now is. Here is where the Christ or Uranus dies, and where the war is settled.

Ezekiel 9: This is the most important part of the prophecy. It says that six men come from the porch near the higher gate toward the north; which is from Switzerland toward the north and is where the United States army is located. These men are prepared for slaughter. The six men are the six great nations of the Allies. It says in verse 3: "And he called to the man clothed with linen, which had the writer's ink-horn by his side," this man is Switzerland. Verse 4 describes the condition of Alsace-Lorraine. At the proper time the American army will destroy the Germans but not the French people there. In verse 5 Uranus is represented as directing the Allies to "Go ye after him through the city, and smite: let not your eye spare, neither have ye pity; slay utterly old and young, both maids and little children and women, but come not near any man upon whom is the mark, and begin at my sanctuary. Then they began at the ancient men which were before the house." This means that the Allies will start "at" Switzerland and destroy the Germans; but the Bible does not say "in" Switzerland. The ending of the fight is really in Alsace-Lorraine. It is apparent that the war will utterly destroy the country, as it is said in verse 11. "I have done as thou hast commanded me."

Ezekiel 10: Begins a new term of expression; the names of the gems or stones representing the new tribes is now used. He (Ezekiel) speaks to the United States as the gem of Sapphire, and tells him to go and bring fire for the other nations from under the cherub which is England. In 10:4 "Then the glory of the Lord went up from the cherub and stood over the threshold of the house." This means that the United States will take charge of the affairs of supplying "fire" (ammunition) to the other nations. The vision described as cherubim, represents the figures of the houses as it appears at this time. The cherub is England; the face of a man is Switzerland; the lion is Germany; the eagle is Austria-Hungary. These houses will occupy the four leading houses of Europe at the end of time.

Austria-Hungary (the tribe Dan) will decide the ending of the war and not Germany or the allies.

Ezekiel 11 describes the condition at the east side of Switzerland when Uranus is in twenty-five degrees of Aquarius. After the surrender in 1918, there is trouble on this side. It will be a caldron and the Austrians will be the flesh. The fight will take place east of Switzerland, verse 8, "Ye have feared the sword and I will bring the sword upon you."

Ezekiel 12 described the closing chapter of the war. The final act of overcoming Germany is described in this chapter. It says that a secret or unobscure transfer of the army will take place. Chapter 12:11, "I am your sign: like as I have done, so shall it be done unto them: they shall remove and go into captivity." This means that Germany will withdraw her army and many will be taken prisoners. In verse 13, "My net also will I spread upon him, and he shall be taken in my snare; and I will bring him to Babylon to the land of the Chaldeans, yet shall he not see it, though he shall die there." This is clear; the Kaiser is to be captured and confined in Germany to the end of his days. Verse 14, "And I will scatter towards every wind all that are about him, to help him, and all his bands; and I will draw out the sword after them. And they shall know that I am the Lord, when I shall scatter them among the nations, and disperse them in the countries." From verses 17 to 20 is shown the conditions within Germany and the allied countries. It is seen clearly that Germany as representing Judah is the opposition in Israel.

Chapter 13 described the Christian Churches and says that "she is a false prophet."

Chapter 15 deals with Europe as Jerusalem; It says they shall go from one fire into another and be destroyed.

Saturn becomes retrograde December 10th, 1918, and remains retrograde to April 28th, 1919. This is the time of the end proper for Germany when this nation begins to retrograde from internal trouble spoken of in chapter 12.

The beginning of the war is described in Ezekiel 21:19 describing Germany's destruction of Belgium and what must result to Germany. The chapters 21-22 show without a doubt that this is the time of the end and Germany is the cause of the war.

France is the head, or sheep, Aries. The French are the shepherds of Europe. Ezekiel 34 explains the ultimate of

France. The United States is to protect France for many years for France will be a dependent of the United States.

Switzerland represents the Holy Mountains and Alsace-Lorraine represents the house in the valley, both are as one and not one. It is represented by Aquarius, the water carrier, a double house as one. Ezekiel 35:36 described these countries. It is shown that the United States army is to play an important part in Alsace-Lorraine for the Germans will be driven from this section of the country. This is Gog and Magog: Meshech and Tubal. The resurrection of dry bones takes place here and is the making of new nations in the United States as is written in chapter 37. In chapter 39 is described the results of the war to Germany—death. In Alsace-Lorraine is where the death struggle will take place It is the place of the porch to the Holy Mountain. Switzerland is the man clothed in linen with a writer's ink-horn; the linen is the snow-capped Mountains, and the ink-horn is the rivers, which start in the mountains.

Greece and Italy represent the two sisters of Libra and Pisces spoken of in Ezekiel 23. They are representing Europe as the Catholic age. This chapter is written with the idea to represent character but the language used is of such a nature that we cannot repeat it here, nor do we care to explain the meaning of the terms used.

Europe corresponds to the land of Egypt. The chapters of Ezekiel 29-36 describe Europe in detail. Pharaoh is Saturn who rules Europe. Germany is spoken of in Ezekiel as Assyrians. It is the house of Leo, the Lion. Turkey is described in Ezekiel 33. Turkey is the mother of nations and is represented by Virgo. It is described as the watchman sitting in the gate of Europe. The resurrection of dry bones spoken of in chapter 37 is the repopulation of the United States after the nations of Europe are destroyed.

CHAPTER 31.

THE BOOK OF REVELATION.

The book of Revelation is similar to the other books of the Bible in that it contains a similar description of the study of the earth and the conditions which would exist at the time of the end. This is the most interesting book of all the books in the Bible for it deals entirely with the time of the end.

Part IV—Chapter 31.

There is a description of seven churches, seven spirits, seven stars, and seven angels, all of which refer to the seven tribes, as nations at war, who are the opposite power to Judah and described in the first chapters.

Chapter 4:6 begins with the description of what he (John) saw "And before the throne there was a sea of glass like unto crystal; And in the midst of the throne, and round about the throne, were four beasts full of eyes before and behind. And the first beast was like a lion, and the second beast like a calf, and the third beast had a face of a man, and the fourth beast was like a flying eagle." This is simply the same description of the horoscope for the time of the end as is given in the other books.

Chapter 5 is the description of Uranus as sitting on the throne with the power of heavens. The sealed book spoken of is the Bible, which describes the great war. The opening of the book describes the beginning of the war, and Judah was the one to open the book. Verse 3, "And no man in heaven nor in earth, neither under the earth, was able to open the book, neither to look thereon." Verse 5, "And one of the elders said unto me, Weep not: Behold the Lion of the tribes of Judah, the root of David, hath prevailed to open the book, and to loose the seven seals, thereof." The tribe of Judah, the Lion, is Germany who is the one to begin the war, and the lamb spoken of in verse 12 is France. He is the one which was slain, but will receive "power and riches," as his reward. Verse 6 describes "seven Spirits of God" which represent the seven tribes of the allied nations.

Chapter 6 describes the opening of the seven seals, which means the beginning of the war. Each seal describes the conditions caused by the war from year to year. In the third year when the third seal was opened, the condition in Europe is described in verse 6, "And I heard a voice in the midst of the four beasts say a measure of wheat for a penny, and three measures of barley for a penny, and see thou hurt not the oil and the wine;" which means the preservation of food for all in Europe at this time.

The fourth seal is the fourth year of the war, and the time the United States sent its army to the front and their mission was death as described in verses 7 and 8. "And power was given unto them over the fourth part of the earth, to kill with the sword, and with hunger, and with death, and with the beasts of the earth."

The fifth seal (year) is described in verses 9, 10 and 11. The white robes referred to represent those who have died from the effects of the war. "And they cried with a loud voice, saying How long, O. Lord holy, and true, dost thou not judge and avenge our blood on them that dwell on the earth. And white robes were given unto every one of them; and it was said unto them that they should rest yet for a little season, until their fellow servants also and their brethren that should be killed as they were, should be fulfilled."

In verse 12, is described the opening of the sixth seal, "And lo, there was a great earthquake, and the sun becomes black as sackcloth of hair, and the moon becomes as blood: And the stars of heaven fell unto the earth." The stars falling unto the earth means the fall of the rulers of the nations and the earthquakes mean revolutions. Verse 15, "And the kings of the earth and the great men, and the rich men, and the chief captains, and the mighty men, and every bond-man, and every free-man, hid themselves in the dens and in the rocks of the mountains; And said to the mountains and rocks, Fall on us, and hide us from the face of him that sitteth on the throne, and from the wrath of the lamb." This describes the conditions beginning after the fall of the Kaiser in 1919, when the revolution begins. The one spoken of as sitting on a throne is Uranus.

Chapter 7 describes the astrological calculations of the degrees in each house referred to as tribes. The tribes sealed, spoken of in this chapter is to show that all the degrees in the twelve houses have been killed. The 144,000 represents the two degrees of 72 years. This chapter is the best and clearest of any in the Bible to show that there is a life after death. Read from the 9th to the 17th verse. In verse 13, "What are these which are arrayed in white robes and whence come they? And I said unto him, Sir, thou knoweth, And he said to me, These are they which came out of the great tribulation, and have washed their robes, and made them white in the blood of the Lamb. Therefore are they before the throne of God, and serve him day and night in his temple, and he that sitteth on the throne shall dwell among them. They shall hunger no more, neither thirst any more; neither shall the sun light on them nor any heat."

Chapter 8 begins with the description of the opening of

the 6th seal and at that time there was peace on earth for half an hour (six months). From this we know that there will be peace from the 5th to the 6th year or from 1918 to 1919.

When the sixth and seventh seals are opened it means that strikes, revolutions and war will start all over again and that all nations will be at war five months, in the revolution described. In chapters 8 and 9 is described this last war in detail and the use of airo-planes.

Chapter 10 describes that an angel (angle) with one foot on the earth, the other on the sea, has a little book open. The explanation of the angel means that a book will be published from that part of the earth illustrated as an angle from land and sea, which is the Pacific Coast division, for this is the only angle which includes the earth and sea. What this book will do is best explained from the Bible; it is written in chapter 10:9 "And I went unto the angel, and said unto him Give me the little book. And he said unto me, Take it and eat it up; and it shall make thy belly bitter, but it shall be in thy mouth sweet as honey." The little book spoken of is the explanation of the Bible for the mysteries of the ages are now to be revealed.

Chapter 11 describes the condition at the end of time where it is and what the conditions would be. The two witnesses spoken of in verse 3 are the two degrees of 144 years.

Chapter 12 describes the prophecy for the United States which began in 1776, when the United States, as the child spoken of, was born. The dragon or Satan is Saturn and Michael is Uranus. It says that the woman fled into the wilderness and was hid for 1260 years. This means that Neptune, representing the church, will be void of power for this length of time, or to 180 degrees west.

Chapter 13 is the continued description of the planet Neptune represented in the Christian Churches. The number 666 is the space of the church. Verse 18; "Here is wisdom. Let him that hath understanding count the number of the beast; for it is the number of a man; and his number is six hundred three score and six." We leave this question unanswered, as we would like to have the Bible students figure the space and end of the Christian nations but it is to 54 degrees east.

It will be observed that the first ten chapters of Revelations deal with the destruction of the government and nations of Europe and the present war. Chapter 13-20 is the description of the church and religions of the world. The same method is used and the same prophecy is made for the church as for the nations. It should be remembered that Saturn represents the nations and that Neptune represents the church and that the churches have not been destroyed as yet and that this takes place after the destruction of the nations.

Chapter 13 describes a general history of the church as written in other books of the Bible, showing that it is the church which is meant and that the end of the church as an organization is near.

Chapter 14 describes the change of cycles. The different angels spoken of, represent new doctrines and laws, coming from the different angles of the earth. This philosophy will produce the condition as spoken of in this chapter. In verse 20 it says, "And the wine-press was trodden without the city, and blood came out of the wine-press, even unto the horse-bridles (Pegasus), by the space of a thousand and six hundred furlongs." This means that there will be a religious war to extend for 1600 furlongs (which equals 160 degrees). This distance is figured for "Zion" and is for Europe. A sudden destruction will take place covering a distance of 160 degrees of the nations of Europe east to the 54th degree.

Chapter 15 gives the description of the religious war which is to take place and describes the seven plagues which are put on the earth. The "sea of glass" again spoken of is the horoscope of all the churches (Neptune). The term used in the next verse that they "sing the songs of Moses," means they are able to read and study the laws as given by Moses.

The 16th chapter describes the seven plagues poured out on the earth in this war; part of this chapter is a repetition of what has already been described. It should be remembered that the war which ends at 1918 has only five plagues and that the sixth and seventh plagues begin in 1919 and are to last thirteen months.

The chapters 17, 18 and 19 describe the Christian Churches and the conditions produced in church worship. The term "beast" is used to illustrate the condition which is produced by the planet Neptune. The Catholic Church headquarters at Rome are called the "City of Seven Hills" or "Seven Waters" as spoken of in chapter 17. These verses are self explanatory and explain one topic and includes all churches. The Lamb is the Savior or Uranus, who will destroy the power of the church.

Part IV—Chapter 31.   151

It is shown very clearly that it is Neptune which is spoken of as representing the church, "And the beast that was, and is not, is himself also an eight, and is one of the seven and he goes into perdition. Verse 11: The explanation of this is that Neptune as well as Uranus is lost to the people of the earth during every dark age, for Neptune is in the middle of the house at that time. He is one of the "Seven and is an eight," planet. He is the one that was and is not known.

The original five tribes of Judah came from Asia called Babylonia as the descendant of Shem. The seven tribes of Israel are the descendants of Japheth as Europe today. From this will be seen the reason why the Germans are called Assyrians and as the Catholic Church originated with the Germans in Asia, the Church is called Babylon. The seven nations of the Allies are the proper nations of Europe and the five nations associated with Germany in war today are the Catholic nations from Asia. The description given in the three chapters, 17, 18 and 19, regarding the Catholic Church is written in such strong language that we do not care to explain the meaning of them. The law and the judgment of the heavens will regulate all things and in the proper time God will explain these chapters in his own way.

The 20th chapter describes Saturn, as Satan, who is to be bound for a thousand years, which means that the power of Saturn is destroyed by Uranus up to the end of the next cycle. It deals with the degrees as calculated for the houses and refers to the earth only. This is illustrated in verse 5, "But the rest of the dead lived not again until the thousand years were finished." "This is the first resurrection" (First cycle). It means that the doctrines, as referred to in the Bible, will be resurrected in one thousand years, when Saturn and Neptune will again be let loose for a season. The first resurrection is the first cycle in the new age. It is the degrees of the houses which are termed dead, for it could not be applied to anything else, when it says: "that the rest of the dead lived not again." In verse 7, "And when the thousand years are expired, Satan shall be loosed out of his prison." This is an astrological calculation for a period of time and is for the next cycle of Uranus, when another destruction takes place.

Chapter 21 describes the New Age beginning with 1921. This chapter is also very simple as it is applied to the government of the United States on the earth and not to heaven. It deals strictly with the material and political affairs of the people here. It should be remembered that it describes a horoscope for the nation and that they were human beings who wrote the Bible describing the conditions seen from an astrological point of view.

The time of the new heaven and the new earth is described in chapter 21. It follows after the description of the great war. The United States is the place described in this chapter and spoken of as "that great city, the holy Jerusalem." From verse 12 is a description of a horoscope, describing the twelve houses by giving the names of the twelve gems instead of the twelve tribes.

The measurement of the wall is the same as calculating in numbers of degrees for this horoscope. It is a similar description as given in other chapters when describing the United States, namely, that it is in four squares and divided into twelve parts. The condition which is to manifest itself in this country is described in verse 26, "And they shall bring the glory and honor of the nations into it. And there shall in no wise enter into it anything that defileth neither whatsoever abomination, or maketh a lie, but they which are written in the Lamb's book of life." The gems or stones representing the twelve tribes are dealt with in another chapter, where it is told what each gem represents, The names of the gems merely take the place of the names of the tribes and other forms of expressions.

Chapter 22 describes the United States as the coming nation of the world. This is the description of a second garden of Eden period. "In the midst of the street of it, and on either side of the river, was there the tree of life, which bare twelve manner of fruits, and yielded her fruit every month; and the leaves of the three were for the healing of nations. And there shall be no more curse, but the throne of God and of the Lamb shall be in it; and his servants shall serve him; And they shall see his face; and his name shall be in their forehead." This is a description of the horoscope for the United States in the coming age.

Verse 10, "And he saith unto me, seal not the sayings of the prophecy of this book; for the time is at hand."

Verse 13, "I am Alpha and Omega, the beginning and the end, the first and the last."

CHAPTER 32.

THE UNITED STATES.

The discovery of the American continent was not an accident or a mere event; but it was according to the laws of the universe. We find in Revelation 12 a calculation for the time when the next nation was to be born. It also gives us the condition which was to exist in Europe at the time of the birth of the new nation for it says: "and there appeared a great wonder in heaven, a woman clothed with the sun, and the moon under her feet and upon her head a crown of twelve stars, and she being with child cried travailing in birth, and pained to be delivered." The entire chapter deals with the birth of the United States and describes the Christian Church and her influence as produced by Neptune. The great wonder is the Roman power, she is the woman, clothed with the sun and the moon under her feet. The power of the sun is religion and the moon is the common people which were under her feet. The war in Europe at the time of the birth of the nation in 1776 is when she suffered to be delivered. The twelve stars are represented as a complete form of independent government for Europe.

In the chapter on cycles is explained that years are calculated by degrees; one degree equaling seventy-two years; half a degree equaling thirty-six years, and two degrees one hundred and forty-four years. The Bible illustrates that the beginning and at the ending of all cycles, ages, nations, or any event which takes place in figuring degrees is symbolically illustrated by one or two degrees; these demonstrate the nature of the event. This we will illustrate with the age of the United States as figured in degrees. The United States was declared an independent nation in 1774 to 1776. We will add thirty-six years or one-half degree and get an event at 1812. This is when there was war and trouble everywhere. Next add one degree of seventy-two years and we have 1846-1848, which is the years of the ending of the Mexican war and of the religious movements all over the United States. This is one of the most eventful periods of the country, when the law was made and the Pacific Coast country taken in. Next add two degrees of one hundred and forty-four years and we have 1918-1920. This will prove to be the real beginning of the United States as a nation. The previous events have been the childhood and in

1921 is the beginning of manhood of the United States. This method of figuring events in the future is used in all ages, as written in the Bible.

It is written "a little child shall lead us;" this little child is the United States and he is now leading the nations of the world. There are two distinct degrees marked for the future which we will describe. Add 36 to 1921 which equals 1957. This is a year for war in Europe which Uncle Sam will settle. The next event is in 72 years from 1921 which is 1993, when the Pacific Coast States want to be a nation. The last date is 144 years from 1921 giving 2065, when the United States proper will be divided. In 4000 France and Germany will invade the eastern part of the United States, and annex the country as far west as Utah. The Bible also says, that Europe shall be forgotten for 70 years, when she again will become a great power.

The United States will be as a new nation in 1921 with a new form of government; when new constitutional laws and amendments will be enacted. The Monroe doctrine will be the first principle for all nations and will be applied internationally.

We have explained elsewhere that the United States was the first country described in the Bible. The original race which inhabited the country was the Hametic, who apparently are the forefathers of the Indian races; as the word Adam means red. The dividing of the races from the time of Noah with the description of the descendants from Shem, Ham and Japeth, show that Ham was the father of the Hametic race of America, that Japheth was the father of the European races and Shem was the father of the Asiatic races, Genesis 10.

There are four distinct races described as belonging to Ham, Genesis 10:6, "And the Sons of Ham; Cush and Mizzain and Phut and Canaan." In verse 15 is described the children of Canaan as a separate race but are the descendants of Ham. When a reference is made to the Pacific Ocean the translator called it the river Euphrates, and the Atlantic Ocean is called the Red Sea, or the "river of Egypt."

It is a singular coincidence that the United States at the beginning of the present form of government was divided into five parts, as territories or concessions, and later into the forty-eight states which again correspond to the forty-eight constellations of the heavens.

There is another very clear comparison and that is that the five states on the Pacific Coast are arranged the same in states as described in the Bible as provinces. The state of Washington is Galilee; Oregon is Samaria and California is Judeah. The state of Nevada was called Perrea, and Eastern Washington, Oregon and Idaho was called a Decapolis. The River Jordan was translated as a river when it is the 120th degree west, and is on top of the Cascade and Sierra Nevada range of mountains. Read "The Acts."

The principle described as the birth of the United States as a man child took place in 1774, when independence was declared in Philadelphia and two years later in 1776 when the government was formed. This period, or cycle, corresponds to the age of Moses and Joshua for their time, and to the age of the Apostle Saul-Paul for the present. The entire history as described, contains two degrees of seventy-two years each or 144 years in all.

In order to prove that the cycle for the United States, as a nation, and the Pacific Coast States, as a division, corresponds to the description which is given in the Bible, we will describe the method the Bible writers used.

The death of the old country and the birth of the new world takes place within this two degrees or 144 years. The beginning of the end as the killing of the Roman Age began in 1774-1776 and lasts to 1918-20. Within this period of time the formation and development of the United States as a well-organized nation, takes place. This is the age as illustrated by Moses and Joshua as the capturing of the country and the locating of the tribes. The events which take place are described by the travels of the planet Uranus in the twelve houses of the heavens. The last 84-year circuit of Uranus began in 1828, when he was in Aquarius and caused war. At this time Turkey lost in the war with Russia. The activity of Uranus from the year 1828 to 1918 is described as part of the life of Jesus, and corresponds to what has taken place in the last century. This can be illustrated in the leading events of the nations. Take 1828-30 and add half of the cycle of Uranus, or forty-two years, which gives 1870-72, when France and Germany had war. To the cycle for the United States, beginning in 1776 add 84, which equals 1860, when the civil war took place. From this can be seen the method used in describing the cycles of time and the history of the nations. It should be remembered that the disciples of Christ are the nations of Europe and that the Pacific Coast division of the United States is described as Judeah, Samaria,

Galilee, Perea and Decapolis. From this can be seen what country and nation is described in the travels of Jesus.

The development and history of the United States correspond to this system of calculation and will be found to be correct. The Bible illustrates that all cycles or nations are first divided into five and seven sections and later into the twelve divisions. This can be illustrated in the history of the United States, as in the formation of the seven and five divisions which later became the forty-eight states. The dates, as given, will be useful in figuring the time for the annexation of territory and for the wars which have taken place. The 84 and 42-year period for Uranus should be used for events and the 72 and 36-year period for time and space representing territory.

The founding and developing of the United States took place in the years, as we have given, in the following order westward. The original thirteen states constituted the territory east of the Mississippi, obtained by treaty in 1783, after the well-known seven years of trouble from 1776 to 1783 when the treaty was signed. The second section is the middle west, known as the "Louisiana Purchase," from France in 1803. The third division is the southeast, including Florida, in the purchase from Spain in 1818-19. The fourth territory is the annexation of Texas in 1845. The fifth section is what was known as the "Gadsden Purchase" of southern Arizoona in 1853. The sixth division consists of the "Oregon Territory," obtained by discovery and treaty from England in 1846. The seventh and last territory is the great southwest of California, Arizona and Nevada, which was obtained from Mexico in 1848. The Pacific Coast section was later divided into five states, which makes the twelve divisions, which in former ages were called provinces.

At the same time when the United States government was formed, it was also the year when the Oregon Country was discovered and named Oregon by Jonathan Carver. It took 72 years for the emigrants to settle in the west and by adding the 72 years to 1774-76, we have 1846-48. These are the years Oregon and California became populated and part of the Union as territory, and also the time when gold was discovered in California, which produced the emigration west.

The age as described as the Apostle Saul-Paul is for the Pacific Coast cycle and begins in 1918-20. California is described as a Jerusalem in Judeah and is to rule first. Oregon is next described with Antioch as a center. Washington is the third division with Ephesus as the Metropolis. The meaning of this description is that California is to be developed first, next Oregon, and last Washington, which means a new Era of progress for the Pacific Coast States. From this illustration can be seen the system used by the Bible writers to describe the ending and beginning of the cycles and the moving with the degrees westward.

The general description given in the New Testament representing the Pacific Coast country is very clear and we will give a general outline of it. The Bible is translated so as to describe the event to take place in Palestine but it is on the Pacific Coast that the New Age is described.

The country was said to consist of five territories, called cities, each section or city is described according to the geographical location and divided by mountains, valleys and rivers.

California is called Judeah; Samaria is Oregon; and Galilee is Washington. Idaho and the country northeast has no special name but is a Decapolis or section by itself. The fifth division is Nevada, which is called Perea. Arizona is not mentioned, for it is in Edom, in the Sodom and Gomorrah district.

Judeah as California is named first. It consists of the territory anciently belonging to the four tribes; Judah, Benjamin, Dan and Simeon. Modern Bible students fail to find the dividing line of Judeah in the north, in Palestine proper.

Samaria is the central province west of the mountains between Judeah and the Galilee country and is northern California and Oregon. Its share of the plains by the sea was known as Sarona (Sharon) and is the Coast Range. The mountain region is described as being held by the Samaritans, who were the descendants of the old Ten Tribes. Later Samaria is included in Galilee.

Washington, called Galilee, is located at the sea of Tiberius, which is the Puget Sound. Phœnicia spoken of is British Columbia and the Lebanoon Mountains are the Cascade Mountains. The Firs and Cedars of Lebanon are the woods of Oregon which again are to become valuable.

The description of the people of Washington was given; that they had the nature of the Jew and not like the people of Jerusalem, which is Southern California. It is written that great work was to be done in this state for the missions in the New Age.

It will be seen that California rules first, then Oregon, and last Washington. In the time of the twelve churches, as described by Paul, the state of Washington ruled and the rest of the country from the Shasta Mountains in the south to Utah east, was subject to the Puget Sound country. The twelve churches included in Paul's travels and which he visits are at first located on the entire coast, but the churches to which he writes the Epistles, are located in western Washington.

"Perea" is Nevada and extends from the mountains in the west to Salt Lake, described as the Dead Sea, and the Desert south and east was called the Syrian desert. Its boundary reached to the river Arnon on the south, which is the Colorado River.

The line was drawn to a place in the north called Pella, which corresponds to the location of the tribe of Dan north of Cœur d'Alene in Idaho. This division represents what was known "from Dan to Beer-sheba" and is from Cœur d'Alene to Colorado River. This territory covers the tribes of Reuben, Gad and Manasseh. The terms used for this part of the country were, "the farther side of Jordan" or "beyond the Jordan." Today it is called "east of the mountains."

The fifth and last territory, as described, is "The Decapolis" and is the section east of the mountains as Oregon and Washington. This section has no given name and is called a Decapolis, which means a nation or headquarters within itself. This section includes the location of the ten tribes. It takes in as far as we can judge, the entire territory east of the mountains, north of the Snake and Columbia Rivers, but the eastern borders are not defined. However, it takes in a lake by the name of "Merom," possibly Cœur d'Alene. The flat country around Spokane was called the "Bashan." The Blue Mountains were called "El Ledja." The Rocky Mountain range in Idaho is called "Mt. Hermon."

It is apparent that the mountains, rivers and country in general have not changed in the last 6000 years, for the description given in the Bible is as good today as it was when it was written.

The names given in the Acts, have been translated from the Greek language and the names of Greece and Italy used to show that Paul lived there.

A good description of the United States as a nation is given in Isaiah, chapters 60-66. It is for the conditions which exist at the present time.

Part IV—Chapter 32.

The Pacific Coast States, when described in the Acts, the years of 1918-1921 is given as 33-35 Anno Domini. The year 1920 is described in chapter 8, and gives the conditions on the west coast of the country which will be far from good.

The cycle after 1920 is figured from the 120th degree west longitude and the disaster which will take place then is for the United States. The first cycle for the United States contains 40 degrees and if the United States has war between the years 1992 and 1996, the country east of the 115th degree will be destroyed and annexed to Europe. There is a prophecy in the Bible that France and Germany may invade the United States as far west as Utah and destroy the eastern States.

The period of time between 1920 and 2992 is called the Millenium age, and during this cycle the conditions and mode of living in the United States will be as a Garden of Eden. The population in the United States will be ten per cent. greater than the entire population of the nations in Europe; according to the description given in the Bible. The 120th degree west longitude is the next center for the world's population and civilization for the next 2000 years.

The disturbances described in the Bible as earthquakes, etc., mean the revolutionizing of the existing national conditions. It has reference to all nations on earth and is described to take place at the time of the end of the world.

The conditions, as described in Europe, need no explanation for the Bible stories give this in detail. The country of the Pacific Coast is described in the Acts, chapters 4-12 and in Revelations as the sixth plague and these predictions will soon come to pass.

It should be remembered that the cycle which begins in 1921 is for new nations under new conditions with new laws and form of government. The laboring and lower classes are to rule and be at the head of the government in America and Asia, as well as in Europe. Before this takes place, however, a great disturbance is to affect all nations; which is the cause of the change in the government. This disturbance as described in Revelations 9:13 as the sixth plague is to begin in Germany and at the Euphrates. All the nations of Europe will change their form of government and the common people will rule this Millenium age.

Up to the fall of 1920 the world is ruled by Saturn as Satan. The nature of the spirit of the age is to be selfish, discontented, destructive and domineering. All seeking to get something for nothing, and if they do not get it their way, they will produce trouble for themselves and others. It will be found that before we enter 1921, that the elements which are ruled by Satan whether rich or poor will do much damage and will upset the present forms of governments. It will be like a cyclone and when it is over the conditions, within all nations, will be satisfactorily adjusted with new and better form of government and living conditions; which is described as the Millenium age.

This disturbance is described as the sixth plague, will last for five months, which will begin in 1919 and will not be satisfactorliy settled until the new form of government is established.

The seventh plague is described in Rev. 10; after the sixth plague has begun. It will take place at the time of the publication of a book explaining the mysterious writings of the Bible.

The eclipse of the Sun and Moon, which took place in the fourth year of the war in 1918, is spoken of in the Bible in a number of places when the end of time was referred to. It is a scientific fact that an eclipse of the sun and moon takes place every eighteen years. The ancient writers figured out, or knew, that at the end of each cycle of time this eclipse and the war comes at a given time. Eighteen times 120 equals 2160 years and this constitutes a cycle of time. From this it will be seen that at the end of every great cycle an eclipse will take place. This is the mystery which the Bible students have magnified and distorted; for all kinds of explanations have been brought forth to show why the sun and moon became dark. The Bible contains the statement that at the time of the crucifying of Christ, the sun and moon were to be darkened. Christ has now been crucified for the past four years, and this is one of the facts to show that Christ is being crucified now and not 2000 years ago.

The United States is represented in the character known as Uncle Sam and corresponds to the eastern or male division of the country. The female principle is represented in the wife of Uncle Sam, who is called Columbia and represents the Pacific Coast States. Uncle Sam and Columbia have a legal family of forty-eight children (48 States) but Uncle Sam has children out of wedlock, his outside possessions. He is doing as Abraham did and has children with his handmaids outside of his own home, which is self explanatory.

For the next age, the United States will, as a power, rule the nations of the world. The end of the cycle and power for the United States is described in John 21:18, "Verily, verily, I say unto thee, when thou wast young thou girdest thyself, and walketh whither thou wouldst: but when thou shalt be old, thou shalt stretch forth thy hands, and another shall gird thee, and carry thee whither thou wouldst not."

The wise men who wrote the Bible were Astrologers. They produced a story of the heavens to show the coming age the law.

CHAPTER 33.

MILLENIUM AND NEW WORLD.

The Bible describes the New World, commonly called the United States. This country is described in the Bible as a real heaven on earth, where living is a perfect dream of happiness. From the beautiful description given in church literature of this New World, and the future home of the races, a real, glorious, heavenly home on earth has been described and not mansions in the clouds. It has been so illustrated that at the end of a given cycle of time, the conditions of the old country, described as the old world, were to be destroyed, and the New World would be the future home for the races. The country of the new world is described as having golden streets and the people living there, playing on harps and singing the songs of Moses; speaking with Angels; and sitting on footstools made by God. It was to be neither night nor day in this heavenly home and they would worship God and work day and night.

What is written in the Bible of the New Heaven and the New Earth is a description of a paradise on earth and is the United States and not a place in the clouds. The place and conditions which were to exist there were described as a perfect life, with personal freedom and liberty without limit. God would live with the people and produce a condition where tears and sorrows should be unknown.

The New Jerusalem is described in Revelation, Chapter 21:1 "And I saw a new heaven and a new earth, for the first heaven and the first earth have passed away; and there was no more sea." The first heaven and the first earth which have passed away are the old conditions in the old country east of Greenwich. The new heaven and earth is the United States and the expression that the sea has passed away is that the Atlantic Ocean is passed, (has been crossed). There is a mention of a third heaven in which is paradise and where the tree of life is located. (2nd Cor. 12:2; Rev. 2:7). This has reference to the third division of the earth and is the Pacific Coast States. This part of the earth is really the paradise described and is the best and healthiest part to live in of all the countries of the earth.

The reason why some people (the church element) at death expect to go to a certain place called heaven, is because of the description given for the new cycle of time. The country was described as a paradise on earth, where the human race lived with God, who also was in a new heaven at this time. An example of the description of this imaginary heaven and earth in the clouds is found in Rev. 21:2, "And I John saw the holy city, New Jerusalem, coming down from God out of heaven, prepared as a bride adorned for her husband. 3 And I heard a great voice out of heaven saying: 'Behold the tabernacle of God is with men, and he will dwell with them, and they shall be his people, and God himself shall be with them, and be their God.' 4 And God shall wipe away all tears fromo their eyes; and there shall be no more death, neither sorrow, nor crying, neither shall there be any more pain; for the former things have passed away." The explanation of these verses is that the bride as described, is the Pacific Coast States, as the female principle of the earth. The bridegroom is the eastern section of the United States. The tabernacle of God is to be with men, which is the true Christian spirit that of having God within. God is to be with men which we call the American spirit today. The expression that there shall be no more death means that the knowledge of that life is eternal will take away the sorrows and fears of death which alone will be enough to call this age a real paradise.

In this Millenium age called Paradise, the Lion and the Lamb, as well as the Bull, Scorpion and the Goats shall dwell together in peace and happiness; that is the tribes as represented by these animals will be peaceful nations living as God's children. The good country of the United States which is God's country on earth and a Paradise from the beginning of time.

The Millenium is the beginning of the New Age history; at this time all nations of the earth will live in peace and harmony. The illustrations, as pictured in the stories of the Millenium, show that there is a law in the universe which rules all things, and that there is an intelligent power above or rather a heavenly power which produces conditions on this earth for good or evil. Take the great war as an example. The war had to be, in order to break up the military or ruling class of Europe for all nations are military, so all the nations had to be destroyed. It is like washing a nation as we would wash a soiled garment. It has to be washed in order to be clean and ready for use. That is what Europe will be in the future, a clean nation, with a clean form of government. Then all the nations will be striving to live according to the golden rule. This will be the millenium age and a New Testament. We are assured that at this time there will be a reorganization of Europe, giving new nations and new forms of governments, and also that the Christian church, as operated now, with its extreme power and rulership over nations and individuals and the collecting of tribute for the salvation of man for the next world, will cease during the time of the millenium. If this form of power were to continue, the Christian church would then rule the world. The Bible states positively that the Christian church will be destroyed. There must be a reason for destroying this great organization, possibly the same reason as the destroying of militarism and capitalism together with other monopolistic powers. If nations are operated justly, the Christian churches will not be allowed to collect a tribute for a life after death, when the fact becomes known that there is no death. The churches of today will be unnecessary and will have to reorganize on the principle of doing good. The people will not go to church to find out what to do to be saved in the next life but to learn the truths of the present life. To correct the adverse conditions and bring about reorganization the great war takes place. It is the working of law, which we do not understand, but before long all will be understood. Peace and war are apparently as necessary as the heat in summer and the cold in winter; so we have no right to condemn war or winter and praise peace and sunshine. One is as essential as the other in this great universe.

If the nations of the world today have violated the laws of God and sinned, they are in hell and have to take the consequences, as every human being does when he violates the law.

If the churches in their teachings stray away from the right path of God and teach doctrines of their own, that is: if they live according to their own desires as do nations and individuals and take the law into their own hand, leading humanity to worship a false God, punishment must follow. This will be endured for a time but not always, so the day comes when the churches, as well as nations, have to reorganize. That is what is meant when it is said that the Christian church and all other churches will be destroyed.

The Catholic Church is called the Mother of Harlots and all the rest of the churches, the daughters. A millstone is to be put around their necks and they are to be thrown into the ocean. So we know God will make quick work in reorganizing these churches and it will be a sad day when it takes place. The creed of the church will go but the spirit of the church will live and be followed. Many a defender of the church will be made white during this calamity, but the soiled garments of the church have to be washed, and it will be washed in blood, as it is written in the Bible. Rev. 17:18:19.

CHAPTER 34.

THE BOOK OF MORMON.

In the teachings of the Mormon church are brought out clearly that the United States has been populated before the present generation. Joseph Smith discovered the writings known as the "Book of Mormon" and is a Bible for mother earth. The writings or slates found by Joseph Smith, buried in an underground vault in the State of New York, are made of metal and are written in the Egyptian language. The writings of the Mormons are similar to the description of the races given in the Bible. It gives the history of the race from the beginning of time.

In the book of Mormon is found a full description of the cycles of the Christian age. The book of Mormon and the Hebrew Talmud come from the same class of writers. It is translated in plain language and easier to understand than the Bible.

In the book of Mormon proper and the book of Nephi are a full description of the time and place of the present war. It describes the present time, better than the Bible, for it gives the degrees for location in detail. The book of Mormon is a part of the Bible and takes up the study of the children of Adam and brings history down to the end at Greenwich. The Mormons' description of ancient time is as clear as the description given in the Bible. In fact it gives information which is not given in the Bible, as it deals with the conflict of the north and south as being the opposition in Israel. We will advise students to obtain the book of Mormon for it is worth the time and money. The contents of the book of Mormon correspond to the laws of Moses. In the "Book of Mormon" is a single book entitled "Book of Mormon;" this book together with the "Book of Moroni," (Moroni is the son of Mormon) represent the heavenly conditions produced by the planet Uranus.

To the Bible students these books are very important for they give the missing link in the history. There is nothing new or important which is not in the Bible but the book of Mormon represents the five tribes, while the Bible describes the twelve tribes.

We believe that Joseph Smith actually found the brass plates and we also believe that Mr. Smith knew that the plates were astrological for we are informed he calculated space and directed the movement of the church in future time. He figured the time of the civil war and many of the national events to come. He used the equinoctial time to place his calculations and must have been familiar with the law of nature.

The action of Joseph Smith in hiding the plates after he had translated them was according to instruction given in the Book of Mormon. The spirits which instructed Mr. Smith how to read the writings of the plates instructed him to hide them for the time being, for there always is a reason for things.

The Mormons are the last church and located at the last degree a church could be located in the old cycle. The church of Mormon is located in the house of Virgo. The Mohammedan church and the Mormon Church correspond for both are in the west end or gate of a cycle of time.

When Moses was in Utah at Mt. Sinai he brought down two slates and when he beheld the "golden calf" he destroyed the first two slates. After a time Moses brings down two more slates out of the mountains to the Mormons and the two slates were adopted as the laws of Moses. We will say that "Moses and Mormon" are the same, and when the first slates were destroyed it is the destruction of the present worship of the Mormons. The golden calf is church worship for church organization is a personal representation of God. This worship will be destroyed and the people of the Mormon church will receive a new set of slates from Moses and they will call him Moroni. These slates are the same as described in the

"Book of Mormon" in the book of Nephi, chapter 13:20 as the "Book of the Jew." Their own Bible tells them what kind of a book it will be and what it will teach. The Jews are the people of Judah in Europe and it will be a man from Europe of the tribe Leo who will write a book which is described in the Book of Mormon. They will accept the teachings of the new book of the Jew, which again corresponds to the two new slates of Moses. This is very simple and it is for the Mormons to figure out from their own book when the new book of the Jew will be published. It is written in very plain, good language following the description of the destruction of the Christian Churches.

The Mormon church proves that the "Garden of Eden" described in the Bible was in the United States. They also believe that the center of the garden calculated in degrees is at 95 degrees west, instead of 90 degrees, to correspond to the location of Salt Lake. The actual place as a center must be where nature divides the country. It will be found at 90 degrees west and 36 degrees north and is in Missouri. At this place within a radius of two degrees the States of Missouri, Arkansas, Tennessee, Mississippi, Kentucky and Illinois are divided. This section of Missouri is a freak of nature and is the center of the "Garden of Eden."

The Mormons are filling in a space in the history of Christianity, they are part of Christ and belong to Christ, but they are of the later day. From this they know they are at the end or last days of Christianity. They have the Christian spirit and are the followers of Moses, and when they get their New Slates in the New Dispensation they can then follow Christ and worship a living God in the eternal universe.

CHAPTER 35.

REINCARNATION AND EVOLUTION.

We have been unable to find in the Bible, or any of the other sacred books, the principles of reincarnation. Every subject or topic we have been able to observe deals with endless cycles of time. The sun and planets are continuous in their eternal revolutions in circuits. They have been given different names at the end of each cycle but a new cycle is not reincarnation. Uranus has been called Adam, Noah, Moses, Jesus and Saul and Paul; this does not mean reincarnation. We do not say that the human race cannot reincarnate, but we have failed to find it in any of the fundamental principles of life written in the Bible. The principle of evolution is the philosophy brought forth in the Bible and not the teachings of man's desire where to live and in what form to exist. The Bible states that the soul and body of man part and that the evolution of the being continues in the next form of expression. The Bible also says that reproduction takes place in our present form of existence and that we do not reproduce in the next life. Reproduction and cycles of time do not go backward.

Our present form is the first expression of conscious life, when memory and individuality are obtained. If individuality and memory are lost in reincarnation, the existence of the being becomes a new expression of life.

If we are not mistaken, there is a continuous change from birth to death and all life is eternal. When the elements of nature have served their purpose, they are discarded and a new expression is taken on. There is not in any expression of life a demonstration that the same life principle exist in the same form twice.

We do not know whether reincarnation is a fact or not, as it is now known or understood, but we do know that the law of nature is regulated and unchangeable; that the same law applies to the smallest as well as to the largest manifestation in existence, because as it is in heaven so is it on earth.

The leaders of Theosophy base their opinion regarding reincarnation on what is written in the book of Matthew 17:10-14, "And his disciple asked him, saying, 'why then say the scribes that Elias must first come' and Jesus answered and said unto them, 'Elias truly shall first come, and restore all things, but I say unto you; That Elias is come already, and they know him not.' Then the disciples understood that he spake unto them of John the Baptist." Read Mark 9:11-13. Also read Malachi 4:5, "Behold, I will send you Elijah the prophet before the coming of the great and dreadful day of the Lord." Elijah and John the Baptist are representations of Neptune. Neptune has again been reincarnated in the furnace of the lion which is the killing and reincarnation of Elijah. Matthew 11:12-15.

CHAPTER 36.

THE ACTS.

The book of The Acts is the description of the events which are to take place in the New Age. We will refer to a few chapters to show what is meant by the travels of Paul and what the names of the different places are. At the beginning of the description of the Apostle's time, new names were given the characters which represent the planet Uranus. A new name was given to both divisions for the name of Saul was applied to the first cycle and Paul to the Pacific Coast section.

The first three chapters deal with the condition in Europe, and the description given is what will take place at the present time. It must be remembered that the disciples of Jesus represent the nations of Europe and when it is said in the Bible that certain disciples meet together, speak, etc., it is really a representation of action of the different nations. When the disciples speak in different tongues (cloven tongues), as is written in chapter 2, it means that all nations are speaking in their own languages. It says that they were "filled with the holy spirit," when speaking; which means that the nations are on friendly terms and have the Christ spirit within.

Chapter 3 describes that Peter heals a lame man sitting at the gate of the temple. In the New Age, Peter is the United States and the lame man is Ireland, who sits at the gate; the gate means near Greenwich degree. This is the same cripple or beggar who has been sitting for ages at the door of the temple. It means that within a few years Ireland will again stand on her own feet and walk as a nation, but it will be by the help of the United States. Verse 6, "Then Peter said, Silver and gold have I none; but such as I have give I thee; In the name of Jesus Christ of Nazareth, rise up and walk." The rest of the chapter is self explanatory, for it shows that the spirit of the age spoken of by Peter is the great American principle of Freedom.

Chapter 4 describes the imprisonment of Peter and John; the imprisonment means war. Peter is the United States and John is either Holland or Belgium. Peter was bold and declared a principle of right and justice, described in verses 8 to 12. This is the American Spirit of the age, called the "Holy Ghost" in verse 8. It also says that the other Apostles were threatened, which means that there was danger of war for other nations.

Chapter 5 is a description of Annanias and his wife Sapphira, who sold some land and did not act honest about it. The characters representing Annanias and his wife are Mexico. The eastern and western part of the country represent man and wife. It is the same story over again at the end of the age, when Uranus, described as a patriarch, goes south, usually called Egypt, to avoid some imaginary persecution. At the beginning of all cycles or ages a trip is made south and at this age it is to Mexico. The story, described in chapter 5, is that Mexico is in some manner involved in a deal to sell part of her country. We are inclined to think that before many years are passed that Mexico will give some other nation part of her territory for money; this will produce war with the United States. It is shown that Peter is the master and will merely say the word, and Mexico from the Atlantic to the Pacific will fall dead at the feet of the United States.

In all the chapters of The Acts, where Peter is used as an illustration, it is the United tates which is meant; as in the first part of The Acts Simon or Peter is the leading character.

In chapter 13:9 Saul is called Paul to show the change of cycles, which takes place after the destruction spoken of in chapter 11:27. This is the end of the age (the first 40 degrees) and at this time Herod dies as described in chapter 12. The age as represented by "Herod the Great" is to Greenwich and is described as belonging to the European cycle.

The rest of the chapters deal with the condition on the west ocast, where the Apostle Paul travels and visits the different tribes described as churches. There are twenty-eight chapters of The Acts and all are repetition of what could and should be done in the different churches, which again is nothing more or less than a representation of the houses of the heavens, describing the philosophy of the universe.

The age of Paul is for the Pacific Coast states and extends across the Pacific Ocean and includes the eastern part of China and Japan. The life of Paul is easily followed, for the Pacific Coast country has been described before, showing the different divisions, as it is a similar history as that described after Solomon's time. When Paul travels across the Pacific Ocean, it is transcribed to be a trip to Rome, when he was shipwrecked as described in chapter 27:10. The shipwreck story is the passing of the 180th degree west. Paul (Uranus) made the trip in the sign for Caster and Pollux which is Gemini, chapter 28:11.

The life of Paul in China is described in chapter 28:8 when he was with the barbarians and healed many in the islands.

This is as far as the Apostle Paul can go and he is at the end of his cycle of time.

The chapters of Paul, written from the Asiatic side of the Pacific Ocean, is described as Epistles to the Romans, Galatians, and others; these letters or epistles are written to the churches on the American side, which were located in the Pacific northwest. In former ages ten tribes used to be described but Paul writes to the twelve churches, representing the twelve tribes.

The ruler, described as Agrippa, in chapter 26, is for the Pacific Coast, described at this time as a nation having a ruler. It is apparent that he was not the highest officer of the nation, for Paul appealed to a higher court above Agrippa. The Cæsar spoken of corresponds to the government at Washington, D. C., in our time, and is represented in Saturn.

Part V.

HEAVENLY CONDITIONS ON EARTH.
CHAPTER 37.
TWELVE TRIBES IN THE UNITED STATES.

The twelve tribes of Israel, as described by Moses and Joshua were located in the Pacific Coast States, and extend over into Japan and China. The Pacific Coast States were described as the promised land and were divided according to the natural divisions of the country, in degrees of latitude and longitude. In this chapter we will describe the principle illustrated in the location of the tribes at a given distance in degrees, called the locating of the tribes and a nativity. The Pacific Coast States have been described as the place for the beginning of Bible history. It was first divided into four parts and later into the five and seven tribes which became the twelve tribes of Israel. The birth of the children of Mother Earth, as described on the Pacific Coast, is the naming and locating of the tribes at the beginning of the cycle. This is the place for the beginning of the history of the age ending at Greenwich. Joshua located the twelve tribes in the Pacific Coast States and Jacob describes the children born in Europe-Asia but does not locate them.

In Solomon's time the country contained five provinces which later were divided into seven and finally into ten tribes. The reason why there should be only ten tribes at this time is that the two tribes of Reuben and Gad are located east of the 120th degree; which leaves the ten tribes west of the mountains. The Pacific Coast Country is described as Eve and the mother of all the children on the earth from which we can see the reason why all cycles should begin at this location.

The Pacific Coast States are by nature, located so that the different cycles within the 120-degree age can be described as tribes. It must be remembered that each age or cycle has a holy mountain. The first age of 120 degrees is represented in Mt. Whitney which is the first holy mountain as the Jerusalem for the five tribes of Judah, which later were called the Jews. The second cycle of 60 degrees consists of the seven tribes north of Judeah having Mt. Ephraim, which is Mt. Shasta, in the Siskiyou Mountains, as the holy mountain for the age. The last cycles of 30 degrees is represented in the two mountains of

Tyre and Zidon, which are respectively the Olympic Mountains and Mt. Rainier in the State of Washington. We will call attention to the fact that the place originally located as the tribe of Issachar constituted the triangular location beween Mt. Rainier, Mt. Adams and Mt. St. Helens in the State of Washington. This is the place which corresponds to Belgium for the cycle for Europe, when the age is killed. It is located between Galilee and Samaria and corresponds to the description given in the Bible. This place corresponds to Alsace-Lorraine and Belgium as the funeral pyre for the cycle for Europe and is called the Armagedden and Golgotha as the end of the cycle for the Christian age.

The International Date Line at 180 degrees has been called the Euphrates and is the location for the tribe of Naphtali. Turkey represents Naphtali for the cycle of Europe and the river Euphrates is located at the 45th degree longitude and is one of the quarter divisions of the earth, called a bad angle. From this can be seen that Turkey represents the end of the cycle and is to Europe the same as the British Columbia boundary line is to the Pacific Coast tribes.

It will be seen that the tribes as located on the Pacific Coast have been located to correspond to the degrees around the earth and the division of the heavens. In order to prove this we will describe the principal angles in the location of the tribes given in the Bible. San Francisco is located in Pisces, near Aries, which corresponds to the meridian in the heavens and is the principal location on the Pacific Coast and called Jericho. In the State of Washington, west of the mountain, is the location for Cancer, called Issachar, and is the end of the first 90-degree cycle and a burying place for the age. The British Columbia boundary represents 180 degrees and is called Naphtali and is the end of the age north. Reuben as Sagitarius is the first born and is located east of the mountains in Nevada and is calculated as 120 degrees east from San Francisco, making the end of the age, as being near the Sodom-Gomorah country. The tribe of Simeon which is Aquarius is located as San Diego County and represents the borders of Mexico and the 60th degree angle from Jericho. Portland, Oregon, is located at a good angle in the upper end of the tribe of Manasseh as Taurus and represents the first 60 degrees of the cycle. The Shasta Mountains divided Ephraim and Manasseh which is Aries and Taurus representing the 30-degree angle.

Part V—Chapter 37.

The holy mountain of Mt. Whitney has been described as Levi, and is Aquarius; (at this age separated from Simeon). It is located 30 degrees from Aries which is the 30-degree of the tribe of Benjamin (Pisces) and is the distance from San Francisco to Mt. Whitney. The tribe of Levi is located at the tribe of Judah which is Leo and corresponds to southern California. The tribe of Judah represents the 120th degree from San Francisco and is the end of the cycle. This tribe extends east to the desert at Death Valley and Arizona and to the Mexican borders. The two tribes of Dan and Asher are located on the coast and are described to extend over into China. These tribes are Libra and Scorpio located respectively 210 and 240 degrees from San Francisco, which explains why these tribes extend to Asia and are located on the other side of the 180th degree.

We realize that the description and location of the tribes are of no value to the students who are not familiar with this study, but this science is known to many who do know and understand the principle described.

The Pacific age begins at 115 degrees, which includes the country from the Gulf of California in the south and north to the Canadian border. The dividing line, described in the Bible as the "Jordan" is the eastern borders of the Sierra Nevada and Cascade Mountains, which is at the 120th degree. East of the mountains was called "on the other side of Jordan," and west of the mountains "beyond the Jordan." The real division is the mountains from the Gulf of California to British Columbia. The description begins with the tribes in the south and goes northward. There are three tribes on the east of the mountains which were divided by Moses and belong to his cycle. These are Reuben, Gad and Manasseh, bounded on the east by the 115th degree.

Mt. Whitney in California is located near the 36th degree north latitude and the tribe of Naphtali as Virgo is located twelve degrees north, at the entrance of the Puget Sound, which is at 48 degrees and corresponds to the meridian of the heavens. From this can be seen the reason why the United States borders do not extend north of the 49th degree.

The Pacific Coast country was divided into four divisions, that is, the 24 degrees from the 30th degree to the 54th degree, were divided into four cycles of six degrees each and were called the twenty-four elders. The first quarter is in the south from the 30th degree in Mexico to the 36th degree at Mt. Whitney; the second quarter terminates at the location of the Siskiyou Mountains at the 42nd degree. The third quarter ends at the 48th degree in Washington and the fourth quarter ends at the 54th degree.

The tribes, described in the Bible and located on the Pacific Coast have been divided by the degrees and this we will prove by the following description. Naphtali is the farthest north and is located north of the 48th degree and east of the 123rd degree. Zebulun is located between the 47th and 48th degree east of the 123rd degree. Issachar is located between the 46th and 47th degree east of the 123rd degree. Manasseh is located between the 41st and 46th degrees east of the 123rd degree. Asher is located along the coast west from the 123rd degree and extends to Asia at the 120th degree east of Greenwich. This tribe is also called Asher in Japan and Chinaa north of the 42nd degree. The tribe of Ephraim is located between the 38th and 41st degree and between the 120th and 124th degree. Benjamin is located between the 36th and 38th degrees. Judah is located between the 34th and 36th degree. Simeon is located south of the 34th degree. Dan is located along the coast and is the coast range from the 35th to the 37th degree. The tribes of Benjamin and Ephraim also extend to Asia. Naphtali, in the north (British Columbia) extends, when making a circle of the tribes, to the south and is then in Mexico and is called Naphtali in the south. The tribes of Reuben and Gad are east of the Mountains.

The virgin Naphtali is located in Galilee next to the two sons of Zebedee and the Sea of Galilee corresponds to the Puget Sound.

The holy mountains in California are located in what is known as Tulare county from Tulare lake to Owens lake, between the 36th and 37th degrees, and include a number of national park reservations. In the Bible this place is called the tribe of Levi.

REUBEN (SAGITARIUS).

The tribe of Reuben is located in Nevada from the Colorado River in the south, west of the 115th degree and north of the 36th degree. Reuben is bounded on the west by the Sierra Nevada Mountains; on the east by the desert and on the north

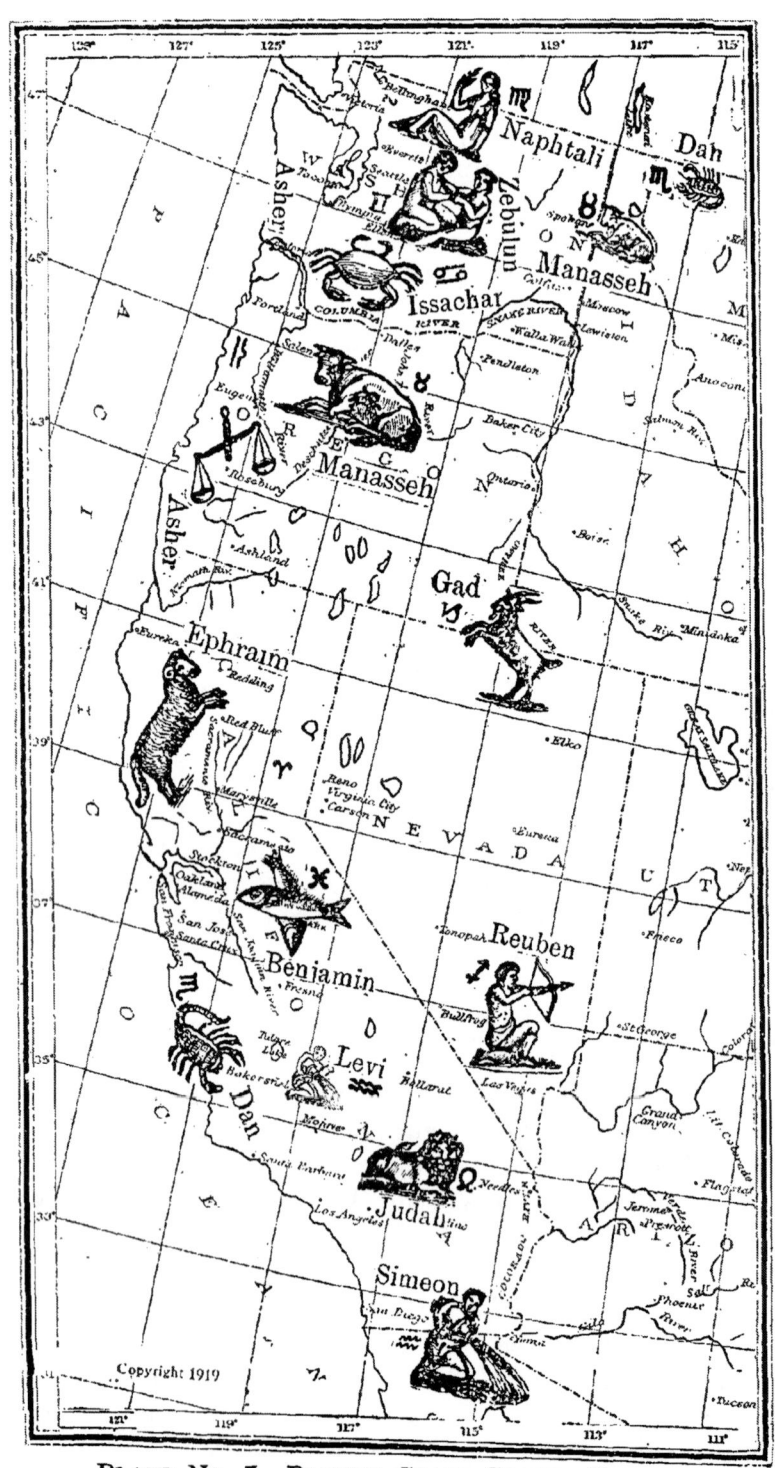

PLATE NO. 7—PACIFIC COAST STATES TRIBES.

by the Humbolt River at the 41st degree. The tribe of Reuben in Europe corresponds to Spain and Portugal.

GAD (CAPRICORN).

The tribe of Gad is located north of Reuben. It is bounded on the west by the 120th degree, on the south by the 41st degree at the Humbolt River, on the east by the 115th degree and on the north by the 46th degree at Columbia River to the Bitter Root Mountains. It takes in the corners of Nevada, Oregon and Idaho. In Europe the tribe of Gad corresponds to Russia.

MANNASSEH (TAURUS).

The half tribe of Manasseh, east is the territory east of the Cascade Mountains, containing what is known as eastern Washington and northern Idaho. It is bounded on the west by the 120th degree, on the south by the 46th degree, on the east by the 115th degree and on the north at the British Columbia boundary in the 48th degree.

This is the section known as Bashan and called "the grainery of Egypt. Manasseh east corresponds to England's outside possessions.

SIMEON-LEVI (AQUARIUS).

The tribe of Simeon is located on the west of the mountains and it received its share of territory from Judah. The tribe of Simeon corresponds to San Diego County, from the Colorado River to the Ocean. It included the northern part of Mexico from the 30th degree latitude to the Gulf of California as a southern boundary. Its northern boundary is the San Bernardino Mountains, south of the 34th degree.

The tribe of Levi is separated from Simeon and is located in what is known as the "Holy Mountains," and is in Tulare County, California. It includes Mt. Whitney and Kaweah Peak, both over 14,000 feet high, and are the highest mountains in the United States. The tribe of Levi includes the Sequoia National Park and is nothing but mountains.

In Europe, the tribe of Simeon corresponds to Alsace-Lorraine, and the tribe of Levi corresponds to Switzerland.

JUDAH (LEO).

The tribe of Judah is described as having the most valuable land and is located in Southern California, west of the mountains. It includes the counties of Riverside, San Bernardino, Los Angeles, Ventura and Kern Counties, up to Tulare and Kings Counties in the mountains. Its northern boundary was the Kings River and Lake Tulare at the 36th degree; the western boundary was the coast range and from Santa Barbara south to the Ocean at the 120th degree. The southern border was at the 34th degree. In Europe the tribe of Judah corresponds to Germany.

BENJAMIN (PISCES).

The tribe of Benjamin is located between the territory of Judah on the south and Ephraim on the north. The eastern border is the mountains; the southern boundary includes Fresno county up to the Kings River and Tulare Lake to the 37th degree; its western border is the coast range, including San Benito County, up to the Salinas River at Santa Cruz, then to the Ocean north of San Francisco to the 38th degree. The northern border is from the bay and the Sacramento River east on the 38th degree 30 minutes to the 120th degree in the mountains. The tribe of Benjamin is the San Joaquin Valley and corresponds to Italy in Europe.

DAN (SCORPIO).

The tribe of Dan is located between Benjamin and the Ocean. It is that part of the state between the coast range and the Ocean from Santa Cruz to Santa Barbara. It includes Monterey and San Louis Obispo counties.

The northern part of Dan described in Judges 13:25 as "the camp of Dan," is in the Phœnician country of British Columbia north of Idaho in the Rocky Mountains at 115 degrees west. The tribe of Dan corresponds to Austria-Hungary in Europe.

EPHRAIM (ARIES).

The tribe of Ephraim is located on the north of Benjamin in the Sacramento Valley and extends over the coast range to the Ocean. The western boundary extends along the Ocean from San Francisco Bay at the 38th degree to the Klamath River in the Siskiyou Mountains at the 41st degree 30 minutes on the north. The eastern border is the 120th degree east of the mountains; and the southern border the San Francisco Bay and the 38th degree. It includes what is known as northern California from Oregon to San Francisco Bay. Ephraim in Europe corresponds to France.

MANNASSEH (TAURUS).

The tribe of Manasseh, west, is located in Oregon from the Siskiyou Mountains on the south to the Columbia River on the north. The eastern boundary is at the 120th degree east of the Cascade mountains. Mannasseh is bounded on the south by the Klamath River in the Siskiyou Mountains, at 41 degrees 30 minutes on the west by the coast range, east of the 123rd degree north to the Columbia River. The north is bounded by the 46th degree. The tribe of Manasseh consists of the central part of Oregon.

Manasseh in Europe corresponds to England. It is described as one with Ephraim; that is, England and France are one and Northern California and Oregon are one.

ISSACHAR (CANCER).

The tribe of Issachar is located in the Cascade Mountains in the State of Washington. The southern border is the 46th degree from the Columbia River, the western border is from the Columbia River at the Coast range eastward to Mt. Rainier at the 47th degree. Its northern boundary is the 47th degree at Mount Rainier and the National Park in the Cascade Mountains eastward to the 120th degree. The Columbia river at the 120th degree is the eastern border. The mountains of Mt. Rainier, St. Helens and Mt. Adams are included in this territory. Issachar corresponds to Holland-Belgium-Denmark in Europe.

ASHER (LIBRA).

The tribe of Asher is located along the coast and is the coast range, from the Siskiyou Mountains to the Strait of Juan de Fuca. On the north it is bounded by the 48th degree, on the east by the 123rd degree, but on the 47th degree it extends eastward to Mt. Rainier and then southwest to the 46th degree at the Columbia River. The tribe of Asher corresponds to Greece in Europe.

ZEBULUN (GEMINI).

The tribe of Zebulun is located on both sides of the Puget Sound in Washington. The eastern borders are the 120th degree at the Columbia River; the northern borders, the Snohomish Divide at the 48th degree and Puget Sound; the western borders, the coast range at the 123rd degree, and the southern border, the upper end of Puget Sound at Olympia on the 47th degree. The tribe of Zebulun corresponds to Scandinavia in Europe.

NAPHTALI (VIRGO).

The tribe of Naphtali is located in the farthest north. It is located north of the 48th degree from the Divide at Snohomish and includes Skagit and Whatcom Counties. It extends from the 120th degree in the Cascade Mountains, west to the 123rd degree, and the north border is the British Columbia

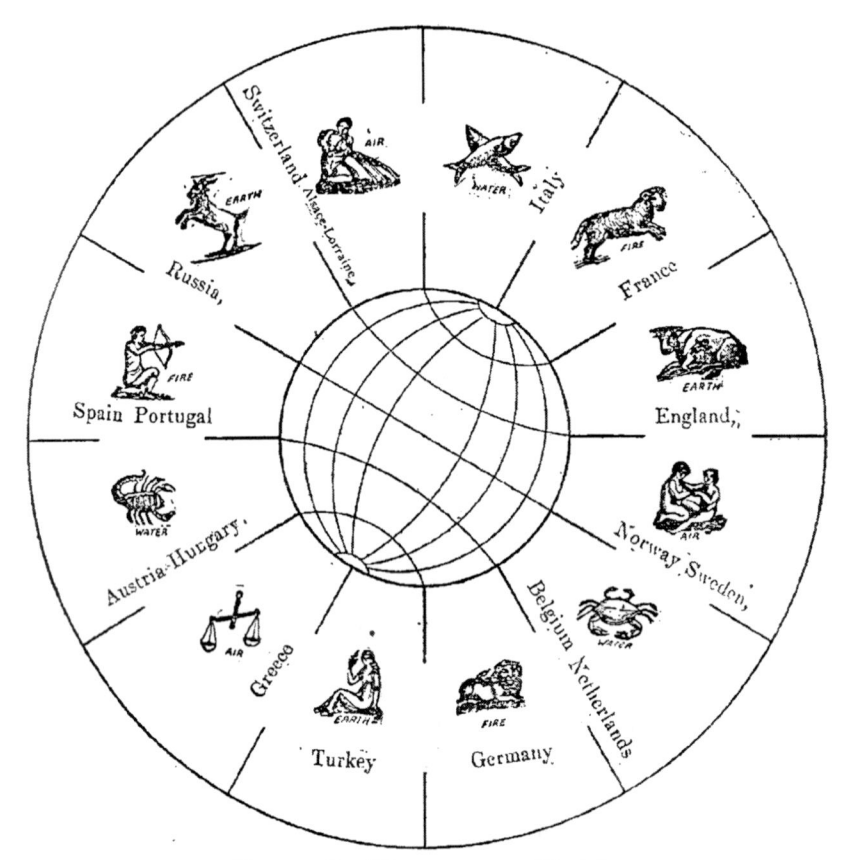

PLATE 8—NATIONS AS TRIBES.

boundary at 49th degree as the Phœnician border. Naphtali corresponds to Turkey in Europe.

CHAPTER 38.

EGYPT, THE PYRAMIDS AND SPHINX.

The country of the Nile Valley, called Egypt, has been referred to in nearly all books of the Bible, but the inhabitants, as a tribe of people, have not been described. It is only at the beginning and the ending of the age for Europe that the principle, illustrated in Egypt, as a thirty-degree space is described. Egypt is located at 30 degrees latitude and also 30 degrees longitude and is the dividing degree for the ages or cycles of time. Egypt has been described as a good location, of a saving or protecting nature, for nearly all the Bible stories described trips to Egypt for the purpose of avoiding persecution from some imaginary enemy. The saving principle in Egypt is that it is located at the angle of 30 degree, which is a good angle.

It should be remembered that the 120th, 60th, and 30th degrees are the good angles of the earth, and from this can be seen the reason why the Pacific Coast States and Egypt are so very important in the Bible stories, as Egypt represents Europe as an age in Aquarius and the Coast States Leo.

The formation of Egypt is similar to the formation of the Pacific Coast States and the same principle in dividing the country was used in both places, that is, the country was arranged as a horoscope and corresponds to the story as described about the Garden of Eden. It was divided into four parts; the tree of life and the tree of knowledge are located in the center of this garden. This principle is described in another chapter but we will explain that the Nile river and the 31st degree longitude represents the tree of life and the 30th degree latitude the tree of knowledge. The Pyramids are located at the 30th degree and represent the principle of the tree of life and a holy place. It is the same principle as described in Mt. Sinai, the tower of Babel and the Mount of Olives, where the patriarch or savior of the age speaks face to face with God. The Pyramids were built to represent the end of the earth's cycle. They are located at the very degree which represents the meridian, and corresponds to a point in the heavens where the ecliptic crosses the equator.

When the philosophy of life, as illustrated in the Bible, and the laws of the universe, as pictured in the principle of the Pyramids, become known, the science of life and death will be a common knowledge and a great blessing to humanity.

It is apparent that it was the Egyptians who were the scientific scholars in the past ages, and built the Pyramids as a silent evidence to illustrate the principle of the science of a universal law. The Jewish race, who formerly inhabited Palestine, has left the Bible as a record of the philosophy of life, illustrating the principle of eternal life, as a God-given law. From this can be seen that the last recorded history for the science of the laws of the universe and the philosophy of life, is the historic records from Egypt and Palestine. These doctrines were later included in the Greek national laws but became a lost art when the Roman powers established a personal God from Rome.

We will briefly explain the system used in Egypt to show the operation of the law of nature, for it is nothing more nor less than the horoscope for the Nile Valley. We will first call attention to the Book of Joshua in the Bible, wherein is described the location of the tribes of Israel in the Pacific Coast States. This part of the country contains a distance of 24 degrees, called the 24 Elders, and was divided into four divisions called Judah, Samaria, Galilee and Phœnicia. These divisions are by nature divided by Mountains and rivers at given degrees of longitude and latitude and are described as the twelve tribes of Israel. The holy mountain for the 120-degree cycle was located at Mt. Whitney in California. The same principle as described for the Pacific Coast section is applied to the country of Egypt, but the tribes in America are described to begin south and end in the north, whereas in Egypt the system is reversed, the beginning is north and the ending is south. The distance in Egypt is from the 31st degree to the 23rd degree latitude, and from the 30th degree to the 34th degree east longitude. This is a distance of eight degrees latitude and four degrees longitude and includes the main part of Egypt. The distance for the Pacific Coast is 24 degrees for a 60-degree cycle and for Egypt the distance is 8 degrees for a 30-degree cycle, which shows that the larger distance is again reduced into three minor divisions.

The valley was divided east from west by the Nile river and the 31st degree longitude. The first section is located as Lower Egypt, between the 31st and 30th degrees, and was called Egyptus Inferior; this division corresponds to Southern California, from Mexico at the 30th degree to Mt. Whitney at the 36th degree.

The second section is located between the 30th and the 28th degrees, north latitude. In this section at the 30th degree east the Pyramids are located. This section was called Heptanomis Arcadia, and corresponds to California from the 36th degree to the Southern boundary of Oregon at the 42nd degree.

The third division, called Egyptus Superior, is located between the 28th and 24 degrees. In this section the Oasis Magna is located (Oasis Dakhla) and corresponds to Oregon and Washington from the 42nd degree to the 48th degree in Washington.

The fourth and last division is located between the 24th and 23rd degrees and is called Dodecaschanus. This section corresponds to British Columbia from the 48th degree to the 54th degree.

That part of the country east of the 30th degree was described as belonging to Babylon, which means Asia, as the 30th degree marks the beginning of the European age. There are many places in Egypt shown on the maps called Heliopolis, Letopolis, Hermopolis and similar names ending in "opolis." These locations illustrate the same principle to Egypt as the names applied in the Bible to the provinces and mean terminal places, representing the cardinal localities.

The writers of modern history have described that the Pyramids were built for the purpose of burying the remains of kings. We find, however, that the location of the Pyramids is the Memphis or holy mountains for Egypt. The Pyramids represent the house of Aquarius which is the home of the planets Uranus and Neptune and were built to illustrate the principle of God's Laws. The Pyramids represent to Egypt the same principle as the Alps do to Europe, Mt. Whitney to America and the Himalaya Mountains to Asia. It is a sacred and holy place being a burying ground for the ages and cycles of time. The Pyramids are located at the 30th degree latitude and 31st degree longitude and is at the dividing of upper and lower Egypt.

The country east of the Pyramids is similar to the country east of Mt. Whitney at 36 degrees latitude in California. The Arizona desert corresponds to the Arabian desert; the Gulf of California is similarly located as the Red Sea; the Nile River was used as a dividing degree as the mountains were used in America. Bath-Sheba was described as the mother of Solomon and is located at the Gulf of California, and Cleopatra corresponds to the country located at the upper end of the Red Sea near the wilderness of Shur; which again corresponds to the wilderness of Zin in Arizona. There is perfect harmony in the nature of the country of Egypt and that of Arizona and California and the law which was illustrated to apply to these locations are the laws of the entire universe. This law has been lost to mankind but it will be found again and the science of life will be a common knowledge to all.

The Sphinx is located near the Pyramids and gives the distance in degrees in the house of Aquarius which is the last house of the cycles for the heavens. The head of the Sphinx illustrates the head of a man and the body of the monument that of a lion. The head represents the house of Aquarius illustrated in the man and the lion represents Leo. At the time of the end of the world the man and the lion are described to be a sign for the ending of time and the three planets Uranus, Saturn and Neptune are in these houses; represented by the Sphinx. We take it for granted that the Sphinx is a sign for the ending of time. The ending of the cycle two thousand years ago corresponds to the location of the Sphinx and the ending of the cycle in 1920 is illustrated by Switzerland and Germany which represents the same houses as the Sphinx, namely: Aquarius and Leo.

The following description gives another illustration of the meaning of the Sphinx: If the head of the Sphinx was the head of a woman and the body of the monument is that of a lion, the head represents the house of Virgo and the body as a lion represents Leo. These houses correspond to the location for the end of the cycle as the place where the age is killed and as this place is located near the 30th degree in the desert, it means the same to Egypt as Arizona does to the cycle for America.

The location of the Sphinx corresponds to the principle illustrated in the International Date Line at 180 degrees. It is a place where space is divided east from west and is the location for the end of time in Aquarius. The heavenly equator crosses the ecliptic in Virgo and is shown in illustrations to cut off the head of Virgo. From this it will be seen that the head of Virgo is added to Leo, which is the reason why the Sphinx may have had the head of a woman and the body of a lion. This shows that the Sphinx illustrates the principle of the 180th degree and represents the end of the age up to the 30th degree east.

Chapter 39.

THE GREAT PLANETS.

The three great planets spoken of in the Bible are Uranus, Neptune and Saturn. The other planets are not included in Bible study. The entire study of the Bible is the description of the nature and movements of the planets Uranus, Neptune and Saturn.

We will give a brief explanation of the character and description of each of the three planets, but the expressions are astrological and not taken from the Bible.

URANUS.

Uranus, also called Hershel, was discovered by Sir John Hershel in 1781. Neptune was discovered in 1846.

Uranus is the strongest of all planets and is called the Son of God. He is described as peculiar and eccentric, outspoken and often violent in manners, original and inventive. He will go to the extreme in anything, as in mercy and love, as well as in hate and anger. Uranus represents a principle out of the ordinary, radical to the extreme; whether for good or bad. Uranus produces artists as well as idiots; also an emotional love nature and the most despondent and sorrowful disposition. Life or death to a Uranus nature is of no value when a principle is involved. The nature of Uranus is human as the first principle. His home is the house of Aquarius, an airy, human house. Uranus governs people in authority, that is, in public office, and controls changes and traveling. The sun is the lifegiver and controlling spirit of the entire Solar System, and reflects the power of the constellations to man. Uranus is as an electric light in a city or a house; it lights the house but is not the life giver of the house. The planet Uranus is the head of the family and he is the one who produces the condition in the home. Uranus is the Son of God and gets his power and wisdom direct from God, which means that the Father and the son of man are one and represent eternal life.

NEPTUNE.

Neptune is about the same size as Uranus but is farther away from the sun. Neptune is spoken of as feminine and is of a watery nature of the lower house of Aquarius. Neptune is lost to our earth except at the beginning and ending of the cycles.

Neptune represents the churches as a whole and as individual. She is a prophet and reformer in doctrines, creeds, and morals. She represents public institutions of the nature of hospitals, orphan homes and fraternal orders. She is neither good nor bad, for her influence is according to the company she is in. If Neptune is with Uranus, it makes the greatest combination for good and if with Saturn she becomes a power for evil. The best explanation to illustrate the power of Neptune is to compare her with a church. When Neptune is good and with Uranus, she is a prophet and helps to build simply for the sake of doing good. When she is with Saturn she will build for the sake of money or for the power there is in it. Neptune will help Uranus to build up an organization for a good purpose and later will help Saturn to kill it. In the Bible Neptune is represented as a prophet. She is the Holy Ghost or the Spirit of things. She is the power behind the throne, whether for good or evil. She is the spirit of the congregation in the church and prayer meetings, as well as the spirit of mob rule or revolt. Neptune will produce a revolution and change a government. If she is with Saturn, it will be rebellion, panic and murder, but if she is with Uranus it is revolution with reorganization. Neptune produces poets, hypocrites and idealists. The leading traits of Neptune is the secret, mysterious and hidden nature of doing things, whether it is religion or murder. The influence of Neptune is of a spiritual or psychic nature and produces doctrines and philosophy.

SATURN.

Saturn is the Satan of old, and his influence is bad. He is envious, jealous, mistrustful, sordid, stubborn, a liar, and is never contented. When Uranus is with Saturn he is harmless and produces a steady, grave, studious nature; a true friend, profound, reliable and patient. Saturn gives a reliable nature to all undertakings, whether good or evil. He is slow, but sure, in love and hate. Saturn's real nature is to destroy. He is the death principle of nature; the winter and old age; the reaper who gathers in the harvest and the wine-press. Saturn destroys but cannot build up except for selfish purposes. Saturn is represented as an old man with skinny fingers, long nails and unkept hair; a miser, fond of digging in the earth, mean and stingy. He is a devil in spirit, mind, and body, and will produce an article according to his own nature and desires. The destructive influence of Satan is the power God gives him to produce.

URANUS, NEPTUNE AND SATURN.

The disposition and character of Jesus as a Savior, as pictured in the Bible, is the nature of Uranus; that of Saturn is the character of Satan, as a Devil; and that of the Holy Ghost, as the spiritual adviser or prophet corresponds to Neptune. These three in combination are a power and the effect of the planets will be according to the house they are in. Saturn and Neptune have the power to kill Uranus when in opposition; Uranus and Neptune kill Saturn when in opposition, and when all three are together a world's power is produced according to the house they are in at the time. The main feature of these three planets is that one is good, one is bad, and one is the spirit to produce results, one way or another. Uranus, Neptune, and Saturn give a combined power to the mind, which is the energy that can produce wonders.

CHAPTER 40.

DESCRIPTION OF THE TWELVE TRIBES.

The description and classification of the tribes is a topic by itself and worthy of detailed attention. We will only give the leading traits and general description of the tribes. The seven tribes of Israel is illustrated as the European nations and Judah is the opposition within Israel. The tribes, as a class of people, did not begin until the time of Abraham, Isaac and Jacob, and from the time of the splitting of the tribes. The first actual dividing of the race took place with Esau and Jacob. Esau goes south and becomes the father of the southern races; (India, Arabia, Turkey, Africa and Mexico), that is, the country south of the 36th degree, which represents the race of Edom and describe the difference of character and disposition of the two brothers. Esau was the cunning, sly hunter, who hunted for the purpose of eating. Esau is to be a servant of Jacob, for he received a material and worldly blessing when his brothers received a spiritual blessing. The children of Esau were called Edom and were given a fundamental trait of character as soldiers or warriors, a traveling tribe, without permanent homes; traders and merchants. They are not tillers of the ground, nor shepherds. Gen. 25: and 37:.

Jacob is of a different nature and belongs to the northern division. Jacob's disposition was to please in a quiet, unassuming way. They were shepherds and cultivators of the soil, with a desire for homes. Jacob is the father of the twelve tribes of Israel, which today are the nations of Europe and are called the Jews and Romans.

Part V—Chapter 40.

Much could be written about the time of the change and where it is found in the Bible, but let it be understood that the races are the country and that the people are divided and live north and south of the 36th degree. The building of the new Jerusalem and the new temple is the establishing of the twelve tribes of Irsael, which consist of the leading nations of Europe.

The tribe of Israel, as the House of Jacob, has twelve tribes. The House of Edom, as the House of Esau, has twelve tribes. The House of Ishmael has twelve tribes. The House of Manasseh has ten tribes. (The tribe of Manasseh is the last).

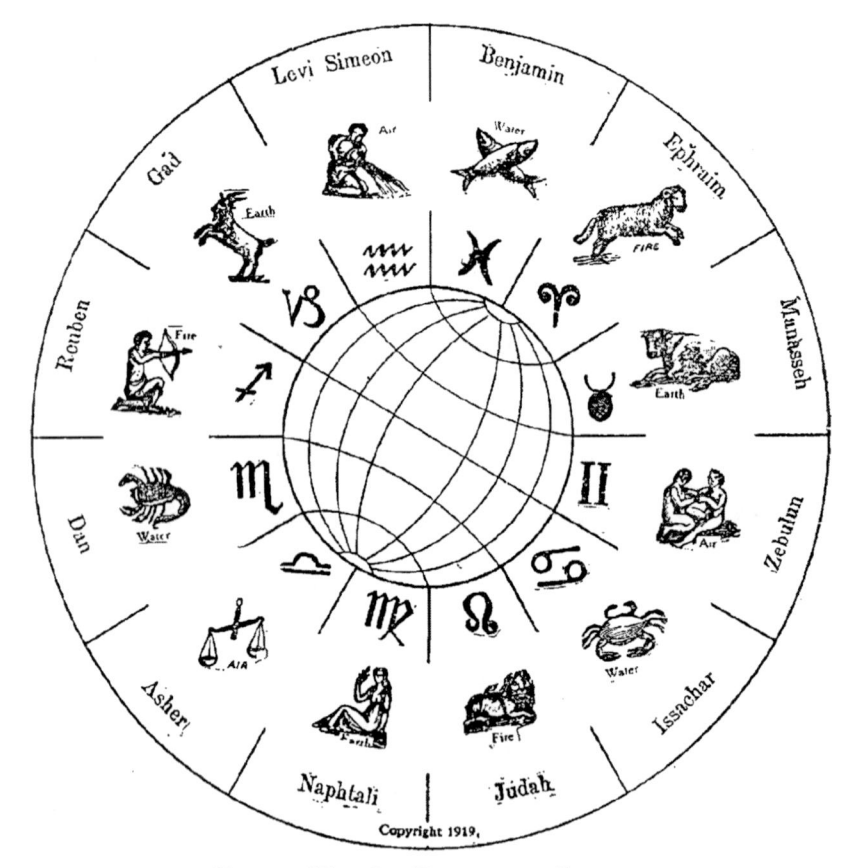

PLATE NO. 9—TRIBES OF ISRAEL.

The twelve tribes of Israel represent the best expression of character and we will combine the tribes with the characters of the nations of Europe and with the houses of the Zodiac. They all represent the same characteristics and disposition as applied to the human race, and as the twelve characteristics represent the twelve months of the year, we can apply the traits as illustrated to individuals.

It should be remembered that the beginning and the ending of the months are not the same as the calendar months which begins on the first day of the month. The influence of Ephraim begins on the 21st of March and ends on April 20th.

There is another very important feature to consider, and that is, when a person is born on the border of the country of a tribe or nation, that he will partake of the nature of both tribes. If a person be born within five days (degrees) from the borders of the month (tribe) he will partake of the nature of both. This is best illustrated by the Swiss people. There are Italian, French and German-Swiss; that is, they represent the border characteristics of both countries, as well as the characteristics of the Swiss nation.

THE TRIBE OF EPHRAIM.

(1)

The tribe of Ephraim is represented by Joseph, the Zodiacal sign is Aries, and its influence lasts from March 21 to April 20. It corresponds to France. It is a double house, indicating a double nature. It represents the Apostle Simon-Peter. In the next generation it will represent the United States, both east and west. It represents the head of man and the leading nation, the mental temperament, the brain worker or schemer, the model and pattern maker, the lawyer and doctor. This tribe is dual in nature and indicates a person who has two natures of opposite character equally well defined. This tribe is the strongest mentally. They are the leaders of all the races of the earth in the development of anything pertaining to the faculty of mentality. They are not one-sided and can produce the good as well as the evil both mentally and physically. The tribe of Ephraim is at the head of the department in whatever it undertakes; their criminals are as brainy as their scientists. They are not religious and take nothing for granted. The tribe is of middle stature, rather lean, with long face and neck, strong limbs, coarse hair and swarthy complexion. In disposition they are violent and quarrelsome, but ambitious, intrepid and determined. The tribe belongs to the fiery elements, giving a quick temper, but they regret and forget as readily. They represent a flaming, blazing furnace. Their passion in love and anger is short, quick and furious, but when the fire is over, peace and order are restored. They live on brain-force and are fed on stimulants, more than on food. Their brain is their work-shop and they produce modes, fashion and ideas. They are neither farmers, sailors nor miners, as their homes and occupations are in large cities in institutions and factories.

Gen. 49:22-23, "Joseph is a fruitful bough, even a fruitful bough by a well, whose branches run over the wall. The archers have sorely grieved him, and shot at him, and hated him;" etc.

THE TRIBE OF MANASSEH.

(2)

The tribe of Manasseh is the partner of Ephraim. She represents the Zodiacal sign Taurus and corresponds to England, (but not to Great Britain). The calendar month for Manasseh is from April 20th to May 20th. It represents the Apostle Andrew, and is illustrated as the neck of man. The tribe represents strength, power and force, quality and quantity. This tribe is the richest in resources of minerals and land, always holding possessions in two or more places, but is not double natured. It is the tribe to manufacture, mechanically and to improve others' ideas. They are conceited, bigotted, ill-natured and unfeeling, great eaters and lovers of ease and home comforts, fond of drink and are sensual. When educated, the bad nature is modified but not overcome. This tribe corresponds to the bull and the nature of the animal cannot be changed. They are short, thick-set, full-face, broad-shouldered and have a heavy neck, dark hair, sometimes curly. The female is a great lover of home, family and children. Whatever the Manasseh tribe owns or controls, looks a little better to them than what others have. Their home is in the mountains and the development of natural resources is their greatest desire. They are not spiritual-minded but are good church-going people, fond of ceremony, rituals and display. Business is transacted in a methodical, systematic, slow and sure way. Their methods are scientific, orderly and reliable. They are of the earth triplicity. **Their home work, and desires belong on earth and not in heaven.** Their greatest and best qualities are in stock-raising and judging of animals, mining and farming; they take in the raw material and produce the finished article, and are one of the leading manufacturers of all tribes.

Gen. 49:26, "The blessing of thy father have prevailed above the blessing of my progenitors unto the utmost bound of the everlasting hills; they shall be on the head of Joseph, and on the crown of the head of him that was separate from his brethren."

THE TRIBE OF ZEBULUN.

(3)

The tribe of Zebulun corresponds to the Apostle James, the sons of Zebedee, and is the house of Gemini. The Zodiacal month is from May 20th to June 21st. It is a masculine, double house and represents Scandinavia, but not Denmark, and corresponds to the shoulders and arms of man. The tribe of Zebulun is the twins in more than one sense, for it represents the duality in nature. It is the principle of Adam and Eve, male and female, mountains and valleys, and a house for harbors and shipping. It is a restless but industrious tribe, fond of sports and hunting. They are scientific, judicious, fond of reading, ambitious of fame, moderate in eating and drinking, generally respected, and good members of society. They are tall and straight with long arms and hands. The tribe belongs to the airy triplicity and make good aviators or succeed with any trade with a perilous position above the ground. They are not miners, for underground work is opposite to their nature. However, they make splendid caretakers of animals and are stock-raisers. They are, by nature, very religious with high hopes and aspirations. They respect old age and parents more than any other tribe. Zebulun is of a domestic nature, fond of family, home and children. They dress in dark clothing and are of steady, sober nature. They make good judges, ministers, and doctors, and are good neighbors and honorable friends.

Gen. 49:13, "Zebulun shall dwell at the haven of the sea, and he shall be for an haven of ships, and his border shall be unto Zidon."

THE TRIBE OF ISAACHAR.

(4)

The tribe of Isaachar represents a double house. It corresponds to the Zodiacal month from June 21st to July 22nd. It represents Cancer, the Crab, and corresponds to the breasts and is a feminine house. The tribe of Isaachar is Holland-Belgium and Denmark and represents the Apostle John. The leading trait of this tribe is that they belong to the watery or liquid triplicity of tribes. All their wealth and possessions must be gained through water, as by shipping, marine insurance, irrigation and condenseries, in fact anything by which liquid is manufactured into commercial commodities. Their home is on the ground and not in the air or mountains. Their greatest desire is for home and family life; they are the cooks and butlers of the world. The number of children they have is immaterial as they can take care of all and the more children the greater the blessing. They are not leaders in intellectual work and soon tire of study, but are the born workers and servants, for they will take contracts to manufacture for others in preference to speculations. There are two distinct traits of character in the Isaachar tribe; one is quick, active, witty, restless and full of life; the other is just the opposite, slow in action, both mentally and physically one who stays home to do the family work in preference to mingling with others. There is no half-way or general disposition for they are either slow or quick. They are usually small of stature, well-developed, with a well-formed figure. They are usually drawn down in the back of the neck, with prominent shoulders and breast bones. They have receding foreheads, prominent chins, large mouths, drooping eyelids, and a peculiar upward, shy look, instead of looking straight ahead. Many of this tribe become round shouldered and hunchbacked from very small injuries. Their complexion is either very light or very dark, hair coarse or exceptionally fine, their hands and feet are also either small or large, and so with their skin it is either coarse or fine. It is a tribe to be trusted, except when they rule over others, when they will make mistakes and dominate. They will always maintain a prominent position in the world's history collectively and individually, for they are one of the cardinal races of the world. The Isaachar nature produces life's necessities and will be as prominently recognized as the life principle illustrated in the woman's breasts.

Gen. 49:14, "Isaachar is a strong Ass, couching down between two burdens; and he saw that rest was good and the land that it was pleasant; and bowed his shoulder to bear, and became a servant unto tribute."

THE TRIBE OF JUDAH.

(5)

The tribe of Judah corresponds to the Apostle Philip; the Zodiacal house is Leo, the Lion, and represents Germany. It is a masculine house and rules from July 22nd to August 23rd. It represents the heart of man and nations and is the tribe of fire, heat, force, vigor and energy. The nature of the tribe of Judah can be illustrated as a complicated engine capable of doing either very delicate or most powerful work. When the engine is in working order it can produce wonders, but when the engine is in the slightest way out of order, the engine stops. The Judah nature is complicated, full of regulations, measurements and divided into detailed organizations. This tribe is a well-formed universe within its own borders. They can do anything, imitate, invent, and work with head and hand as well. They are industrious, economical and practical. Their greatest detriment is their conceited nature, for they know that they have power and feel that the world and all in it depends on them. They do not work alone but must have partners or work as an organization. Their greatest strength is in their method of doing things, more than in actual work. The nature of Judah is fire, and when anyone gets near they get burned or stung. Their lower nature is of a violent form, with the whole heart or none, hot-tempered but not revengeful. They are happy, musical and congenial among their own, but out of place among strangers. The Judah tribe can attain to anything, for they excel in science, literature, arts, mechanics, and in professions. They are usually of medium stature with strong, set features; big bones; broad shoulders; well-set, strong chins; gray eyes; quick sight; light hair; large, round head; slanting forehead; complexion ruddy. Their disposition is bold, firm and generous; ambitious and aspiring; fond of sports and recreations; active, intrepid and very determined. The best illustration of Judah is to compare it with Germany. It is a fiery furnace, a melting pot or manufacturing plant, but when the rest of the nations put out the fire Germany, as an organization, is ruined.

Gen. 49:8-11, "Judah thou art he whom thy brethren shall praise; thy hand shall be in the neck of thine enemies; thy father's children shall bow down before thee. Judah is a lion's whelp; from the prey, my son, thou art gone up; He washed his garments in wine, and his clothes in the blood of grapes."

THE TRIBE OF NAPHTALI.

(6)

The tribe of Naphtali represents a feminine house. It corresponds to the Apostle Bartholomew; the Zodiacal house of Virgo, the virgin, ruling from August 23rd to September 23rd. It represents Turkey. It also represents the bowels of man. The tribe of Naphtali is an earthy house of material elements; its strong points are eating and these people eat only what they want and not what they can get. Naphtali people will produce only what appeals to them as good; they are neither mechanics, farmers nor miners. Science, literature and research appeals to them. They always want the reason for this or that and have a full share of the ability to contrive and find ways and means for doing things. They are eminent as philosophers, judges, officers, composers, inventors and workers in arts. Their description is: a slender body above medium height; a ruddy dark complexion; round face; dark hair and eyes; well-formed but not handsome; a long crooked nose, and closed narrow lips. They are fond of learning; are ambitious, quick and active; given to study of languages and are good, graceful speakers. The tribe of Naphtali is like a hotel; it is a transcient stopping place, and only good for one thing or purpose at the time; for if they eat, they do nothing else and if they work they cannot eat. Their aim, hope and aspirations lie in their stomach and bowels and when feeding stops—friendship stops. They are good cooks, bakers and pastry-makers, but not home-makers. Their religious views are peculiar; if they think they are right, no power on earth can change them; they are reverently and religiously inclined but for ceremony only. The leading trait of Naphtali is that her life's work, be it religion, science or business, has to come to her through her stomach.

Gen. 49:21, "Naphtali is a hind let loose; he giveth goodly words."

THE TRIBE OF ASHER.

(7)

The tribe of Asher corresponds to the house of Libra, illustrated as a pair of scales. It means to balance and signifies the reins of man. The Zodiacal time is from September 23rd to October 23rd. It represents the Greek nation; is a feminine cardinal house. The Apostle Matthew represents this tribe.

The tribe of Asher belongs to the mental and airy triplicity; they work with their head, are good managers, having the ability to judge and reason. They are inclined to go to extremes in happiness and sorrow and are rather unstable; they always look to the future to bring something unexpected to them. They have great mental and physical endurance; are original in thought and are not followers; they are by nature intuitive and make writers, poets, translators, editors, lawyers and speakers. They have a tall, straight body, rather slender; hair black or brown, and smooth; a well-featured round face; a straight nose, and a clear complexion, dark eyes, and are very good looking. They are spasmodically ambitious, talkative and fond of the opposite sex, with an even temper except when ill. They are not farmers nor mechanics, and dislike dirt or soiled garments. For employment they are best adapted as judges, editors, stenographers, clerks, milliners, music teachers and photographers. They are not good mothers nor housekeepers but prefer a public position instead of housework. Their strongest trait of character is their intuitive and inspirational nature; their tools and ability come from within and they usually follow their natural inclinations.

Gen. 49:20, "Out of Asher his bread shall be fat, and he shall yield royal dainties."

THE TRIBE OF DAN.

(8)

The tribe of Dan represents the house of Scorpio, the Scorpion or Eagle. The Zodiacal month is from October 23rd to November 22nd. It is a watery house and illustrates the reproductive parts of man. The tribe of Dan is Austria-Hungary, as a nation; and was represented as the Apostle Thomas. It is a feminine house and is a double or two-natured house, similar to Isaachar. It represents the male and female principle, as a divided nation. The Scorpion and the Eagle are two distinct classes of animals, each with distinct traits, so also is the tribe of Dan. They are fruitful and are the parents of nations and man, through the generations of Naphtali and Dan must pass all future generations. It is a strong, healthy, vigorous tribe, stubborn and self-willed; determined in action and unforgiving in spirit. They are reliable and make splendid managers and financiers, as they live up to their word and want others to do the same. The tribe of Dan is of a middle stature, thick, well-set body, strong and robust; face large and broad, dark, palish complexion; thick, dark curly hair; short thick neck; ill-made and large feet; sometimes bow-legged. Their general disposition is not agreeable as they are conceited, void of feeling, and brutish. When educated they become reserved, but as they have the nature of the scorpion, the real nature cannot be hid. They have resources and applications but the method of using their gifts is crude. They have not the human motherly feeling for their children as others; for it is more of a matter of breeding stock than of having a family. Later in life, after experience and sorrow have been felt keenly, they become the best of citizens and friends. They are then the most reliable characters but do not like to be reminded of past transactions. The judgment of the old men of this tribe is as reliable as a life of experience can give and is usually given honestly.

Gen. 49:16-17-18, "Dan shall judge his people, as one of the tribes of Israel. Dan shall be a serpent by the way, an adder in the path, that biteth the horse heels, so that his rider shall fall backward. I have waited for thy salvation, O Lord!"

THE TRIBE OF REUBEN.

(9)

The tribe of Reuben represents the house of Sagitarius, illustrated as a bowman or archer. It represents the thighs of man, also Spain-Portugal as a nation. It is a double house in the sense of having double possessions; either in land, wealth or intellect. It rules from November 22nd to December 21st. The tribe is represented by the Apostle James (Alpheus). This tribe is of a fiery nature, but neutral in disputes and troubles. These people are natural mathematicians, teachers and scholars. This is the tribe for ministers, priests and college professors. They are the born prophets for the next world and are superstitious and want information ahead of time. They have an exceptional love nature, and a kind, good-hearted disposition; are high-minded, honorable and are true friends. They are apt to run to extremes in their moral ideas. They get their experience early and their wealth later in life. All that a Reuben nature undertakes will come back to him in double measure, be it good or evil. They are well formed and good looking; rather tall, with slanting forehead, bald at the temples; free and open countenance. They are bold, active and generous, fond of sports and recreations. They are honorable and can be trusted and depended on. They are fairly good business people and like to be independent; and dislike to take orders. The Reuben nature is not one to accumulate wealth or possessions, but they live for what there is in life, let it be education, travel or religion. Their desires are high, their road long, and with limited means they never reach their goal.

Gen. 49:3, "Reuben thou art my first born, my might, and the beginning of my strength, the excellency of dignity, and the excellency of power, Unstable as water, thou shall not excel; because thou wentest up to my father's bed; then defilest thou it: he went up to my couch."

THE TRIBE OF GAD.

(10)

The tribe of Gad is called the house of Capricorn and represents a Goat. It is also shown as the knees of man. It represents Russia as a nation and the Apostle Thaddeus (Judas). The Zodiacal month is from December 21st to January 20th. It is an earthy tribe, of a very material mind and disposition, dissatisfied, unstable and discontented. They can be lead in any and all directions and will follow blindly. When aroused to anger they become wild and uncontrollable and when in danger they lose their reason entirely. They belong to the serving class of labor, in mines, farms, and industries of nature. Their thoughts and desires are for worldly goods and personal comfort. When this tribe is educated they want to change and reorganize; they will tear down and want complete destruction before they begin to build again. Their strong trait is their rural desires for agricultural life, whether in the woods or mines, or fishing, hunting, or in the mills. They are not musical and tire of study; they can learn from illustration easily, but not from books. They are not intelligently independent and their religion is handed down to them ready made. This tribe is a great eater and likes strong drinks and tobacco. Their weakness is in their kidneys and they are subject to rheumatism. They are built short and slender with long thin face, straggling beard and hair; long chin; coarse hair; narrow chest; long, small neck; weak knees and walk with a peculiar gait. Their entire appearance is of a bony nature; wiry, tough and strong. The real nature of the tribe of Gad is like a truck horse or a goat, they must be looked after, fed and driven in order to be productive.

Gen. 49:19, "Gad, a troop shall overcome him: but he shall overcome at the last."

THE TRIBE OF SIMEON-LEVI.

(11)

The tribes of Simeon and Levi are one. It is a double-natured tribe and represents the house of Aquarius. It is illustrated as a water carrier and represents the legs of man. The Apostle Simon, and Tubel-Cain as well as the holy tabernacle illustrations describe the tribe of Simeon. The Zodiacal month is from January 20th to February 19th. The countries of Switzerland as Levi, and Alsace-Lorraine as Simeon represent this tribe. The nature of this tribe is double in the sense of an upper and lower portion, a spiritual and material, as well as a saving and destructive nature. The upper chamber or brain is the spiritual or airy nature of the house; the lower is the killing and destructive place where death becomes a birth. Their profession or business is to divide heaven and hell as places. They are either in the salvation of man as ministers of the gospel, or as church workers, undertakers, or are butchers, all dealing with death. Their life thoughts and desires are on life and death. The higher type of the Levi nature gives the real philosophers. Their natures are not selfish and they live simply for the purpose of doing good. It is the good samaritan as expressed in General Booth of the Salvation Army. The lower type are the historians, surgeons, taxidermists and caretakers of cemeteries. One desires to live in the mountains and the other in the valleys. They are of middle stature, well-set, have strong, long visage; sanguine complexion; are generally handsome, especially the females. They always look sad and worried, but determined; are good and kind-hearted with an even temper. They are scientific, fond of learning and are reserved. They are adapted for a professional career and nothing else, for they have no mechanical or industrial ability. Their strongest points are their intellectual and moral nature. It is easy for them to distribute the waters of life and give out salvation as free as air. Their mind is on heaven and hell; the church and the cemetery.

Gen. 49:5-6-7, "Simeon and Levi are brethren; instruments of cruelty are in their habitations. O my soul, come not thou into their secret; unto their assembly, mine honor, be not thou united; for in their anger they slew a man, and in their self-will they digged down a wall. Cursed be their anger, for it was fierce; and their wrath, for it was cruel: I will divide them in Jacob, and scatter them in Israel."

THE TRIBE OF BENJAMIN.

(12)

The tribe of Benjamin corresponds to the house of Pisces and is illustrated as two fishes. It is called the house of the fisherman, and is the feet of man. The Zodiacal month is from February 19th to March 21st. It represents Italy as a nation and is a watery house. It is the house of Judas-Iscariot. This tribe is double in every sense of the word. It represents church and state; honor and dishonor; wealth and poverty; intelligence and ignorance. There is no middle class, as a happy medium, in this tribe. They are either one or the other. The best illustration is given in the nature of Italy, as they have church and state in one and yet divided. The church is a spiritual organization, but has become commercial; the government is for the benefit of the people but is operated for the good of the few. There is no one nation of Europe which can produce as complete a double nature as Italy. It is the priest and Judas as honor and dishonor. The general make-up of the tribe is a low stature, short limbs, inclined to be stout; ill-shaped and large feet. Their disposition is indolent, dull and lazy; caring for nothing, for they love ease and comfort. When educated they become specialists but are neither scientists nor philosophers. The brainier class is quicker in action, and may become clairvoyant and some have inventive ability but it is a case of individual ability and not as a tribe. The tribe of Benjamin is not a good nature; there is always something underhanded or tricky about them. They do not fight openly but will come back and stab you in the back. It is not the question how much good they can do in the world, but rather how much good they can get out of it. Always remember the Benjamin people are fishermen; they hand out a bait or put out a net to catch others.

Gen. 49:27, "Benjamin shall raven as a wolf; in the morning he shall devour the prey, and at night he shall divide the spoil."

CHAPTER 41.

HEAD OF MAN.

It is a known fact that the Universe is formed globular, which is illustrated in the Sun, Stars and the earth. The Bible says that man is made in the image of God, and that heaven is within man. We will now explain what is meant by these expressions.

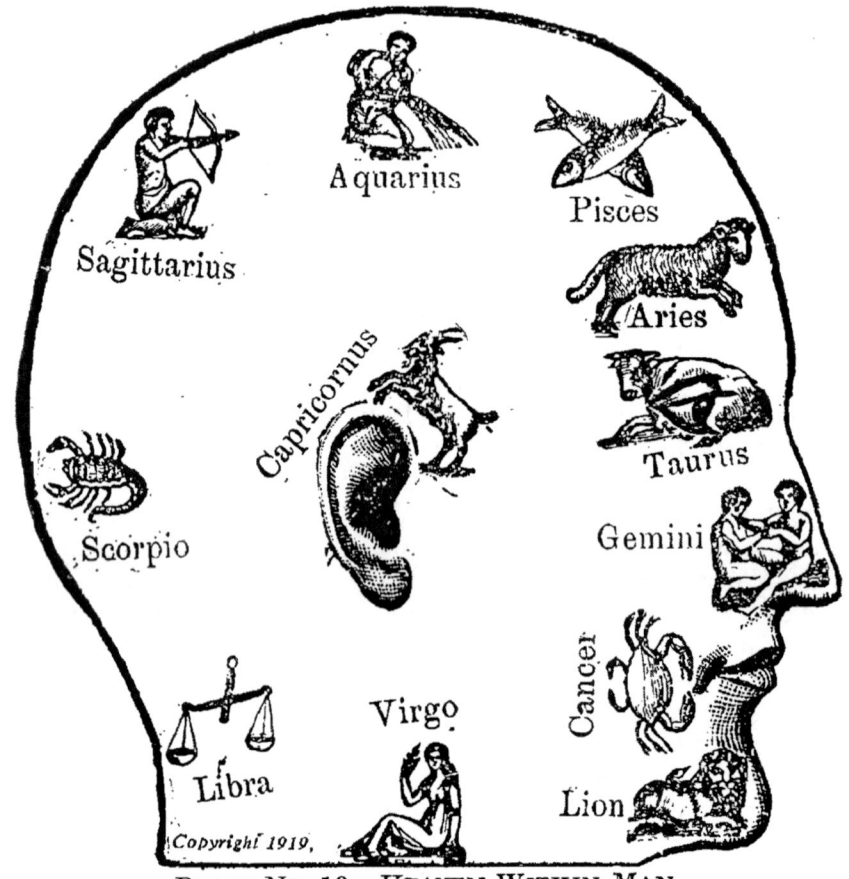

PLATE NO. 10—HEAVEN WITHIN MAN.

The head of man is globular and the principle applied to the heavens and the earth is also applied to man. The location of the twelve houses in the heavens are correspondingly located in the head of man as it is in the heavens.

The two axis of the head are located at the front-top of the head and the throat. The axis at the top of the head is located in the benevolent and intuitive faculties and corresponds to twelve o'clock and the point in Pisces where the equator crosses the ecliptic. The opposite pole to Pisces is Virgo, which is located in the throat at six o'clock.

The path of the ecliptic and the locating of the houses begins at Pisces in the front or upper part of the forehead, going downward over the face to the throat and neck, then up the back to the top of the head. In this circuit of the head the twelve signs of the Zodiac are located and represent faculties and character of man, the same as it is given in the heavens.

The beginning of the houses in the heavens are at the vernal equinox and located at Pisces in the front-top part of the head. This part of the head represents benevolence and churchology and is illustrated as the fishes, being a double watery house.

Greenwich and Aries are located in the forehead above the eyebrows, at the reasoning and intellectual part of the head. It is illustrated as a sheep and is a fiery mental house.

The eyes represent Taurus, the Bull, and the eyebrows the horns of the Bull. The faculties of the eyes are both spiritual and material.

The airy house of Gemini, the Twins, is located at the Nose and is self-explanatory, as the nose is double and for air.

The watery house of Cancer, the crab, is the mouth and the teeth correspond to the claws of the crab. The Bible says that Cancer is a place of destruction.

The Chin represents the strength of the Lion and corresponds to the fiery house of Leo. Force and strength of character are shown in the shape of the chin.

The house of Virgo has been called a Virgin sitting in the gate and as Virgo is located in the throat, it is another description of a gateway in man. It is the place from where time and space are calculated and is a boundary line for east and west.

The double house of Libra is located at the base of the brain and is indicated as a pair of Scales. This house is the opposite of Aries, located on the forehead and these are the cardinal points of the head. The oil in the lamps, so often spoken of in ancient literature, is located here.

The double house of the Scorpion is located above the base of the brain in the back of the head. Scorpio is a watery house representing sex, conjugality and love.

Sagitarius, the Archer, is located where the faculties of self esteem and continuity are placed in the upper back part of the head and is a double fiery house.

Capricorn, the Goat, is located at the ears, in the faculty of destructiveness. It is a cardinal and earthy house and is described as a prophet.

The house of Aquarius, the water carrier, is located on the top of the head between Pisces and Sagitarius, where the faculties of morality, hope and spirituality are located.

Much could be said regarding the location of the twelve houses and the description of character, disposition and ability, but as this has been described in the chapter on tribes, it will not be necessary.

We will call attention to the four cardinal points of the head. They are Aries, the forehead; Cancer, the mouth; Libra, the base of the brain, and Capricorn, the ears. This is a very peculiar arrangement in nature and corresponds to the location of north, east, south and west.

The Bible says that the Ox, the Lion, the Scorpion and the Man would be located at the four corners of the earth in the time of the end of the world. It will be seen that the location of these four houses is at the four corners of the head, and these four correspond to the nations at war described elsewhere.

It depends on what house the planets were in at the time of birth whether the faculties and character of man are developed or deficient. The house or organ the planets were in will be developed and it depends on the planets' aspect to each other whether it is for a good or detrimental purpose. Saturn produces strength but for evil purposes. Uranus will always give a good character and develop the organ for good uses. Neptune will give reasoning or inspiration in the use of the organ she is in. This can be explained by comparison. If Neptune is located in Aries it means an inspiring mind or reasoning by intuition. If Uranus is located in Gemini the nose will be well developed and if Saturn is in Leo, the party will have strong broad chin but bad temper and disposition. When the planets pass from one house to another the organs or faculties will be affected according to the nature of the planets and at the time of the change. If it is known what house the planets were in at birth, it will be an easy study to follow: as Uranus stays seven years; Neptune, fourteen, and Saturn, two and one-half years in each house.

CHAPTER 42.

ASTROLOGY.

For the benefit of those familiar with the study of Astrology we will give a brief explanation of the system used in setting up a figure, as given in the Bible. The difference between the ordinary geocentric system and that used in the Bible is, that the Bible divides the 360-degree space into minor cycles, and

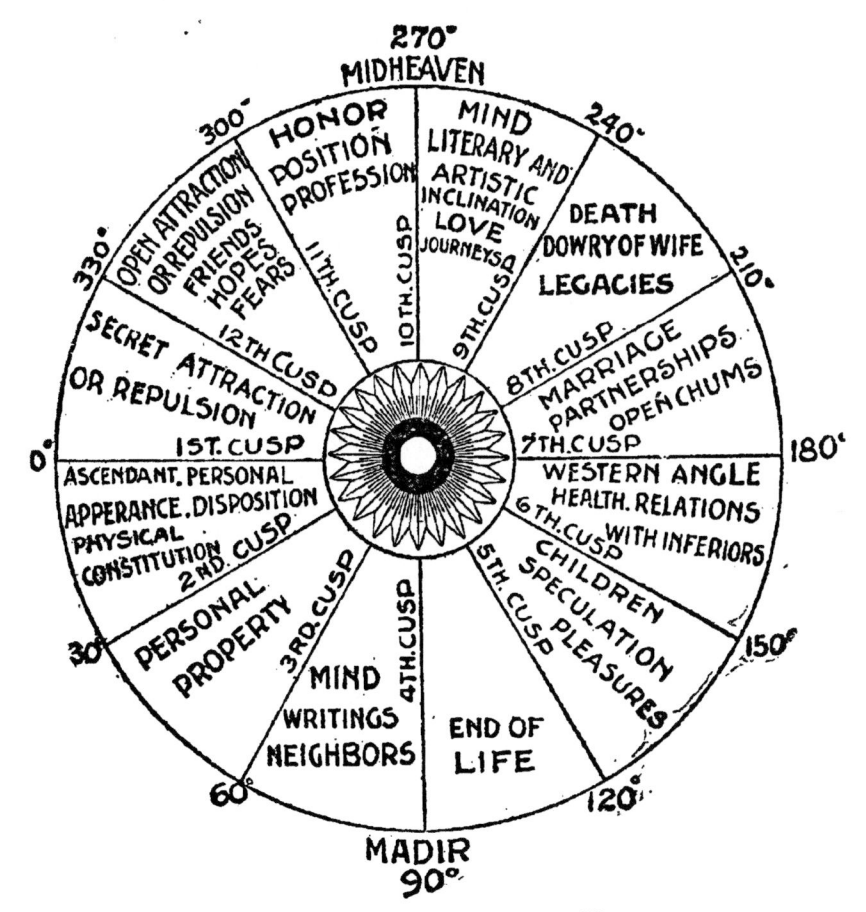

PLATE NO. 11—ASTROLOGICAL HEAVEN.

divides again the minor cycles into sideral units of clock time of 360 degrees as a unit of one. Another difference is, that Uranus and the Sun, is used as the leading power of the heavens from which to calculate time and events; and the aspects of Neptune and Saturn give the answer to events in the different

Part V—Chapter 42.

houses. Time is calculated in the usual way by the sun, moon and the houses as well as from the planets. The first two and the last two degrees of the houses occupying the cusps of the three 120-degree angles were calculated for eventful periods. Attention is called to the nature of the 4th, 8th and 12th houses illustrated in Plate No. 11. These houses represent the three 120-degree cycles and in the nature of the houses, they illustrate the end of the cycles. This shows that the prevailing astrological system of explaining the houses are the same as used in the Bible. The planet Uranus represents the male principle; Neptune, the female principle, and Saturn the earthly or Satanic elements.

The cycles of time as calculated in the Bible correspond to the system used at the present time. The great or Solar cycle consists of 360 degrees as the basic number and 72 degrees as the unit of one. This is the system used today in all scientific calculations, as in the measurement of the heavens, the earth, years, months, days, hours, minutes and seconds.

In all descriptions the Bible divides the cycles into four divisions and into twelve parts; this division corresponds to the four seasons of the year and the twelve months. This cycle of one-twelfth is again subdivided on the principle of days, hours, minutes and seconds. The unit of 24 hours consists of 144 degrees; and twelve hours equal 72 degrees, which corresponds to the solar or clock time. From this it will be seen that a complete cycle is figured from the units of 72 and 360 degrees, and is calculated from prime units of seconds of clock time, to the great cycle of 25,920 degrees and up to an endless distance of space. The great or heavenly cycle of 25,920 degrees equals 360 degrees and these cycles are divided into a 120-degree cycle containing a period of time of 1008 years. The minor or 60-degree cycle contains a period of 500 years. This cycle is used when the conditions of the heavens are applied to the earth. The earth's distance of 360-degree cycles are also divided by the same method into smaller divisions, as the distance of 30 or 40 degrees or any other minor cycles called angles.

The distance of Europe and also the distance for the Ten Tribes is for the 30-degree space cycle. A horoscope is set up for each cycle and calculated as a complete cycle of 360 degrees. This method was described as "wheels within wheels" and corresponds to seconds within the cycle of minutes.

The placing of the planets Uranus, Neptune, Saturn, Sun and Moon are the same as used in the Geocentric System and deductions are then made according to the laws which were given by Moses.

The Israelites represent the ages on the earth and we will briefly explain what the meaning of the cycles of the heavens are which produce the condition on the earth. The students, who are not familiar with the Zodiac, should look at the illustrations to get the meaning of this part of the study.

The beginning of time for the earth is at Aries and the cycle for Adam represents this house, which is illustrated as a ram. The second house is Taurus, as Eve, and is illustrated as a bull. The third house is Gemini, represented as twins and described as Cain and Abel. These three houses represent the first cycle around the earth and illustrate the nature of the three planets in the three houses spoken of. Adam represents Uranus in the first cycle, Aries. Eve illustrates Neptune as a spiritual age in the second cycle of Taurus, the bull. The third cycle represents Saturn in Gemini, a double house, illustrating a two-sided nature in a good man and in a murderer as demonstrated in Cain and Abel. From this will be seen that Adam, as Uranus, represents creation in the cycle west of Greenwich, as Aries. Eve illustrates a spiritual life and philosophy which is represented in the Pacific Coast cycle. Saturn rules the cycle for Asia and Europe and represents the carnal nature. This principle is the foundation for all cycles which repeats the circuit around the earth, each cycle containing 360 degrees.

It takes Uranus 84 years to travel in a cycle of 360 degrees; it requires 42 years to the cycle of 180 degrees and 28 years for a space of 120 degrees; 14 years to 60 degrees and seven years for 30 degrees. The other distances or angles in proportion to the length of space calculated. The 30-degree cycle is figured as a complete cycle of 360 degrees and Uranus makes a circuit of the 12 houses of this cycle in seven years; the other planets in proportion to their time in covering space. As an example we will say that we want a figure for a space of 30 degrees which corresponds to one house. A figure for the time is set and calculated as a 360-degree horoscope and divided into houses in the usual way. Uranus stays in each house seven months; Saturn in each house about two and one-half months and Neptune stays in each house a little over one year. This system will apply to man as well as to nations and all who are familiar with the prevailing system will readily see the principle of operation.

The system as used in the Bible is corrct as can be seen from the accurate calculations made for the formation and destruction of nations and in the description of the present war.

From the method of measuring time and space as described in the Bible we can see that the entire universe is measured as space on the same principle as a watch or clock and when the planets pass in the space of the heavens by looking at a watch or clock the location of the planets can be placed in the year, month, down to seconds of time.

The scientific study of the Bible is to obtain a knowledge of the laws of the universe. It requires neither praying nor singing to understand the Bible, but common sense application, with the object in view of learning to understand it. The Bible is a text book for both the science and philosophy of life. Use the Bible as a guide and avoid the literature of those teaching a personal God and Devil, for their literature is misleading. Learn first what the heavens mean and what produces the condition which is in the heavens, for the conditions in the heavens are the same as on earth and the method of applying them to the earth becomes a matter of simple repetition.

The Bible has been sealed and considered to be a mystery, but it is now an open book. Study it and write about it for the guidance of others but avoid criticizing others' opinion; all are subject to mistakes, the writer as well as the reader. The Bible contains the Laws of God, so do not intentionally teach or write anything contrary to the Words of God.

The Author is not at liberty at the present time to give any reason for and what the cause, method and from what source he has obtained the information contained in this book, but he may do so at some future time.

CHAPTER 43.

THE MEANING OF BIBLE NAMES.

The concordance of words and names given in the Bible is not the names of persons as human beings, but each word or name represents a principle describing the condition of the people, places and cycles of time. The names given in the Bible have similar meanings to the terms used in geographical and astrological literature, and describe locations, space and conditions implied by the nature of the name given. We will describe some of the most common words and names to show the system used, and what the meaning or significance is. It should be remembered that the Bible described the conditions of the houses in the heavens, the fixed stars and planets, and not an actual description of the earth. The condition in earth is reproduced from the heavens as it is in the heavens, so is it on earth; from this it will be seen that the Bible is an Astrological text-book.

Aaron; a teacher. Abel; vanity, mourning. Abi; my father. Abimelech; father of the king. Abram; a high father. Abraham; the father of a great multitude. Absalon; father of peace. Aceldama; the field of blood. Achish; thus it is, or how is this. Achor; trouble. Adam; earthy man, red. Adami; my man, red, earthy, human. Agrippa; one who causes great pain at his birth. Alexander; one who assists men. Alpheus; a thousand, learned, chief. Amalek; a people that licks up. Ammon; a people, son of my people. Amorite; bitter, a rebel, a babbler. Ananias; the cloud of the Lord. Andrew; a stout and strong man. Antioch; speedy as a chariot. Antipas; for all, or against all. Apollyon; one who exterminates. Aquila; an eagle. Arabia; evening, wild, and desert. Ararat; the curse of trembling. Arcturus; a gathering together. Arimathea; a lion dead to the Lord. Asher; happiness. Asia; muddy.

Baal; he that rules and subdues. Baalim; idols, masters, false Gods. Babel or Babylon; confusion or mixture. Bar-Jesus; son of Jesus or Joshua. Bar-Jona; son of Jona, or of a dove. Bashan; in the tooth, or in ivory. Bath-Sheba; the seventh daughter, or the daughter of satiety. Beer; a well. Belshazzar; master of the treasure. Benjamin; son of the right hand. Bethel; the house of God. Bethlehem; the house of bread. Beulah; married.

Cain; possession or possessed. Cainan; possessor. Caleb; a dog, a crow, a basket. Calvary; the place of a skull. Canaan, trader, one that humbles and subdues. Chaldea; as demons, or as robbers. Cush; Ethiopians, black. Cushau; blackness, heat.

Damascus; a sack full of blood. Dan; judgment, or he that judges. Daniel; judgment of God. David; well beloved, dear. Didymus; a twin or double. Dothan; the law or custom.

Easter; the passover. Eden; pleasure or delight. Edom; red, earthy, of blood. Egypt; that troubles or oppresses. Eliazar; help of God, court of God. Eli; my God. Elijah; God, the Lord. Elymas; a magician. Endor; fountain, eye of generations. Ephesus; desire. Ephraim; that brings fruit. Ephron; dust. Er; watch or enemy. Esau; he that acts or finishes. Ethiopia; blackness, heat. Euphrates; that makes fruitful. Eve; living, enlivening. Ezekiel; the strength of God. Ezra; help or court.

Felix; happy, prosperous. Festus; festival, or joyful. Fortunatus; lucky or fortunate.

Gabriel; God is my strength. Gad; a band, happy. Galatia; white, the color of milk. Galilee; wheel, revolution, heap. Gaza; strong or a goat. Gilgal; wheel revolution. Golgotha; a heap of skulls.

Ham; hot, heat, brown. Haran; mountainous country. Havilah; that suffers, pain, that prings forth. Hebrews; the descendants of Heber. Heber; one that passes, or anger. Heldai; the world. Hermes; Mercury; gain or refuge. Herod; the glory of the skin.

Isaac; laughter. Isaiah; the salvation of the Lord. Israel; who prevails with God. Issachar; reward.

Jacob; that supplants. Jerah; the moon or month. Jericho; his moon or month. Jerusalem; vision or peace. Jordan; the river of judgment. Joshua; the Lord, the Savior. Jews; Judas; and Judah; the praise of the Lord. Jupiter; the father that helpeth.

Kedemah; oriental. Kittim; they that bruise, or gold, or coloring. Korah; bald, frozen.

Leban; white or a brick. Laish; a lion. Lebanon; white or incense. Lot; hidden, covered. Lucas, Lucius, Luke; luminous. Lucifer, bringing light.

Magdalen; elevated, magnificent. Mamre; rebellious, or bitter. Mannasseh; forgetfulness, he that is forgotten. Mara; bitter. Memphis: by the mouth. Mercurius; an orator or an interpreter; Michel; who is perfect. Moses; taken out of the water.

Nahash; snake or serpent. Naphtali; that struggles or fights. Niger; black. Nod; vagabond.

Olympas; heavenly. Paul; small, little. Peniel; face or vision of God. Peor; halo or opening. Persia; that cuts or divided, or a nail, or horseman, gryphon. Peter; rock or stone. Pharaoh; that disperses, that spoils. Phinehas; aspect, face or trust. Pilate; who is armed with a dart. Pontius;

marine, belonging to the sea. Potiphar; bull of Africa, a fat bull.

Rachal; injurious, or perfumer. Rachel, sheep. Ram; elevated, sublime. Rebe; the fourth or square. Rehoboth; spaces, places. Reuben; who sees the son, the vision of the son. Rome; strength, power. Rufus; red. Ruth; drunk.

Salem, Salmon, Salome; peace, complete, perfect. Samaria; his prison, his throne, his diamond. Sarai, Saraah; lady, princess of multitude. Satan; contrary, adversary, enemy, accuser. Saul, demanded, lent, ditch, hell. Sheba; captivity, old age. Shem; name, renown. Shiloh; sent, peace, abundance. Shinar; watch of him that sleeps. Shittim; that turn away or divert. Sidon, Zidon; hunting, fishing, venison. Silas; three or the third. Silvanus; who loves the forest. Simeon; that hears, that is heard. Simon; that hears, obeys. Sin; bush. Sinai; a bush, enmity. Sion; noise, tumult. Sirion; a breastplate, deliverance. Sivan; a bush or thorn. Smyrna; myrrh. So; a measure for grain. Sodom; their escort, their cement. Solomon; peaceable, perfect.

Tamar; palm, palmtree. Tammus; concealed. Tarsus; winged, feathered. Teman; the south. Teritus; the third. Tertullus; a liar, an imposter. Tetrarch; governor of a fourth part. Thomas; a twin. Tubal; the earth, the world, that is carried or led. Tubal-cain; worldly possessions. Tyre, Tyrus; strength, rock, sharp.

Ur, Uri; light, fire, a valley; Urim and Thummim; light and perfection. Uzzah; strength, goat.

Vashni; the second. Vashti; that drinks.

Zarah; east, brightness. Zebedee; abundant, portion. Zebulun; dwelling. Zenas; living. Zillah; shadow. Zilpah; distillation. Zion; monument, sepulchre, raised up. Zoar; little, small.

Part VI.

THE UNIVERSAL LAW.

Chapter 44.

SCIENCE OF THE HEAVENS.

The heavens constitute the eternal space of the Universe, wherein our solar system and millions of other solar systems are located. The law governing the movements or operations of the elements in the heavens is called the will or word of God and is described as the science and philosophy of life. The scientific study of this universal law is called astronomy and the philosophical principle is termed theology. This universal law of the heavens and the science of life have been given in the Bible and illustrated in the stories describing the life of the patriarchs as the leaders of Israel. This same law or principle has also been described in all ages of the past by tribes or races of people in all parts of the world in what is known as mythological tales. The best and most scientific description of this law is given in what is known as Astrology, excluding the mundane or fortune-telling part of the study.

The description of this law, as given in the Bible, is perfect, but the peculiar method employed in illustrating it is misleading, for a system adhering to a personal worship is described. It is apparent that the Bible was written in one of the Uranian (Uro-anna) cycles of time when the population of the earth could get this knowledge from a heavenly source. And in order to preserve this law for future generations, the peculiar method of describing it, in the Bible, was employed. The system used in the Bible is described in other chapters and given as the history for a particular race of the earth for a period of 6,000 years. The scientific or astronomical description of this law is described in the chapters on heaven.

It may not be out of place to state that the science of Astronomy is the outgrowth of the ancient study called Astrology. The word "Astro" or "Astral" means stars and the word "logy" means logic. The study of the stars is called Astronomy and today the logic study is called Theology and these two studies together are called Astrology.

The ancients illustrated the heavens in maps or charts giving names to the different constellations which are used today.

The system used at the present time in dividing the heavens and earth into cycles of 360-degree periods is of ancient origin and is described in astrological books. The location and description of the constellations of fixed stars were given to the very degree but the method employed by the ancients to measure the heavens has not been known for centuries. The key to this knowledge will be found in the Bible and anyone familiar with the study of Astronomy or Astrology will readily see the system used. It is not for us to say, or give a reason why, this knowledge should not be known or understood. The Bible says, that God in his wisdom would reveal this knowledge to man in his own way and in the proper time, and the very year is described. From this can be seen that the law of the universe is not controlled by man and that the elements of nature including man are simply tools in the fulfillment of the law.

The elements of nature produce a life-giving principle on this earth, as well as on the rest of the planets and in the operation of this law the human being is born, lives and dies. God in his wisdom did not make this law for the glorification and comfort of one and for a hell punishment to others as this law is based on the universal principle in creation. The beginning or creating of life is to change a former condition into a new expression and the length of time for the manifestation and growth of this life depends on the nature of the being. When this life principle has made its manifestation in whatever form it may exist, it unfolds, grows and decays; wherein it again changes the existing conditions and produces a new form of expression. It depends entirely on the nature and character of the being, at the time of the change, in what form the next expression of life will manifest. It is the law of the universe that all life manifests from the lower to a higher form of existence, which can be compared by the life of Jesus, as he left a material life to live a spiritual life in the heavens. This principle is also described in the stories about the children of Israel; they were represented as human beings, but it is the principle of life which is described. The characters described in the Bible as the children of Israel, represent a living creative principle, comparatively illustrated in the movements of the planets and is the actual description of the law for all life. It should be remembered that the law of the heavens is to manifest in cycles, which is described in the movements of the planets. And this law is comparatively the law for all life, illustrating that man lives after passing out of the body, as death means the end of a cycle. From the stories given in the Bible describing the operations of the three planets in cycles of time can be seen that the life of man on earth is comparatively the same as the life of the planets.

The planet Uranus has been described to illustrate the conditions in the heavens and is spoken of as a man who lived and dies as a human being. When his cycle of time was complete, and the patriarch represented in him had finished his life work, he ascended to heaven where he continued to live with his father. This story is similar to the old Greek and Roman mythological fables, when their myth life was finished on earth, someone prosecuted them and killed the leading spirit of the age. In these myth stories are described, that when the party spoken of had terminated the life on earth, he or she, went to heaven and became one of the fixed stars of the constellations. The topic in the stories of the Greek Gods is well known and we will only say that the story described in the life of Jesus corresponds to the myth Gods of old. The life work of Jesus was to live right and to teach man the philosophy of life, but his Christian principles and doctrines were not understood and at the end of his time he was tortured to death. The multitude who crucified Christ was the same people who had listened to the doctrines of Christianity. He said the law had to be fulfilled and he had to die and go to his father in the heavens. The life story of Jesus as given in the Bible, is a very lamentable description of a perfect life and is a fairly good illustration of the life lived by the average human being today; for, the life of Jesus is a comparative description of the life lived by man in the flesh. We can see that after the termination of the life in the flesh, the human beings take on the form of a spiritual being and live in the heavens in the realm of spirits. This is one of the best illustrations of what the philosophy of life teaches and that life is not destroyed in death.

The scientific study of the Universe called Astronomy, consists in the actual measurement of space in the heavens and the movement of the different solar systems and planets in their respective orbits. The science of Astronomy can be compared with the science of geography, as one measures the heavens and the other the earth, but neither of these sciences deals with the influences of the elements of nature, which produce the conditions in the heavens and on the earth. Geographers pay no attention to the conditions in the heavens which produce the climate and the seasons of the year, as their work consists of the measurement of the physical earth. The same can be said of Astronomers, as they simply measure time and space and do not realize that there is a universal law which produces all conditions in the heavens and on the earth. In the study known as Astrology, the principles of life promulgated by both Astronomy and Geography, as well as Theology, are included. These three sciences combined, teach the law in its completeness and are described in the Bible as the word or God. From this it will be seen that the Astronomical study consists of the physical science of the heavens. The geographical study describes the nature of this earth and the theological study consists of the philosophical conclusions of what life is, as produced by the elements in the heavens and on earth.

The science of Astrology teaches what are the elements of nature, which produce the conditions and life on this earth. The fundamental principle of the science of Astrology is not understood any more than the other sciences, and a personal system has been adopted instead of a universal. So also with Theology; both sciences apply the principles as taught to man, whereas they should be applied to the universe. When this mistake is known, and corrected, it will be found that the sciences of astrology and theology will become exact sciences and not before.

It is not our intention to criticize and find fault with others, but to correct mistakes as we see them. Our aim is to make statements of facts and to explain what is meant by these statements, in comparing them with the erroneous teachings of the past.

The idea that Jesus was a human being is not a fact, as he was a Christ or Savior in principle and represents the Christian era. The Christian theological conception of what constitutes the heavens is as much a mistake as the doctrines they teach. The principle described in the Bible of the trinity of God in the heavens simply means the dividing of the heavens into cycles of three divisions. The trinity of God in the heavens is at the present time scientifically described in the different magnitudes of the stars. The stars in the heavens are described to be in the first, second or third, etc., magnitudes from each other. The different magnitudes, therefore, means the many heavens referred to. In order to get the distance and number of stars in each of the different magnitudes or heavens, the ancients multiplied or divided each magnitude by three and the result obtained is the number of stars in each magnitude.

From this it will be seen that the heavens described in the Bible consist of the trinity of God and that this same God-given principle is expressed in every living form in existence. The trinity of life has been expressed in many terms, such as father, son and holy ghost; or heaven, hell and eternal life. It is also called Astronomy, Geography, and Theology, or Saturn, Uranus and Neptune, and many other names, which consists in dividing the universal law into the expressions of three. Let it be distinctly understood that life in the heavens and on earth consists in the trinity of God.

We have described what constitutes the different cycles of time and space and how many degrees there are to each period. We wish to call the attention of astronomers to this system of calculating space in the heavens. It is a known fact that the exact degrees in years in the celestial sphere are not known. As far as we know it is a guess between 70 and 83 years to each degree. We have proved without a question or doubt, that this cycle consists of 72 years to each degree. From this can be seen, that the great cycle consists of 25,920 years and not a speculative figure from 25,000 to 27,000 years. There is also another very important fact we will call astronomers' attention to and that is, that in 1920 the pole of the celestial ecliptic will be a little over one degree (80 years) from the pole star. This is the time which is described in the Bible as the passover, and it will be found to be the exact degree of the celestial pole and corresponds to the sideral degree of the north pole. In the year 2000 the celestial pole will be on the very degree of the pole star.

We have repeatedly made the statement that the law of the universe is written in the Bible and that this law is not understood. We will describe the fundamental principles as given in the Bible and it will be found to be the description of our solar system's revolution around another centre.

The Bible described that there are three heavens to calculate time in and that they are called the Terrestrial plain, the Celestial plain and the Earth or natural plain. The heaven or plain of the earth consists of the space wherein our earth and seven other planets move around our sun. The Celestial heaven is the circuit of our solar system among the constellations called fixed stars. The last and great Terrestrial heavens is the space or circuit in the heavens known as the "Milky Way," "Galaxy," or "Light of Heavens." The three distances, circuits or spaces of the heavens have been calculated on the same principle as we calculate the earth's orbit around the sun. The heavens have been divided into twelve houses and ordinarily called the twelve signs of the Zodiac. Each of these distances is calculated on the Universal principle which is described in the chapter on cycles of time.

The creative law of the heavens is the same as the laws which govern the human races on earth. This creative principle can be compared with our solar system and the life on earth. The sun, comparatively speaking, has a family of eight children; the seven planets and the earth. Each of these planets has again children which are the moons belonging to the planets. The principles shown in the operation of the solar systems are the same which govern the human race; for each child of the heavens and earth represents part of the great unit for all, called God. The Bible illustrates this creative principle of the heavens in the stories described to take place on this earth and at the same time says that a similar condition exists in the heavens. The sun is given as the cause or father of creation on this plain of existence and the three planets Uranus, Neptune and Saturn represent the effect or condition produced. In the three planets, a descriptive illustration is given showing what the nature of the planets are and the conditions produced on this earth by them. We have previously mentioned that the study of the operation of the Universe consists of the three principles described in Astronomy, Geography and Theology. The three great planets represent the principles given in these sciences and are spoken of in the Bible as the word of God. The laws of the heavens are described to correspond to the law governing the planet Uranus and this study is at the present time called Astronomy. The principle illustrated in the planet Saturn corresponds to the condition the earth produces and is called Geography. The planet Neptune is described to give reasoning or inspiring conditions and represents the study of Theology.

The period of time, as calculated in the heavens, consists of a cycle of one thousand years and is called an ecliptic period. This ecliptic cycle of the heavens corresponds to the cycle of Uranus in his orbit and also the ecliptic period comparing the relation of the north pole to the pole star.

Part VI—Chapter 44.

The precession of the equinoxes are described in the Bible by the travels of the children of Israel westward around the earth, and the different cycles represent the ages of the patriarchs. The ecliptic distance of the heavens is calculated on the earth from the orbit of Uranus around the sun and corresponds to a belt, around the earth at 36 degrees north latitude, of 120 degrees longitude each. The ecliptic period at the pole consists

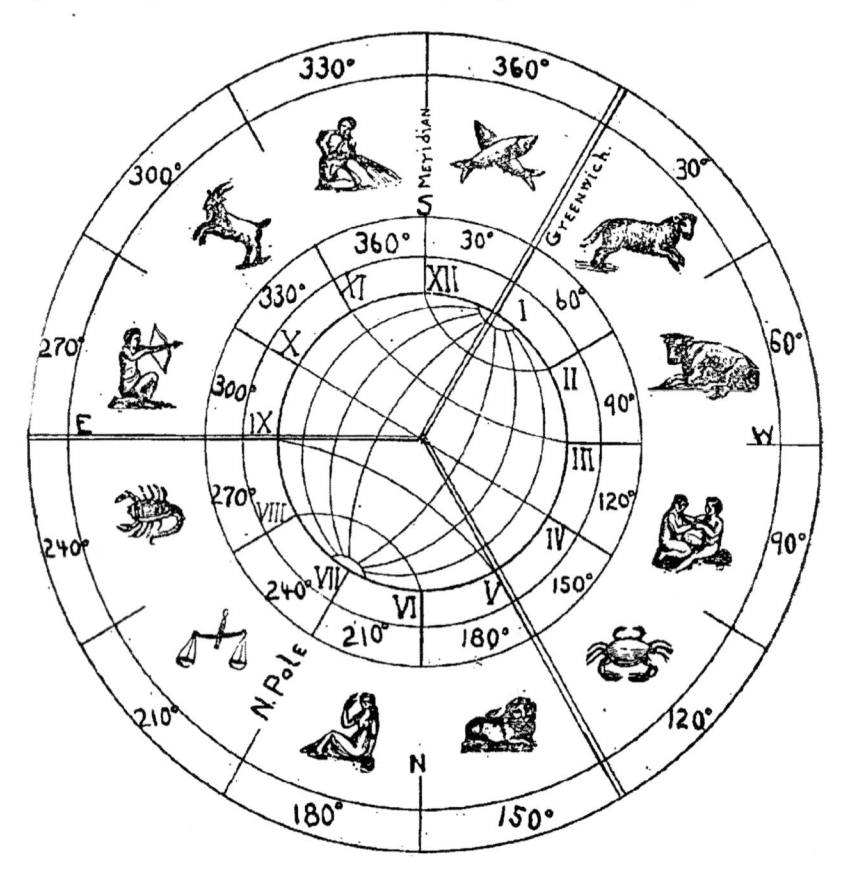

PLATE NO. 12—SPACE, TIME AND CYCLES.

of 24 hours, Astronomically calculated, but it takes the celestial pole 24,000 sideral years for a complete circuit. The distance calculated for the earth by the precession of the equinoxes at 36 degrees north latitude consists of 25,920 years as figured in degrees.

The principle illustrated in Saturn corresponds to the law as described in the circuit of Uranus. Saturn represents the earth and his circuit around the sun corresponds to the Moon's complete cycle around the earth. Saturn requires 29½ years to complete his circuit around the sun and the Moon encircles the earth in 29½ days. Saturn and the Moon's cycles correspond, that is, the Moon's sideral time of 27 1-3 days from new moon to new moon corresponds to Saturn's period. The years as here given are from equinoctial calculations. The planet Neptune makes a circuit of the heavens in 164 years and this time corresponds to six times the circuit of Saturn and the Moon, as six times 27 1-3 equals 164 years and this is the cycle of Neptune.

From this comparative description can be seen, that the entire universe is figured in cycles and that there are cycles within cycles all based on the same law.

The conclusions to be reached from the study of the Bible and the heavens are, that the heavens are a real place or space and not an imaginary location somewhere in the clouds.

Chapter 45.

Equinoctial Influence.

The science called the precession of the equinoxes for the earth is a very common topic and we will only say, that it is caused by the earth's motion and revolution in space around the sun. The method of calculating the precession of the equinoxes in the heavens and for the earth for spring and autumn is the same, and consists in the measurement of space on the ecliptic for the sun and the earth. The Modern astronomical calculations divide the distance of the heavens and earth into four periods of 90 degrees each and when the earth's polarity strikes one of the four dividing degrees, the seasons of the year are changed and this is called the precession of the equinoxes. The four cycles for the earth are called spring, summer, autumn and winter, and are calculated from Greenwich in 90-degree angles.

The ancient Bible writers describe that the heavens and the earth, beside being divided into four divisions of 90-degree cycles, were also calculated in three cycles of 120 degrees each and called the ages of the patriarchs. The method of dividing the heavens into three cycles of 120 degrees each is in the system called precession of the equinoxes. The place in the heavens from which to calculate time and space is the point where the ecliptic crosses the equator in Pisces. From this it will be seen that the precession of the equinoxes is figured on the ecliptic from Pisces westward in cycles. The first ecliptic cycle for the earth is calculated from Greenwich to 120 degrees west and as the ecliptic circuit is apparently located at 36 degrees north latitude, the degree from which to calculate will be 120 degrees west longitude and 36 degrees north latitude. The second 120-degree cycle is calculated to and from the 240th degree west longitude. The ancient Bible writers describe cycles containing a given number of degrees, by the precession of the equinoxes, but only the cycle of 90 degrees is used by scientific astronomers at the present time.

The time required for the precession of the equinoxes in cycles for the earth, corresponds to the time in which the planets Uranus, Neptune and Saturn make their respective circuits around the sun. The life history of the patriarchs which is described in the Bible is given in the circuit of Uranus as an age, in the precession of the equinoxes and illustrated in the travels of the children of Israel westward. The planets Neptune and Saturn are shown to describe the conditions and influences which existed at the time, caused by the change of the equinoctial seasons. From this it will be seen, that it is the law of the heavens and earth, which is described in the Bible and that the conditions produced by the planets and by the precession of the equinoxes, constitute the law and word of God.

The six ages described in the history of the patriarchs given in the Bible, corresponds to the six great constellations, located near the pole and represent a period of time for 6,000 years. The names of the six constellations are given in the same order as described in the Bible for the patriarchs. The constellations are named in the following order: Cassiopeia, Camelo Pardalis, Ursa Major, Ursa Minor, Draco, and Cepheus. The six cycles of Bible time are named, Adam, Noah, Abraham, Moses, David and Jesus.

The six ages represent 1,000 years each and describe the changing of the earth's polarity by the precession of the equinoxes. It begins with the birth of Adam in the beginning of time and terminates with the destruction of the Christian age. The new cycle after the Christian age is called the Millenium and describes a new heaven and earth, after which time the cycles of Bible history will be repeated. The Old Testament describes the changing of cycles for Asia and Europe, and the New Testament describes the destruction of the old cycle and also gives the conditions of the New World in the United States.

The change in the cycles of time from Europe to America, is caused by the changing of polarity in an angle of 120 degrees westward, commonly called the precession of the equinoxes. This changing of polarity is based on a universal law, for all the equinoctial time and space in the heavens and on the earth corresponds. From this it will be seen that the Moon's cycle around the earth, as well as the cycles of the earth and sun are measured by the same system and the precession of the equinoxes for the Moon and the earth correspond to the equinoxes for all cycles in the heavens. The Bible describes the precession of the equinoxes as the passover and at this time a peculiar condition is produced on the earth. The old cycle east of the changing degree is described as destroyed, when the new or western cycle begins. The period of time required for the earth to change polarity in this passover is 216 years; which corresponds to a distance of space in the heavens of three degrees of seventy-two years to each degree. This time is divided so that two degrees of 144 years are calculated before and 72 years after, the actual change of polarity takes place.

It should be remembered that the heavens and the earth are calculated in cycles of 360 degrees divided into minor ages, and that this 360-degree cycle represents 6,000 years. There are three 120-degree cycles which represent 2,000 years each, and six 60-degree cycles representing a period of time each of 1,000 yars. The 30-degree cycle contains twelve cycles of 500 years each, which are subdivided into twelve minor ages of 40 degrees in space, making the 24,000 degrees in all.

The distance in the heavens is measured from the point where the ecliptic crosses the equator in Pisces and is called "right ascension." The earth is measured from Greenwich which is 30 degrees west of Pisces and is calculated in degrees of longitude west. At the present time, Greenwich is the dividing point from which the polarity of the earth is calculated, but by the precession of the equinoxes the polarity of the earth will change to the 120th degree west longitude in the year 1920.

The conditions produced by the changing of polarity are being fulfilled in the development of the United States by the emigration from Europe to America. The first 144 years (2 degrees) represent the time from 1776 to the passover in 1920 and the second period of 72 years represents the cycle west of the changing degree, which is given in detail in the chapter on the United States.

Part VI—Chapter 45.

The ending of the cycle for Europe takes place in 1918 and the beginning of the cycle for the American continent is in 1920-1921. This is the period of time described in the Bible in the death of the Christian age and as the beginning of time in a new heaven and earth. A similar condition is described in the Bible at the passover for the ages of Abraham, Moses and David. Their cycles extended from Europe to the Pacific Coast and each age is repeated when the precession of the equinoxes takes place.

The cycle described in the New Testament is for the Pacific Coast west, at the 120th degree of longitude, but as the Pacific Ocean is west of the 124th degree, this cycle is described in latitude beginning at the 24th degree in the south and ending at the 54th degree in the north. A distance of 30 degrees is also given from the 30th to the 60th degree and contains twelve houses. The description for the space south of 32 degrees 30 minutes latitude is written as belonging to the cycle of Europe. The space between the 30th and the 50th degree represents the two 120-degree cycles from Greenwich to 240 degrees west. The 40-degree space from the 26th degree to the 66th degree, was divided into cycles of 10 degrees each by the usual angles, the same as the 40-degree distance of Europe. The main distance or space is from the 30th to the 54th degrees, which are divided into four cycles of six degrees each, and called the twenty-four elders. This space corresponds to the center of the ecliptic circle and within this radius is described the location of the twelve tribes in the Book of Joshua and also the provinces called Judah, Samaria and Galilee.

The following description will show how the 360-degree cycles are reduced into minor cycles. The space of 30 degrees from the 30th to the 60th degree represents a cycle of 360 degrees divided into twelve houses. The space of 15 degrees from the 30th to the 45th degree equals 180 degrees and from the 30th to the 37th degree 30 minutes, a 90-degree space. The space of 360 degrees is divided into angles of three, the same way. The distance of 30 degrees from the 30th to the 60th degree is divided into three cycles of 10 degrees each and represents a distance of 120 degrees. From the 30th to the 40th degree is an angle of 120 degrees and from the 30th to the 50th, an angle of 240 degrees. The space of 5 degrees from the 30th to the 35th degree equals an angle of 60 degrees and from the 30th to the 32nd degree 30 minutes equals an angle of 30 degrees or one house. From this it will be seen that 360 degrees equals 30 degrees, 180 degrees equals 15 degrees, 90 degrees equals 7 degrees 30 minutes, and 45 degrees equals 3 degrees 45 minutes. The distance of 120 equals 10 degrees, 60 degrees equals 5 degrees, and 30 degrees equals 2 degrees 30 minutes, and 15 degrees equals 1 degree 15 minutes degrees of latitude.

The books of the New Testament from Matthew to Revelation describe a distance from the 26th to the 96th degree and misled the translators to believe that these books were written in the years, which were described as degrees, in the New age. The book of Revelation is calculated from the 96th degree west longitude from the 120th degree and corresponds to the location at 216 degrees west or 144 degrees east longitude; which again corresponds to the very year when the cycles of time changed by the precession of the equinoxes. The book of Revelation describes the three cycles beginning in Asia including Europe and terminates in the New World in America. The year 35 A. D. corresponds to 1920 and as all Bible ages end at 96 A. D., the difference of 60 years will be added to 1920, which is 1980. The year 1980 is divided by the cycle of 360 and leaves us at 180 degrees west which is at the International Date Line at the end of time given in the New Testament.

The period of time given in each of the books of the New Testament contains 32 years; which represents the distance of 32 degrees. The time is calculated from the death of Christ in the 33rd year to the end, which is described in the different distances in degrees. Each of the books describes a given distance and represents space. This is a positive proof that all the books of the Bible are figured in degrees. The books were not written in these years, as pertaining to the age, but were written for the degrees constituting the Christian age.

The law of the Universe, spoken of in the Bible as the words and will of God, is the law which governs the life-giving elements in the heavens and on earth, and this is the God-given power ordinarily called the influence of the Sun, stars and planets. This law or influence may be expressed in different terms and called dinamic, magnetic, electric, force or power, and consists in the automatic transmission or polarization of the will of the creator, also called the infinite mind of God. We do not know of a better word to use in expressing this law than the term "influence of the elements," which expresses this power in whatever form it may manifest. The law of the universe

Part VI—Chapter 45.

which produces this influence on the earth can as an example, be compared to an electric generating plant. We will, as an illustration, say that the 48 great constellations in the heavens compare to that many electric dinamic headquarters and that the fixed stars within these constellations become transformers, being separate solar systems within the constellations. Our solar system can be compared to one of these dinamic substations producing a wireless energy to the eight planets of this unit and this energy is the word of God which is termed influence of the elements.

It is supposed to be a scientific fact today that the sun's rays produce a direct heat and life-giving power on this earth, but it will be found that the sun does not produce this energy as it consists of a reflected magnetic influence from other greater solar systems. From this it may be seen that our sun is one of many suns in the celestial heavens and when our solar system passes through space in its circuits, it gets its power from other solar systems similar to the energy the planets, earth and moon gets from the sun. As this dinamic energy is reflected through space it must necessarily strike the objective point in given angles of degrees and this measurement of space in the heavens is given in the Bible as good and bad angels.

We have stated that it is not the direct rays of the sun which produce the life-giving principle on this earth, but that it is a reflected energy operated similar to a wireless electric-magnetic instrument, which sends and receives messages according to the angle of adjustment. The distance from the sun to the earth is 93,000,000 miles and if it is the actual direct heat of the sun, which heats the earth, the entire surface of the earth where the sun's rays strike would obtain equal light and heat after passing this great distance. But instead of an equal distribution of the life-giving power it is reflected on this earth into zones which today are termed the life regions or belts. The heat and cold atmospheric waves strike within a few miles of each other; which proves that it is not the direct rays of the sun but a megnetic influence sent to a place atuned to this infinite law. One of these magnetic belts has been described in the Bible as the 24 Elders, which corresponds to the temperate zone of the life regions of the earth and the influence of the elements have been described within this zone in the history of creation for 6,000 yars.

We have described the comparative location of this ecliptic

belt around the earth in degrees and within this belt can be applied the conditions of the heavens which is produced on this earth. It may be earthquakes, cyclones, rain, or sunshine according to the angle which the different parts of the earth are atuned. Many systems of calculating climatic conditions are used today and Almanacs published giving approximate weather forecasts, but as the houses of the heavens have not been known and applied to the circuit around the earth, the calculations necessarily have been general instead of specific.

The universal principle of calculating in angles from the fixed stars and planets, to the different locations on the earth will give the climatic and weather conditions on this earth. The nature of the stars corresponds to the influence described for the planets and the nature of the houses the fixed stars are in also corresponds to the nature of the houses around the earth, as well as to man which is described in another chapter.

It should be remembered that the law of the Universe is harmonious and that the law of the elements of the heavens will equally apply to man as a God-given principle. A message from the Pleiades corresponds to a message of love and good will from Venus. A message from Antares corresponds to a call from Mars with war and pestilence. Messages from Alphard and Regulus correspond to those sent by Saturn meaning destruction, death and the end of the cycle, and so on with the rest of the stars. The magnetic energy or influence which the constellations and fixed stars produce on our sun is in harmony with the power which the sun sends to the planets and earth, as a reflected energy can only produce what it received. So also with the conditions which exist on this earth, as the elements of nature produce the conditions here and if man cares to observe this law, he may study it and know the will of the eternal father.

There is a principle illustrated in the description given in the Bible of the place "Peniel." The place Peniel is located in the constellation Scutum Sobiesii at the beginning of Sagitarius and indicates that this place is endowed by nature to produce spiritual gifts if developed. These psychic or spiritual gifts have been known and used in all ages, but during the Roman age, the development of these natural gifts for spiritual purposes have been prohibited by laws. The principle described in Peniel means vision of God or to obtain knowledge of God; which again we call spiritual development, clear-seeing and clear-hearing, etc. The ancients also called the principle illustrated in Peniel the "philosopher's stone," the "light within," and "Urim and Thummim." Many scientists called alchemists have for centuries been experimenting in chemical laboratories to find the philohopher's stone, not knowing what they were looking for, but expecting to find a mineral stone. The law or power hidden in the terms used as the Philosopher's stone and Peniel is not for a material or earthly use, but for the purpose of developing the inner or soul principle of man while in the flesh. God in his wisdom has hidden this law as well as the knowledge and power which can be obtained by the use of these gifts. It is, however, a universal law, and to those whose aim is not entirely of a material nature and who do not live for self alone, these gifts can be developed, but for others they cannot.

During the change in the cycles of time the elements of nature produce an influence on this earth when this soul-building power within man is intensified and the human race becomes the most enlightened in both spiritual and material knowledge. This God-given power is a reflected energy from the heavens, produced in cycles or waves and it depends on the physical condition in which man is, when this energy strikes him and what he does with it after he receives it.

The proper use of man's vitality is illustrated in the term "Peniel," and the abuse is called, "The unpardonable sin against the Holy Ghost," which means that when man lives in material, sensual pleasures and abuses the law, he sins against the most precious gifts of God. The reason why this kind of sin is called "unpardonable" is, that the life-giving power is wasted, and cannot be restored, because God has given this power as a life-building principle for an eternal life.

If man lives according to the law of God, this power becomes a blessing, but if man's vitality, as a soul-building power is abused, he becomes a mere animal and lives now and hereafter in environments to correspond to his nature.

As there is a creative power of the heavens so is there also a destroying or counteracting influence to harmonize the law of creation. And it depends on man's physical condition at the time when this influence is produced, if it builds or destroys his body. This detrimental influence of the elements has been shown very clearly at the present time in the disease called "Spanish Influenza." This same influence was also described in the Bible as Reuben's Mandrakes, and in the many diseases and pestilences spoken of for the time of the end. It is illustrated as the work of Satan who destroys the power of the Holy Ghost which God produces in man on this earth. We should realize that the Holy Ghost spoken of is Neptune and that the power of Satan is the influence which the planet Saturn produces. From this we may learn that in the laws of God a principle is involved and if we know this law, we may live according to his will.

It is God's will that this knowledge shall only be given to those who seek it, as it is said, "Seek ye first the kingdom of heaven and all other things shall be added unto you;" which means that the philosopher's stone shall be found only by those who seek after the kingdom of God. If this knowledge is worth having it is worth looking for; "Seek and ye shall find, knock and it shall be opened unto you." From this it will be seen that God in his wisdom has given laws and ordinances which must be followed, and in obeying God's laws the rewards will be a heavenly condition both now and hereafter.

Some of the teachers of the philosophy of the Christian and other religions, do not understand this law of life, but in the new dispensation this law will be revealed to them and they will see God and know his will.

We have mentioned that the angels (angles) of the heavens produce a given influence on the earth and that this influence would be according to the conditions and nature of the place where this influence is produced. The places in the heavens called angels (angles) which produce the conditions on earth spoken of, consist of living intelligent beings and the influence they produce is according to the laws of nature. If an influence is produced from the angles of 90 degrees, at the poles of the earth, warm and pleasant climatic conditions could not be expected, and so also from places in the heavens where darkness and ignorance prevails. Good cannot come from a place where there is no good, any more than to expect darkness to produce light. There are places in the heavens to correspond to every environment and form of life and the places where the human and other beings live in the heavens, is according to the nature of the beings. From this will be seen that the angels of the heavens are in the environments of the place and that the being who lives at the different angles in degrees corresponds to the nature of the place.

This can be illustrated in the nature of Germany which produced a German environment and also to the influence produced by the people of the United States, as they produce an American influence. In emigrating to another nation one becomes an influence of that nation on this earth as he does when emigrating to a life in the heavens.

The Bible states that life in the next form of expression in the heavens is rewarded according to the nature and environments of the being here, and that men and others in the next life will live according to his desires and reap the harvest of that which he has produced in the flesh. If man lives in ignorance, as animals, and produces evil conditions for himself and others, he will find his level when he enters the next world and get his reward according to what he is, and so also for those who aim to do good and live according to the law. We should remember that man after passing out of the body, enters a life in the heavens and that the place where he then lives is calculated in angles of degrees the same as it is on the earth, and that he, as a being, becomes one of the spirits within this angle. From this it will be seen, that man becomes one of the angels of the heavens according to his nature and that he is as much of an angel of God on earth now, as he will be after passing out of the body of flesh.

We have reproduced charts of the heavens copied by G. P. Serviss from Heis's Atlas Celestis. These charts are apparently the best illustrations of the heavens in existence today, and will be of great help in applying the locations of the constellations to the earth.

These charts will show the comparative locations of the constellations and fixed stars on the earth and can be used as reference when reading the Bible and the old mythological stories.

It is apparent that mineral and other valuable resources can be discovered at the corresponding location on the earth to where the fixed stars are located in the heavens. In Europe the locations of the tribes are the nations and the stars can readily be located there. In the Pacific Coast States we have described the location of the tribes from the book of Joshua and the twelve charts will illustrate where the fixed stars are located within this area. For the sake of comparison, the location of the nations of Europe can be compared to the location of the tribes on the Pacific Coast, as the fixed stars are correspondingly located. When it is known what are the natural resources of the nations in Europe, it can be applied to the Pacific Coast

States and the hidden wealth of the country discovered. The **mines of England, France and Belgium can be comparatively** located within a radius of a few miles in the Pacific Coast States. So also with the copper and iron mines of Scandinavia, which are comparatively located in the State of Washington and so with the resources of the rest of the nations of Europe. This can also be illustrated in the stories from the Bible where it says, that in the foot of the tribe of Asher will be found oil, iron and brass. The foot of the tribe of Asher is located in the western part of the State of Washington near the coast and south of the Olympic Mountains. Another good comparison can be given in the great Pleiades located in Taurus, corresponding to the location of the Blue Mountains in eastern Oregon. In this locality will be found one of the most valuable undiscovered mineral deposits of the world. In the State of Washington north of Mt. Adams and Mt. St. Helens will be found valuable coal deposits. In Death Valley in California will be found gold, silver and oil which is located within a triangular or wedge-shaped formation of the valley. When oil is discovered in Death Valley it will produce trouble for the other oil fields in California as this is the place Achor spoken of in the Bible. From this it will be seen that the nature and conditions in the heavens are the same as on earth, and that this knowledge can be applied in a practical scientific way for the guidance and benefit to man. We must remember, that as it is in the heavens so is it on the earth. God's words are the same when spoken in the heavens as when they are expressed on the earth.

God, the Universe and man is not part of a part but is part of the whole unit of one.

CHAPTER 46.

THE HEAVENS AND EARTH.

The "celestial heavens" is the name given to the path of our solar system in the twelve houses of the heavens and within this path or circuit are located other solar systems, known as constellations or fixed stars. The name, nature and location of these fixed stars are copied from ancient records and given in a separate chapter.

The method of applying the aspects of the fixed stars to the sun is the same as used by astrologers when calculating locations for the sun and planets in relations to the earth. It is in the well-known method of calculating the influences or aspects in angles of trine, squares, conjunction, parallel and opposition, etc. When calculating space in the heavens, the center or ecliptic point is located in Pisces and not, as it is on the earth, at Greenwich. From this point in the heavens, all longitude of right ascension for all stars is calculated. In the heavens Pisces is the first constellation of the Zodiac and Aries is the second and so on; but on the earth Aries has been called the first house. This distinction is very important as the location of the constellations of the Zodiac for the heavens and earth will not correspond if this is not considered.

It is apparent that the fundamental principle of the law of the heavens is not understood by Astronomers today, as they do not realize that the constellations and fixed stars move in circuits around a given center. However, they know that the stars move and call it "Star drift." Astronomical text books contain some very surprising and far from scientific statements, as will be seen from the following extract copied from a modern text book: "The constellations have in consequence of the precession of the equinoxes, drifted out of connection with the framework of the Zodiac which is formed with the signs as a basis. Thus the sign Aries becomes Pisces and Taurus becomes Aries, etc." We will only say that there is no drifting in the heavens and that the constellations could not be out of connection with the Zodiac, because the Zodiac consists of twelve constellations and the Zodiac cannot drift out of place any more than the Sun, planets or the earth. We will call astronomers' attention to the distinction we have spoken of between Greenwich in Aries and the Meridian in Pisces and they will readily see their mistake.

The original division of the heavens into constellations described by the ancients was in the dividing of the Terrestrial heavens into twelve houses or hours called the twelve tribes of Israel. These twelve tribes were divided into three groups of four tribes to each division. The first four houses consist of Sagitarius, Capricorn, Aquarius, and Pisces, and these four houses represent the space called 4 B. C. The next four houses begin with the dividing of space and time east and west and are Aries, Taurus, Gemini and Cancer, making the second cycle. The third and last division contains the houses of Leo, Virgo, Libra and Scorpio. These divisions of the heavens are again subdivided into many minor ages and called the descendants of the children of Israel.

228   *Key to Bible and Heaven.*

The three cycles consisting of the four houses each are calculated from Greenwich for the cycles of Europe, and from the first degree of Leo for America, and the first degree of Sagitarius for Asia. The dividing degree for these houses is at the 120th degree east and west from Greenwich and is the dividing of the earth into three cycles of 120 degrees each, making 360 degrees in all.

The four degrees or houses east of this dividing point were called B. C. which means they were located east of Greenwich or east of one of the other 120-degree divisions. Each of these 120-degree divisions consists of twelve houses and is figured as a complete cycle. The first degree of Aries begins at the 120th degree and in the cycle for Europe this is at Greenwich. For the American cycle, the first degree of Aries begins at the 120th degrees west longitude in Leo and is the same to America as Greenwich is to Europe. This dividing line given at Greenwich simply divides east from west. The Christian cycle described in the heavens began at 4 B. C. and for the earth it is described to have begun at 40 B. C. and to extend to 70 or 80 A. D. This means that all ages, the Christian age included, extend four houses east and eight houses west of Greenwich and illustrates that the Christian era consists of twelve houses as a complete age.

The Christian cycle of time terminates in 1920 and the new age for America begins in 1921. The center from which to figure time and space for the coming age is the 120th degree west longitude. The same system is used in America as was used in Europe and there will be another 40 degrees east and 80 degrees west from the 120-degree dividing line. The 40 degrees east extends to the east coast of the United States and is the same place where Adam lived in the Garden of Eden and where Abraham and Moses had their troubles. The 80-degree west extends to the 200th degree west longitude. This system of measuring 40 degrees east and 80 degrees west to every 120-degree cycle also applies to the cycle for Asia. The Asiatic age will begin in the year 4080 A. D. at the 120th degree east longitude.

It will be found that in the study of the heavens, a system of parallel locations was described. This means that two or more planets or constellations which are located on the same degree of longitude are in parallel positions. As an example, we will say that the constellation Ursa Major and Leo are parallel, being located on the same degree in longitude. The planets or stars may be in either north or south declination and still be in parallel position to each other. From this it will be seen that a constellation located within the same degrees of longitude as a house, is termed to be in parallel position in that house. When our solar system passes through the twelve houses of the celestial heavens it becomes in conjunction and **parallel position to** all the constellations of the heavens. This is very important to know for when the sun is in the different locations, a condition or influence is produced and this influence is again reproduced and called aspects. The law of the heavens including this influence of the Stars is the word of God and in this manner God speaks to man on this earth.

There are still in existence some of the old maps or charts showing how the ancients illustrated the conditions in the heavens and implied that the conditions of the heavens were the conditions on this earth. We have copied some of these charts to show that it contains the same system as described in the Bible. As an example, we will give the names of the three great divisions illustrated in the charts and it will be found to correspond to the stories given in the Bible.

The constellation Cepheus is pictured with the well-known features of Jesus of Nazareth. The space covered by the picture is from 55 degrees east to 70 degrees west representing the location of Europe and the Atlantic Ocean. The constellation Cepheus represents the Christian age as a period of time which is described in other chapters.

The constellation Camelo Pardalis is illustrated as a Camel and covers the space from the 45th degree to the 200th degree west longitude. The distance of the Camel extends from the Atlantic Ocean and includes the American continent to past the International Date Line in the Pacific Ocean.

The constellation Draco (including Ursa Minor) represents the third division and is illustrated as a great dragon. Draco covers the space from the 140th degree to the 300th degree west longitude, and is the space from the west coast of the American continent across the Pacific Ocean and Asia, to the 60th degree east at the dividing of Europe and Asia.

The location of the constellations in the heavens measured in degrees on the ecliptic, corresponds to the location on the earth as figured in degrees east and west from the meridian.

From the old illustrations of the heavens can be seen the

exact location of all the constellations and will help in memorizing the names for the different localities in the heavens as well as on earth. Detailed description of the scientific meanings of these ancient charts will be found in nearly all Astronomical books and in the Greek and Roman mythological story books. These books are very common and are found in all public libraries. It should be remembered that these books do not contain myth stories but that it is a description of the heavens and earth similar to that given in the Bible.

In studying the charts of the heavens it must be remembered that the first and the 360th degrees are calculated from Pisces and that this house contains the 30-degree east of Aries. We find that Casiopeia and Andromeda are located in parallel position with this house. The story that Andromeda was chained to a rock means that the age representing the house Pisces as Andromeda would be chained. This house represents the mind of man and it shows that during this age the mind of man would be chained to the rock of ignorance. The house of Pisces represents the Roman power which has ruled Europe in ignorance during the Christian age.

The house of Aries is located from Greenwich to the 30th degree west and in this house are located the Triangle and Persius. The house Taurus, extends from the 30th to the 60th degree west longitude and includes Orion and Auriga. From this it will be seen that Aries and Taurus cover the distance from England across the Atlantic Ocean and that the head and the horns of the bull, Taurus, are located in the Ocean east of the United States.

The two houses of Gemini and Cancer cover the distance of the United States from the Atlantic to the 120th degree west longitude. The constellations of Auriga, Monoceros, Canis Minor and Major, Argo and the Lynx are in parallel with these houses. The location of Eridanus corresponds to the Gulf of Mexico. The house of Gemini covers the space in the eastern part of the United States, and Cancer represents the country west of the Mississippi to Utah and Arizona. In the house of Cancer is the place where the age is destroyed and as this is at the end of the cycle, it is located at what was known as Sodom and Gomorrah.

The house Leo is located west from the 120th degree in the Pacific Coast States and from this degree the calculation for a new cycle of time is made. The constellation Ursa Major is located at the 153rd degree west, which corresponds to the 123rd degree for the earth. This constellation and the Pleiades contains seven stars each from which the seven tribes or churches of Israel were located. Leo contains five stars and gave the location for the five other tribes of Judah as the tribes of the Lion. These two divisions of five and seven were originally given from the Pacific Coast States.

The 120th degree west is at the Pacific Coast States and west from this location we find the constellation Hydra containing most of the evil fixed stars of the heavens. The entire space of Hydra covers the distance of the Pacific Ocean because it extends from America to Asia and in this distance Leo, Virgo, Crater, Centourus, Bootes and Coma Berenices are located. Special attention is called to the location of the Sextans at 150 degrees west at the equator.

The houses of Libra and Scorpio are located in the Pacific Ocean and extend to the Coast of Japan and China. In this part of the world the Serpent, Ophiuchus, Hercules and Corona are located. Scorpio is the last house of the cycle, and is located east of China in the Ocean.

Sagitarius is the first house of the third cycle and begins in the Southeastern part of China, terminating in the Himalaya Mountains. In the parallel of Sagitarius is located Sagitta, Aquilla, and Scutum Sobiesii. This is one of the most peculiar locations of all the places described in mythology, astronomy and the Bible. It is the birthplace or first house for all cycles. The location of the Archer's bow corresponds to the 120th degree east longitude and in the heavens it is located at 210 degrees west. The bow Noah placed in the heavens at the time of the flood is the bow of Sagitarius and not a rainbow.

Capricorn, in the heavens, begins at the 300th degree west and extends to the 330th degree west, which again corresponds to the location from Thibet to Persia and from the 90th to the 60th degree east longitude. The two houses of Capricorn and Aquarius overlap each other and as these houses represent the dividing section of Asia and Europe the illustrations are peculiarly arranged. Capricorn and Aquarius cover the distance from the 90th to the 30th degree east longitude which is from Thibet to Egypt. The constellations Pisces Austrinus, Delphines, Cygnus and Pegasus are located within this parallel.

Aquarius is located from the 60th to the 30th degree east longitude and illustrates the end of the cycles with the termination of Aquarius at Pisces. This house covers the distance of Persia and Turkey in Asia and is the place described in all Bible stories as the headquarters for the patriarchs. The Caspian Sea is located here which was called the well of Haran. The twelve children of Israel were born to Jacob, Rachael, Leah and the handmaids from this place. The closing or ending of the cycle is at the 30th degree east longitude where Pisces begins as a new cycle. The flying horse, Pegasus, does not extend into Pisces and that is the reason why the back part of the horse is cut off. Pegasus represents to the heavens the same as the Sphinx of Egypt does to the earth. The Pyramids are located at the 30th degree east longitude and have been given as the place where the cycles end.

It is shown in the stories described in the Bible that all cycles begin at the 40th degree east, but the main events of the cycle or life of the person described does not begin until the 30th degree westward was reached. We have observed that the last 10 degrees of the age is where destruction of the cycles takes place and also where the party described begins to rule. From this we conclude that there is 10 degrees allowed for the old age and the same 10 degrees are used for the beginning of the cycle. The new and younger patriarchs of Israel became leaders before their forefathers died. From this can be seen, that the 10 degrees between the 30th and the 40th degree is where the change takes place. The city of Jerusalem in Palestine is located at the 35th degree east and that is the reason why the Ancients said that the Christian age would begin from this locality. The last ten degrees of the cycle extend east from Egypt to the Arabian desert and this is the location where the age previous to the Christian age was killed and from where the new or Christian age began. Pegasus is located at 20 degrees in Aquarius at this location.

The Christian age began 2000 years ago and we know that each age consists of thirty degrees and from this we can figure that the Christian cycle of time represents the new generation of Pisces for the space of Europe. At the time of the termination of the old age at the end of the Aquarius cycle, the years were divided to be B. C. and A. D. and the cycle changed at the 30th degree east. The dividing of time into B. C. means before the Christian era and A. D. stands for after date or means during the Christian age. This division is calculated from the sixth degree of Pisces, being the ecliptic pole or Meri-

Part VI—Chapter 46. 233

dian of the heavens. In the year 1921, the ecliptic pole corresponds in location to the 120th degree west, whereas the old cycle was calculated from Greenwich which again is from Aries.

The Christian age began at 40 B. C. with the beginning of the Roman power and extends to 70 A. D. This is the space recorded for the cycle in Europe covering a period of time for 2000 years. The nations of Europe from France and England to Turkey have been described as the disciples of Christ and represent Christianity as an age in the fishermen and Pisces as a cycle for the heavens.

We have described the Zodiacal circuit around the earth, its divisions into twelve sections, called houses, and each house is described according to degrees on earth, corresponding to a similar location in the heavens. The distance for the Christian cycle is described in the same manner but for this age a space of 30 degrees longitude is figured to contain the twelve houses and in this space the twelve nations of Europe are located. The nature and locations of the nations of Europe correspond to the nature of the constellations and the houses described around the earth. In another chapter, we have given the names of the nations and the corresponding names for the houses of the Zodiac, the names of the twelve tribes and disciples of Jesus, etc., to show who they are and their comparative nature.

At the termination of all cycles when the earth's polarity is changed the cycle or age is killed. The destroying of the age takes place during the last seven years of the sideral cycle of 2000 years. The Bible describes that at the end of the Christian age a great destruction is to take place, and gives a detailed description of the conditions which would prevail during this calamity. The predictions given in the Bible for this destruction are being fulfilled in the present world's war. The time, place and the nations involved, are correctly described, showing that a condition would exist which would produce the war.

The destruction of the Christian age takes place within ten degrees east of Greenwich, which is the location where the present war really takes place. The holy mountains for Europe are in Switzerland and represent the house of Aquarius which is the home or mansion for the planet Uranus. It is a scientific fact that Uranus has been passing through the house of Aquarius in the heavens during the world's war. Uranus entered Aquarius in 1912 and he will not be entirely out of this house before 1920 and as the change of cycles takes place when Uranus leaves

Aquarius and enters Pisces, the new cycle will begin at that time. The Bible describes that at the end of the Christian age, which is illustrated in the life of Jesus as a man on earth and as the planet Uranus in the heavens, the earth is to be destroyed. The life or age of Jesus, corresponds to the period when our solar system passes in the heavens, through the house of Pisces representing the period for Europe. At the termination of this cycle of 1920 years and at the time when Uranus leaves the house of Aquarius, is the end of the age. The last seven years of this cycle is the time when the destruction of the age takes place, and the time when Uranus and Saturn are in direct opposition in the heavens. When Uranus is in the house of Aquarius, Saturn must be in Leo, in order to be in opposition to Uranus and as this is at the end of the age, Saturn kills Uranus. Leo is the house of Judah and corresponds to Germany and as Saturn has been in this house during the war, Germany is the cause of the war. Uranus was in the 25th degree of Aquarius and Saturn was in the 25th degree of Leo in October, 1918, when the war terminated, which means that the earthly life of Christianity came to an end at that time.

The three days described in the Bible as years from the death of Christ to the passover, representing the passing into the new age, are the three years from 1918 to 1921. It is during this uncertain period that Uranus is both direct and retrograde in motion which is described as the time that Jesus is in the grave when the old cycle dies and the American cycle begins.

We have said that the Christian age begins at 40 degrees east and terminates at 70 to 80 degrees west. The location for the 80 degrees west is on the east coast of the United States. The Bible says that in forty days after the death of the Christian age, that Christ ascended to heaven and began to rule in his spiritual kingdom. This means that the forty days referred to, represent the forty degrees across the United States from the 80th to the 120th degrees. A description is given that a spiritual Christian doctrine will come from the west coast of the United States and that Christ will rule his Millenium age from his home in the heavens. The cycles were calculated in degrees of longitude from 40 degrees east to 80 degrees west, and when this principle was applied to the Pacific Coast section it was figured in latitude from Mexico to British Columbia. The distance in Mexico from the 26th degree to the 33rd degree, corresponds to the distance of Europe from Greenwich east to Turkey and

Part VI—Chapter 46.

that is the reason why Mexico has been translated to correspond to the age of Egypt. This distance again corresponds to the seven years when the age is killed and is the border distance from the Rio Grande at the Gulf of Mexico to the Pacific Ocean.

The distance of 30 and 40 degrees east of Greenwich has been described as the space for the Christian age, but for the time of the end, the space was figured up to the 45th degree at the Euphrates river. A figure or horoscope was set up for this space and the houses of the heavens were applied to the nations of Europe. The names of the nations and the corresponding houses and tribes of Israel have been given in another chapter. The constellations of fixed stars were also applied to the nations and when the planets, Uranus, Saturn and Neptune passed through the different houses of the heavens, the conditions produced were applied to the nations.

The ancients describe four fixed stars as the principal constellations and these fixed stars have been referred to by nearly all astronomers as the leading stars of the heavens. They are Aldebaren, in Taurus; Regulus, in Leo; Antares, in Scorpio, and Fomalhaut, in Aquarius. In the Bible these same stars have been described according to the names of the houses they were located in, and given the name of the Bull, the Lion, the Scorpion, and the Man. The four fixed stars described, represent the four leading nations at war at the present time. The Bull, and Aldebaren represent England; the Lion and Regulus stand for Germany; the Scorpion and Antares for Austria-Hungary; the Man and Fomalhaut is representing humanity in Switzerland. We have illustrated the location of these houses and constellations showing the reason why the ancients located them at the four cardinal houses for Europe at the time of the end. Anyone familiar with this study can readily see that the nature of the four fixed stars is applied to the houses as nations in which the stars are located.

The next point to be considered is the distance of Europe as a horoscope for the twelve houses. The twelve nations of Europe represent a house of 30 degrees each and the distance figured in angles of a given number of degrees shows the relation between the different nations. It should be remembered that the good angles are the spaces divided by three or triangles and that the bad or evil angles are the spaces divided by four or the square distances in space. We will give a brief explanation of what is meant by the nations being in friendly or antagonistic relations to each other. When two nations are 30, 60 or 120 degrees apart, they are friendly, but if 45, 90 or 180 degrees apart they are antagonistic to each other. This method is called the figuring of aspects of the houses and is called good and bad angles.

The conditions produced within the nations are caused by the movements of the planets through the houses and the different aspects are caused by the nature of the planets in their position toward other planets. This can be explained by Saturn, who has always been a regular Satan, and when he is in a house representing a nation, that nation will act as a devil toward others. Saturn was in the house of Germany during the principal part of the war. These principles will be readily seen by those who understand this study and it will not be understood by others even if it were described in detail.

We have described that the crucifying of Christ is illustrated in the opposition of Uranus to Saturn which took place in October, 1918, and we have also said that the religion of the world is to be changed and the Churches destroyed. We will now give the reason why the Christian and other Churches are to be destroyed and the date when it is to take place.

It is written that when the sign of the son of man is seen in the heavens that it is a sign for the time of the end. The planet Uranus represents the son of man and was discovered by Sir John Hershel in 1781 A. D., five year after the beginning of the time of the end. This is self explanatory and is a sign for the time of the end. In the year 1920 Uranus will be in the house of Pisces, representing Europe and Italy as a nation, and this is the year when Italy and the Church will be ruined. Saturn and Neptune are in Leo and Virgo which is located in the Pacific Coast States and from this place the destruction of the church takes place. The war stopped at the time when Saturn and Uranus were in the degree of opposition, so we take it for granted that the war on the Church will be over by August, 1920, and not before.

It is written that there will be great suffering and crime in Europe from the year 1919 to 1920 and that this year is the most important in the history of the world. Peace will be restored in Europe when the international convention is held in Switzerland after the revolution has taken place. The delegates will not represent the government as in the peace conference in 1919, but will represent the common people. The

Austria-Hungarian nation will not take part in the meetings in Switzerland when these meetings are first held, but later. (John 20:24.) We calculate that peace on earth and good will to man will begin in 1921 and that all nations will aim to do right after this year.

The conclusion to be reached from the study of the heavens and the Bible is, that the law of the Universe has been lost to the human race, and is found in the Bible.

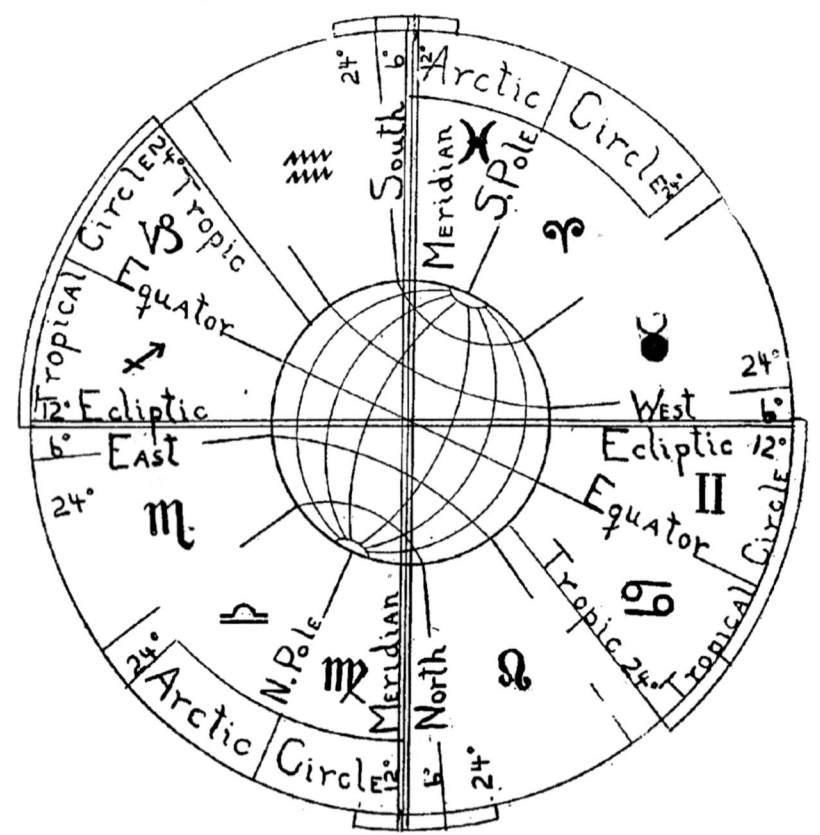

PLATE 13—PRECESSIONAL ZONES.

CHAPTER 47.

TIME AND SPACE IN THE HEAVENS.

The twelve houses of the heavens correspond to the twelve hours of the clock. The Meridian, in the heavens, is the point where the ecliptic crosses the equator and is described to be in

Pisces and corresponds to the top of the head of man. This point is located as twelve o'clock and the house Pisces corresponds to the time between twelve and one o'clock. Astronomical charts illustrate the twelve houses to contain two hours each.

Time is figured from Aries and Greenwich, (the first house of the heavens) at one o'clock and calculated from the Meridian at twelve o'clock. This illustrates the reason why the mistake was made by the astronomers in locating the fixed stars and constellations in the houses, as they were figured from the Meridian at twelve o'clock and located in the houses from one o'clock. That is, observation is taken at England and calculated for the meridian in Egypt

The rest of the houses are located in the regular order: Taurus, at two o'clock; Gemini, at three o'clock; Cancer, at four o'clock; Leo, at five o'clock; Virgo, at six o'clock; Libra, at seven o'clock; Scorpio, at eight o'clock; Sagitarius, at nine o'clock; Capricorn, at ten o'clock; Aquarius, at eleven o'clock; and Pisces, at twelve o'clock.

It will be found that there is harmony in all the arrangement that nature makes, which can be seen by the dividing of the heavens and earth, into time and space by the vernal and autumnal equinoxes. Time and space have been divided into angles of a given number of hours or degrees and in the Bible these angles have been called good and bad Angels. When man comes to realize that this system of dividing time is made by nature, he will not have to strike for shorter or longer hours of work. The good angles are formed by the division of the heavens into angles based on the multiple of three and the bad angles by multiples of four. From this it can readily be seen what is meant by the different angles or distances spoken of in the measurement of the heavens. The space in the heavens and the distance around the earth is figured by the same method as the hours of the clock.

We have given a description of the earth, that it was laid out in a space of twelve houses and that each house counted as thirty degrees. This is a very simple arrangement as it means the same to the earth as if we were to arrange the twelve hours of the clock and call them houses. We will again give a general outline of what part of the earth corresponds to the time given by the clock. The Bible describes a circle around the earth where this calculation was made and this is at 36 degrees north latitude, which corresponds to the Mediterranean Sea in

Europe, passing Thibet in Asia, and the Mason and Dixon line in the United States. In this line or circuit around the earth, we place the twelve hours of the clock and call them houses. Each one of these houses has 30 degrees which takes the place of minutes of the clock.

The beginning of time is at one o'clock which is called the Greenwich degree of longitude. This line crosses Spain, England and France and from this point distance is counted east and west. We will first explain that the distance of Europe east of England consists of one hour of 30 degrees and if we look on an Atlas of the world, we find that 30 degrees east strikes at Egypt where the Pyramids are located. This distance corresponds to the time between twelve o'clock and one o'clock and has been called Pisces, the fishes. The time is changed at twelve o'clock and corresponds to when the sun in the heavens passes the point where it changes the seasons of the year and is called the vernal equinox. From this it will be seen that the time of twelve o'clock corresponds to Egypt and is the place for both the ending and beginning of time and is the meridian.

The Atlantic Ocean, from England to the United States, contains about 70 degrees which is over two hours and this space is covered by the two houses of Aries and Taurus. It should be remembered that each house consists of 30 degrees and if we add the two houses of Gemini and Cancer, it brings us to the 120th degree west longitude, at the mountains on the Pacific Coast. It is now four o'clock and the end of the first cycle of time. West from the Pacific Coast States are the houses of Leo, Virgo, Libra and Scorpio and all four of these houses lie in the Pacific Ocean. The Bible describes this distance as the home of the Dragon where all the bad elements of the heavens are located. In the middle of the Pacific Ocean is the location on the earth opposite to the degree described as Greenwich in England and the Meridian in Egypt. These are located as six and seven o'clock at 150 degrees and 180 degrees west. This makes eight houses, or 240 degrees west from England and four houses or 120 degrees east from England. We are now at 120 degrees on the east coast of China and the time is nine o'clock in the house Sagitarius. This is the place described in the Book of Daniel as the beginning of the time of the end and where Nebuchadnezzar began to rule. The house of Sagitarius is from the east coast of China to Thibet in the Himalaya Mountains. The next 30 degrees is from Thibet at 90 degrees east, to Persia at 60 degrees in the house of Capricorn at ten o'clock. The third house of the cycle is Aquarius at eleven o'clock from Persia at 60 degrees, to Egypt at 30 degrees. If we figure in degrees from Greenwich west, the east coast of China would be 240 degrees, Thibet 270, Persia 300, and Egypt 330 degrees west. We have now completed the circuit back to Egypt which is at twelve o'clock where Pisces begins. From this it will be seen that Aquarius is the house between eleven and twelve o'clock and is the end of all time.

For the past 1920 years the center of population and civilization have been west of Egypt. The time previous to the Christian era up to 2000 B. C., the earth's center was east from Egypt to the east coast of China. In the time previous to 4000 B. C., the center was in the United States. This is the period described in the Bible as the Garden of Eden age and as far back as Bible history goes. The beginning of time is for the United States west from Greenwich, and the ending of time is the destruction of the Christian age east of Greenwich. This completes the age and illustrates what is meant by time and space.

The books of the New Testament describe time as being divided into thirty-two years each and the spiritual life of Christianity is described to represent the Pacific Coast States. In all the books in the New Testament from Matthew to The Acts, the conditions on the Pacific Coast and the years given for that portion of the country, represent degrees of latitude; which means that when events are described to take place in a given year, it is the place in degrees of latitude which is described.

The life story of Christ represents the space of Europe as an age, and includes Mexico as far north as the 32nd degree 30 minutes latitude; and this space in all cycles has been called Egypt or Europe. Christ, as a cycle of time, died when at the 32nd degree 30 minutes latitude, or as a man in his thirty-third year; which means that the cycle for Europe including Mexico, ends at the 32nd degree 30 minutes latitude when the new age begins at the Mexican borders of the United States as the spiritual life of Christ.

This is best described from the book of St. Luke, where the first two chapters describe the time up to 8 A. D., which means the 8 degrees east of Greenwich, the location of the Alps Mountains and corresponds to 24 degrees latitude. Chapter 3 begins at 26 A. D., meaning the 26th degree north latitude, in Mexico.

The fourth Chapter of St. Luke ends at 31 A. D., which makes the four degrees called 4 B. C., for the beginning of all cycles of time and proves that it is the degrees referred to. In the cycle for two thousand years ago, Egypt was used as the dividing line and the degrees north of the 30th degree in Palestine illustrated the same to Egypt as Mexico is to the Pacific Coast cycle.

The life of Christ given in the New Testament contains seven years, beginning at 26 A. D. and ending at 33 A. D., which are the seven years when Uranus is in Aquarius. The years from 26 to 33 A. D. represent Europe and Mexico, and from these degrees, as years, begins the Pacific Coast Cycle.

The years given as the Julian Calendar age are figured in cycles of 360 degrees longitude calculated west, and the year 1920 corresponds to 120 degrees west from Greenwich. The years given from 26 A. D. in the New Testament are in degrees of latitude for the Pacific Coast cycle and when the Christian age dies at the age of 32 degrees 30 minutes, it is the beginning of a New Age with the boundary line at the Mexican borders. The three days after Christ died is represented in the three degrees from San Diego to Mt. Whitney, and when the age reaches the 36th degree, it corresponds to the year 1920. From this it will be seen that the 36th degree latitude and the 120th degree longitude correspond to the year 1920.

The book of Acts gives the locations of the country and events on the coast and the description given is perfect. The first seven chapters describe the time up to 1919; the ending of the old age. Chapter 8 describes Southern California at 34 A. D. and also describes what the conditions are on the coast in this year. Chapter 9 describes the 35th and the 37th degrees as 35 and 37 A. D., and the 10th Chapter includes as far north as the Shasta Mountains at 41 A. D., or 41 degrees north. The description for Oregon begins at Chapter 11:22, ending at the Chapter 13. The State of Washington is described in Chapter 14. In Chapter 15:2 begins the description of British Columbia, showing the change of nationality; and the rest of the Chapters from the 16th to the 28th describe the country extending to the 63rd degree north latitude. The names of the cities on the coast are given where the location is referred to in years.

The Christian age came to an end in 1918 when Christ was 32 years of age and the next two or three years are described as very uncertain in events. The year 34 A. D. corresponds to 1919 of the present age and this is figured the same as all other years given in the Bible. Divide 1919 by 360, which equals five circuits around the earth and leave 119 degrees (years) west from Greenwich. The 120th degree longitude, west is at the beginning of the New Age in the Pacific Coast States and corresponds to 1920 A. D. as a year. From this, alone, can be seen that the new cycle of time is for the Pacific Coast and that the description given in the Bible for the years after 34 is for the happenings there.

It is not advisable to explain the prophecies for the New Age as it may be considered as premature propaganda for the Millenium. We are, at the present time, living at the end of the time of the end, and the events described in the Bible will shortly come to pass in the Pacific Coast States.

CHAPTER 48.

THE CONSTELLATIONS.

The Bible says that the heavens are divided into three divisions, and are illustrated as three separate heavens within the unit of the one great universal heaven. The greatest space of the heavens are called the "Terrestrial Heavens" and within this space is the "Celestial Heavens." The third or lowest heaven consists of the Zodiac of our solar system. The universal law governing the conditions in the heavens is operated on the same principles as the law controlling the Moon's circuit around the earth and the earth and planets' relations to the sun in the sun's travels around the ecliptic within the Zodiac.

The dividing of the great heavens into three parts illustrates the principle of the trinity of God in the heavens; being divided into three parts and yet remaining as one eternal power. The trinity of God as a unit of one in the heavens is manifest in all the minor divisions of the entire creative universe. The divisions of the unit of one into three parts is demonstrated in the three planets of Uranus, Neptune, and Saturn. The law or power of God has been illustrated in the influence as produced by these planets and is called the word of God. From this can be seen, that there is a law in the universe and in the operation of this law, a condition is produced which is called the influence of the Sun and planets, as the word of God.

The law of the universe has been very carefully written in the Bible and described in the stories as pictured there. It is not the astrological aspects or influence of the planets which is explained, but it is the law of God as explained in the stories illustrated by the planets. We have been ignorant of this law but at the beginning of all new cycles of time, God reveals his will to man so that the human race will know his will and live accordingly.

We will describe some of the ruling principles of the celestial heavens and what the reasons are for the conditions produced, which are spoken of in the Bible. In the book of Job, Chapter 38: 31 to 33, a reference is made to the celestial heavens as a "God given law."

The stars are mostly suns, the nearest of them at a distance from us more than 500,000 times our distance from the sun, are of a size we cannot estimate, but are believed to be 300 times larger than the earth; they are of unequal brightness, and are, according to this standard, classified as of the first, second, down to the sixth magnitude; those visible to the naked eye include stars from the first to the sixth magnitude; and number 3,000, while 20,000,000 are visible by the telescope; of these in the Milky Way alone there are 18,000,000; they are distinguished by their colors as well as their brightness, being white, orange, red, green, and blue, according to their temperature and composition; they have from ancient date been grouped into constellations of the northern and southern hemispheres and of the Zodiac.

The planets, unlike the sun, are all dark bodies, having no light of their own, and are seen and shine only by the light they receive from the sun. Those visible to the unaided eye are Mercury (rarely), Venus, Mars, Jupiter, Saturn and Uranus, but not Neptune, and these are readily distinguished by their clear steady light, so different from the twinkling light of the fixed stars. Six of the planets have satellites or moons revolving around them in the same manner that the planets do around the sun, and they serve to light their respective planets at night in the same manner that our moon gives light to the earth.

Our earth has but one satellite, the familiar Moon, which is 238,000 miles distant from us. It is 2160 miles in diameter and circles around the earth once in 28 days.

The twelve divisions of the Zodiac consist of groups of stars, lying within 8 degrees on either side of the celestial ecliptic; which is the great circle where the sun appears to move in the heavens, and corresponds to the line around the earth as the course of the moon.

244 *Key to Bible and Heaven.*

The fixed stars, or groups of stars and the ecliptic circuit have been illustrated in Plate No. 2. The nature of the illus-

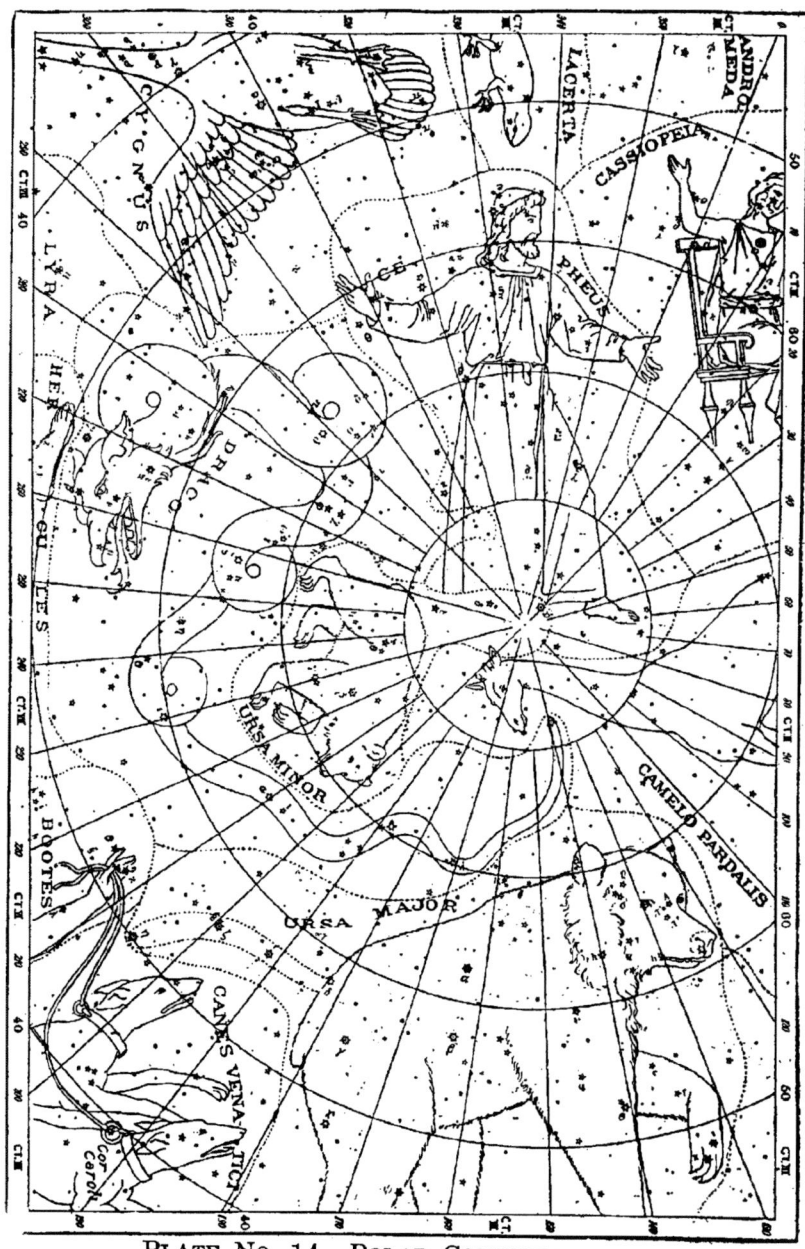

PLATE NO. 14—POLAR CONSTELLATIONS.

tration indicates the nature of the influence which the stars produce.

Part VI—Chapter 48. 245

The fixed stars do not produce any influence on the earth, except at the beginning and ending of the cycles, when polarity

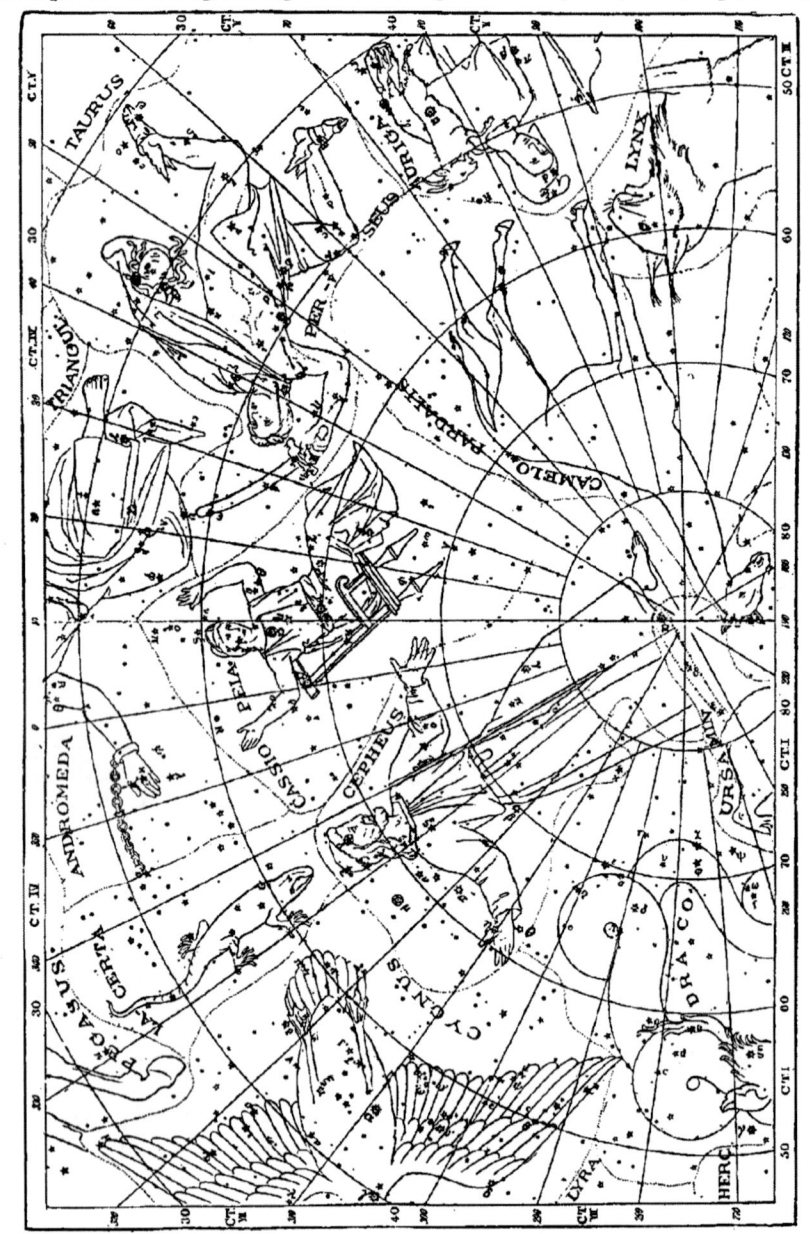

PLATE NO. 15—POLAR CONSTELLATIONS.

is changed, and when the planets Uranus, Saturn and Neptune pass from one house, or mansion, to another, and are in aspect to each other and to the fixed stars. The length of time for these aspects is 3 degrees.

The distance or space, of the heavens is figured in degrees and calculated on and from the ecliptic. Longitude is the distance in the Zodiac east and west of Pisces 0 degree, measured on the ecliptic. Latitude is the distance as measured north and south of the equator. Declination is not considered in Bible study. Right ascension (R. A.) is the correct time for a given place calculated from Pisces.

The fixed stars are classified in the order written and the influence or condition produced by the stars are explained according to the method as used by the ancients. The names of the stars are from Arabian, Babylonian and Greek records, some of the expressions used are literal translations of the indication as used by the ancients. The descriptions and calculations given in the Bible are according to the location and nature of the stars as here given.

We have described that there are five circuits or belts of stars and that these constellations encircle the heavens. There is one belt of stars located south of the Zodiac and three north of the Zodiac. The first belt at the pole contains three constellations; the second belt, three and the others contain twelve constellations each. It is apparent that each belt contains eighteen degrees; five times eighteen equals ninety, which is the distance from the pole to the equator. These five belts have been applied to the earth and divided by three in the usual way into five belts of six degrees each; the ecliptic at the 36th degree represents the twelve houses of the Zodiac. From this it will be seen that the distance from the pole to the equator has been reduced from 90 degrees to 30 degrees in width and is calculated from the 24th degree to the 54th degree north latitude.

The heavens and the earth are described to contain twenty-four degrees in width, termed in the Bible, "the twenty-four elders," and is the temperate zone of the earth today, varying from the 24th to the 54th degree.

We have described the locations of the twelve houses of the Zodiac in 30-degree distances around the earth and the ecliptic circuit as pictured in the heavens should be applied to the houses. The travels of the patriarchs are described in the movements of the planets, according to the location of the houses on the ecliptic.

It is apparent that the heavens containing the three constellations of Ursa Minor, Cepheus and Camelo Pardalis, which are located nearest to the pole, were figured as pole stars for

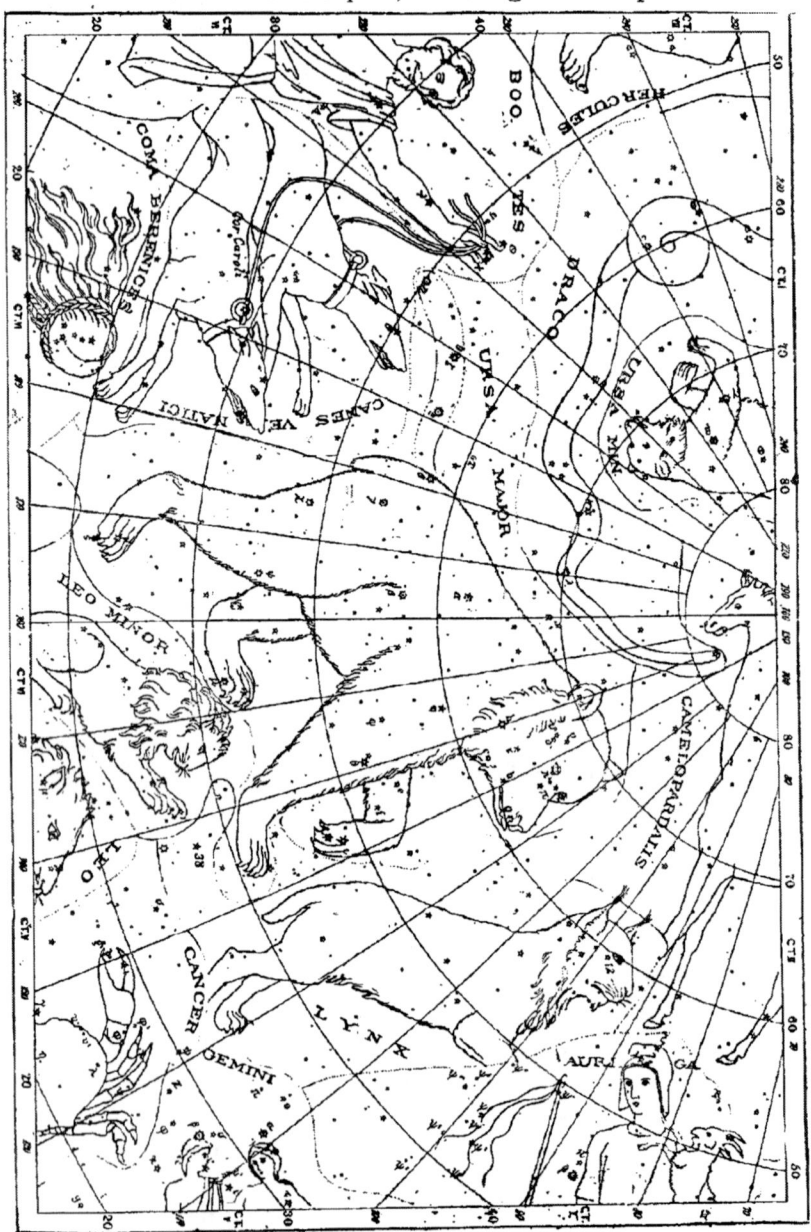

PLATE 16—POLAR CONSTELLATIONS.

two thousand years each. The six constellations of Ursa Minor, Draco, Cepheus, Cassiopeia, Camelo Pardalis and Ursa Major were calculated as pole stars in one thousand-year cycles. The twelve constellations located north of the Zodiac from Andromeda to Pegasus represent two thousand years each, constituting the 24,000-year cycle. The twelve houses of the Zodiac contain 2,160 years each, which equal the 25,920 years as a complete cycle of space for the earth.

The ancient Bible writers illustrated the law of the universe by picturing the constellations and described the different parts of the heavens as living beings. The constellations were illustrated to contain a given number of degrees and to rule or produce an influence on the earth for a given length of time. We have copied some of these charts and will explain the system used in describing events. The recorded history given in the Bible is for 6,000 years and is described as the six days of creation constituting a complete cycle for the earth. The 6,000-year cycle was divided into six 1,000-year cycles, which was again subdivided into many minor cycles.

The meridian of the earth in the year 1920, taken at the 120th degree west longitude, will correspond to the meridian of the heavens taken at 150 degrees in the constellation Sextans. At this time the meridian of the heavens and earth will correspond to the very degree of the poles in the heavens and on earth. The crossing or passing of this degree is called the passover and is the changing of the polarity of the Universe. When this change takes place, the old heavens and earth are destroyed and it is the beginning of time for the new heaven and earth. We have learned that previous to the time, when the polarity is changed that seven years of famine, disaster and pestilence, caused by the elements of nature, takes place on this earth. The location of this disaster takes place in the degrees on earth corresponding to the location of the pole star in the heavens for the age.

Near the pole is pictured the three constellations of Cepheus, Camelo Pardalis and Ursa Minor and these three represent the Celestial heavens. The 6,000 years of Creation are represented in the three constellations which contain 2,000 years each as a cycle of time. It takes 6,000 years for our solar system to make one-fourth of a revolution of the Celestial heavens and during this period the three constellations are figured as pole stars for our earth. From this it will be seen that there are three pole stars in the celestial heavens and that each constellation remains as a pole star for 2,000 years. At the present time the pole star is the star Polaris in the constellation Ursa Minor.

In the year 1920 the earth's meridian position to the Celestial pole is on the very degree of the pole and in the year 2,000 A. D. the earth's pole will be on the degree of the pole star Polaris. At the time when the north pole of the earth is on the corresponding degree of the poles in the Celestial and Terrestrial heavens, the change in the cycles of time takes place. This is called the passover or the end of the world and the beginning of a new heaven and earth. From this it will be seen that the pole represents the Terrestrial heavens, the three constellations represent the Celestial heavens and that the other constellations and the Zodiac represent our solar system and the earth.

The location of the houses and constellations in the heavens are calculated from the ecliptic circle, and the conditions illustrated in the constellations are literally applied to the earth. This is best illustrated in the constellation of Cassiopeia and Andromeda which are located north of Pisces and represent the distasce of Europe from Egypt to France. Pisces is the ruling house and Italy has been described as representing this house and the Roman Empire as a power illustrated as two fishes. The distance of Pisces begins at 30 degrees from Greenwich and Aries, where the Triangle is located and includes Persius. The rest of the houses contain 30 degrees each, making 360 degrees in all.

Within the great constellations are located what is known as fixed stars and the location of these stars are calculated from the first degree of Pisces. This distance is called Right Ascension and is figured on the ecliptic westward in the heavens within the 360-degree radius. From this it will be seen that the name of right ascension in the heavens is the same as degrees of longitude when applied to a similar circuit on the earth. The fixed stars are described to be located at a given degree of R. A. or longitude west and correspondingly located in the houses. After having located the constellations and fixed stars in the heavens they were then located on the earth as they were in the heavens.

The Bible describes the great constellations as the continents and the fixed stars as the nations; which means that the continents are the parents of the nations and all are the children of mother earth. In the stories about the patriarchs and the children of Israel, the Bible illustrates, that when they were at a given place on the earth, a certain condition prevailed. The place described is in degrees of longitude and the conditions produced at the place are in the nature of the place, planets and stars. The age of the patriarchs is in degrees and the words spoken by them is the influence which the planets, stars and constellations produced on the earth. The influence or conditions produced on the earth by the constellations, fixed stars, sun and planets are called the words or laws of God.

It is described in the Bible that "a day is as a year and a year as a thousand years with the Lord," and this states in specific terms what a cycle of time consists of. The time referred to is calculated from the travels or circuits of the earth and Uranus around the sun in cycles. It is ordinarily termed that the sun moves one degree per day through the twelve houses of the heavens. It is, however, the motion of the earth in its orbit around the sun, which is meant. The earth travels in the twelve houses around the sun at the rate of one degree per day; which makes the 360 degrees or days to a complete cycle; making "one day as a year with the Lord." Uranus makes one revolution of the twelve houses around the sun in one thousand years (12 X 84—1008) and these years as degrees are as "a thousand years with the Lord." The system of dividing the heavens into sideral time and space is in the well-known method called precession of the equinoxes. By this method the cycles of the heavens are divided into the four seasons of the year and the twelve months.

The Milky Way is the ecliptic path or highway of the heavens and corresponds to the ecliptic circuit of the sun and earth. It begins with the twelfth degree in Casiopeia which corresponds to the 12th degree of Pisces and contains twelve houses. The nature and shape of the Milky Way is similar to the Zodiac, the ecliptic circle around the earth and man as a universe. The creative and other elements of the heavens are correspondingly located in the Milky Way and constellations, as it is locatd in the Zodiac and in man.

Astronomers' attention is called to the constellations located near Sagitary and Scutum Sobieskii; they will find that the black space named "Coal Sack" in this region represents the creative elements of the Milky Way. And that the "Shooting Stars" coming from this part of the heavens, usually in November, are the creative or birth-giving elements making new worlds. Anyone familiar with this study will readily see that the universal law of God is similarly applied to the Milky Way, as it is to the earth and man. We should remember that "man is made in the image of God" and that "as it is in the heavens so is it on earth;" from which we can reason that the Milky Way, solar system, planets, earth and man are made in the image of God as a universe.

We believe that the following method can be applied in calculating the great distances in the heavens and that it will prove to be scientifically correct. The same method is used as in calculating the earth's cycle on the ecliptic.

The celestial heavens contain 25,920,000 degrees as miles, which is divided into three cycles of 864,000 each. This cycle of 864,000 is again divided by twelve and equals 72,000 miles for each degree. The cycle of 25,920,000 is also divided into six parts containing 432,000 degrees each, which is again subdivided into three parts containing 144,000 each. The cycle of 25,920,000 is divided into twelve parts of 2,160,000 each.

Time and space in the heavens are calculated on the ecliptic circle from the pole of the heavens and called the meridian. This can best be explained by our earth as a globe, the center for the earth's circle being the North Pole. In the Celestial heavens the pole star in Ursa Minor is figured as the Polaris for this heaven and from this point all time and space on this earth is measured. From this it will be seen that all space is figured from the center of one circuit to the center of the other circuits. In other words, the north pole is the center from which to calculate for the earth, and the center of the path or ecliptic of the twelve houses for the earth, is the sun. The celestial heavens make a circuit of the terrestrial heavens and the center of each heaven is the pole. The observation or measurement of the different distances from pole to pole in the heavens were figured in degrees and is called angles.

There are 6,000 years or degrees at the poles, each containing 72 years, making 432,000 years, which are divided into the three cycles. The 432,000 divided by three equals 144,000 years, which were described in the Bible as the population of the new heavens and earth, Rev. Chapt. 7:4.

The grouping of the planets in the western heavens in December, 1919, is a peculiar arrangement, which takes place only in every 2000 years. Astronomers' attention is called to the position of the six planets within 30 degrees of a perfect opposition to Uranus and all in square to the Earth. There is going to take place some unexplainable phenomena and we venture to say that the sun will be the most interesting to observe. The ecliptic belt of the sun is where the sun spots are located and in the changing of its polarity there should be a sunspot visible of unusual magnitude. These sun spots should be visible between November, 1919, and December, 1920. If earthquakes take place during this period it will affect the entire earth and do a great deal of damage. It is our candid opinion that some natural disturbance will take place during this year, which will change the opinion of many regarding the operation of God's Laws.

CHAPTER 49.

ASTRONOMY.

The changing of cycles of time, which is described as the passover, is the changing of polarity for the earth, sun and the heavens. The cycles of time described in the Bible consists of 6,000 years which is the time required for our solar system to change pole stars. In the celestial heavens a cycle of time consists of 6,000 years which is an ecliptic cycle by precession, from one pole star to another.

The North Star, Polaris, is at the present time pole star, but this star is not located at the very degree of the pole. The polarity is changed in the year 1920 when the celestial pole will be one degree distant from the pole star and at this time the earth and sun's polarity will be on the very degree of the pole. When the earth and solar system passes the degree of the pole it is called the passover, when the old heavens and earth are destroyed and a new cycle begins.

The time required for this passover is 216 years, divided into three periods of 72 years each. When the earth's polarity gets within two degrees from the celestial pole the earth and all life on earth is influenced and a peculiar condition is produced. We have described elsewhere the effect of the changing of polarity in detail, which is best shown by the history of the United States.

The distance described as the universal pole contains three degrees, which is divided first in three great divisions of one degree each, and subdivided into six divisions of one-half degree each. The three degrees are also divided so that two degrees are calculated as one cycle and that the second cycle contains

Part VI—Chapter 49. 253

one degree. From this it will be seen that the pole consists of 3 degrees of 72 years each and that 144 years represent one

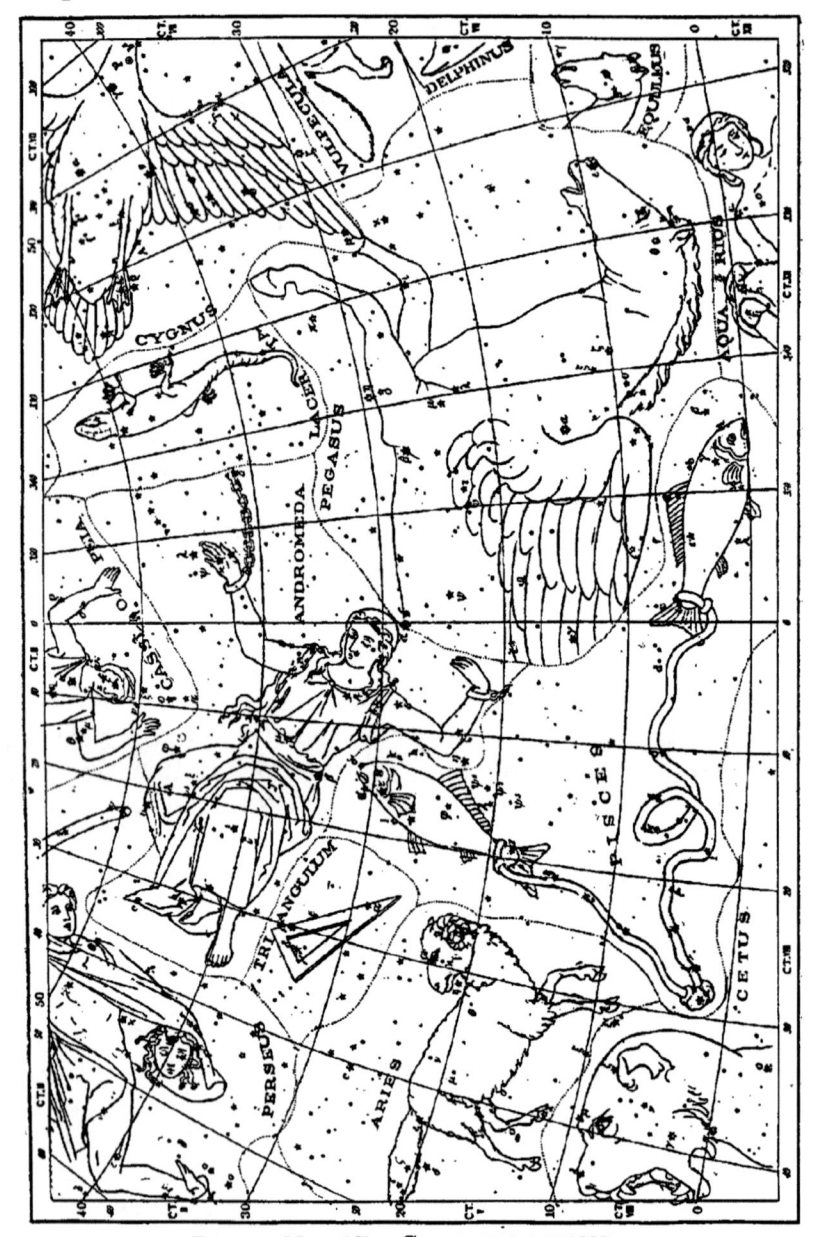

PLATE NO. 17—CONSTELLATIONS.

cycle as a period of time and also that the second division contains 72 years. At the time of the changing from the 144th to the 145th year, which is between the second and third degree, the polarity is changed, and at this degree is the exact location of the pole for the celestial heavens. The earth, sun and the entire celestial heavens are at the present time changing polarity and when the sun is in the 6th degree of Sagitarius in November, 1920, is the time of the change.

A condition is produced by the changing of polarity which will last for 72 years beginning in 1921 and terminating in 1992. This influence or condition which is produced on earth and the time required is self explanatory. The time for the beginning of the change is 144 years previous to 1920 which is 1776 A. D. The condition then produced was the making of the United States as a new center for the earth's population. The condition produced after 1921 is termed the Millenium age which is described in another chapter.

The description given in the Bible regarding the travels of the children of Israel and in the ages which were given in latitude and longitude, are the description of a given location on the earth. It describes the ecliptic circuits of the sun, moon, and planets in the precessions of the heavens. The given distances are calculated by the precession of the sun and moon in cycles of a given number of degrees and as the precession of all the stars and planets takes place at the same time, the calculations made on the earth will correspond to the space in the heavens.

The ecliptic circuit is located on the earth as it is in the heavens and extends one-half degree north and south of the Equator, which again corresponds to the location of the horizon. From this it will be seen, that the sun, moon and each of the stars and planets have ecliptic circuits and that it is similarly located in all parts of the heavens as it is on the earth.

The conditions produced which is described in the travels of the children of Israel around the earth are the conditions produced by the precession of the equinoxes, when the sun and planets are correspondingly located in the heavens as the children of Israel were at the time described on the earth.

It is a known fact that by the precession of the equinoxes, the seasons of the year are produced and it will now become a proven scientific fact, that when the earth and the rest of the elements of the heavens change polarity that a given condition is produced, which man has no more control over than he has in the changing of the equinoctial seasons.

Part VI—Chapter 49.   255

The ecliptic circuit is known as the path of the sun in the heavens and also as the path of the moon around the earth.

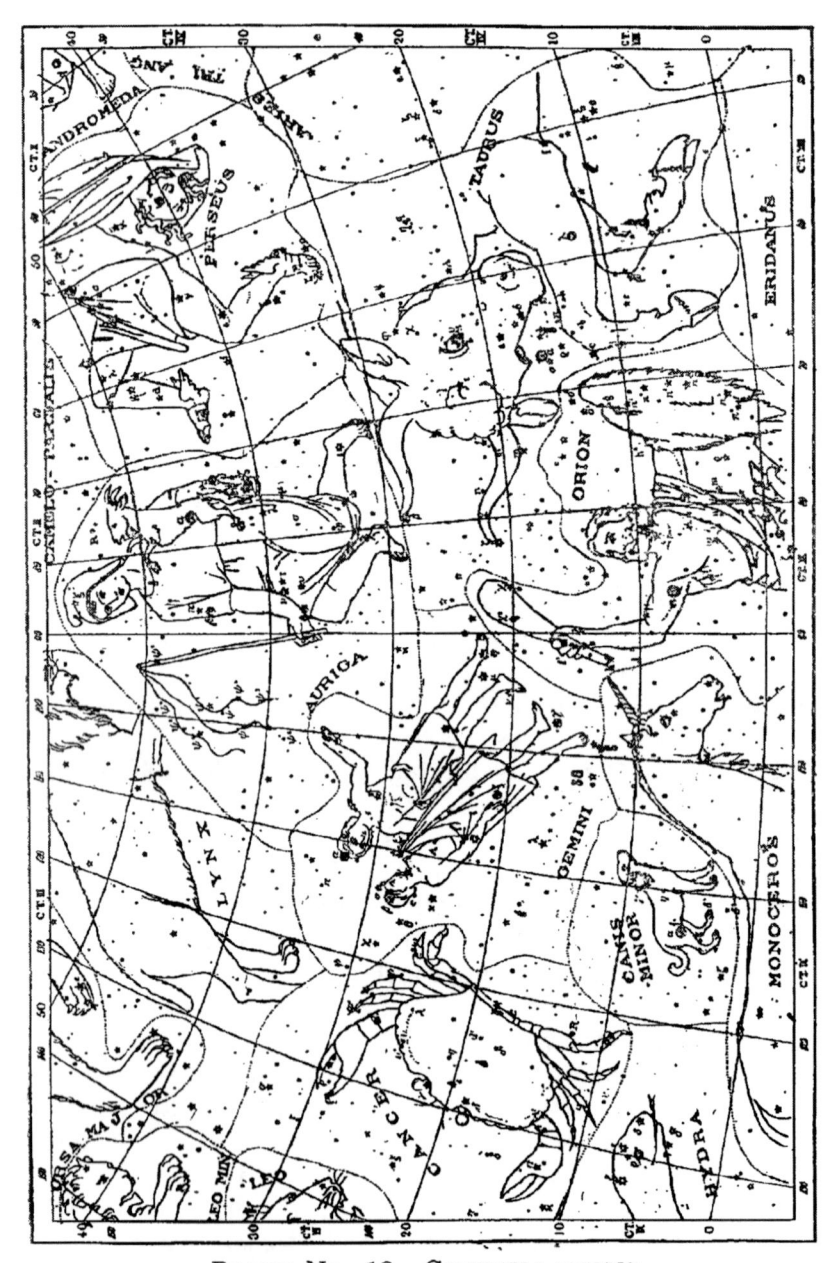

PLATE NO. 18—CONSTELLATIONS.

On Saturn it is located where Saturn's rings appear to be and on the sun it is where the sun-spots are located, which also encircles the sun.

The circumference and diameter of all the heavenly bodies correspond and the same system of measurement can be applied to the sun, moon and the planets as is used for the earth. All measurements for space and dimensions are to be calculated on and from the ecliptic circuits of any of the heavenly bodies, as well as on the circuit of the sun.

There is no difference between the present astronomical method and that described in the Bible, astronomers calculate from the equator as a center and the Bible gives all dimensions from the ecliptic circle.

It is very difficult for us to obtain the exact degree for the different measurement of the heavens, sun and planets and if we have made mistakes it should not be criticised, as it is in the principle involved and in the method employed we are interested and not in the exact degrees, but we believe we are correct in all instances.

The distance of the solar circuit is divided into 12 signs of 30 degrees each making 360 degrees, which contain 72 miles each and equal 25,920 miles as a complete cycle. One-third of this distance contains 8,640 degrees and one-twelfth equals 2,160 degrees.

The sun's daily rotation is 25 degrees 92 minutes calculated on the sun's ecliptic. The sun rotates on its axis similar to the spinning motion of the earth and this peculiar action produces what is known as the short and long ascensions in the signs of the Zodiac.

The sun's diameter is 32 minutes which consists of 864,000 miles and three times its diameter is its circumference, which is 2,592,000 miles. The sun's diameter of 864,000 miles is divided into 12 signs of 72,000 miles each.

The sun's diameter 32 minutes is multiplied by 72 degrees and equals 2304 degrees as years and corresponds to the ages of the patriarchs given in the Bible. This distance is calculated for a 40-degree cycle, as follows: The sun's diameter of 32 minutes X 3 equals 96 degrees, which we will make into a space of 30 degrees X 96 degrees, giving 2,880 miles or 40 degrees of 72 years each.

The sun's diameter of 32 minutes X 60 minutes equals 1920 degrees as years. These dimensions represent a cycle of time, which can be understood by all. The age of Jesus as a man was

Part VI—Chapter 49.   257

32 years and the cycle for the Christian age contains 1920 years and is self explanatory.

The solar precession of the equinoxes consists of 72 years and 14 precessions makes 1008 years, this was termed a complete cycle and called 14 generations in the Bible. This cycle corresponds to the circuit of Uranus around the sun, which was described in the stories of the pariarchs as an age.

The sun, moon, and earth's cycles consist of 25,920 degrees of 60 minutes each, which equals 432,000, that is, the celestial heavens contain 60 minutes X 72 degrees which equals 432,000, which is again divided by three and equals 144,000, and spoken of in the Book of Revelation as the population for the earth at the beginning of the new age.

The earth's circumference at the ecliptic is 25,920 miles and the earth's diameter is one-third of this distance or 8,640 miles. The moon's diameter is one-twelfth of the earth's circumference and equals 2,160 miles. The moon's circumference is three times its diameter at the ecliptic and contains 6,480 miles, divided in 90-degree cycles of 72 degrees each.

Saturn and the moon's time and space correspond, that is, the moon's measurement is applied to Saturn and multiplied 100 times. Saturn's diameter is 72,000 miles multiplied by three and equals 216,000 miles which are the dimensions of Saturn.

The precessions of the equinoxes, in seven-year cycles, for the moon also corresponds to the precession of Saturn, Neptune and Uranus. The precession of Saturn is calculated in 90-degree, Uranus in 30-degree and Neptune in 15-degree cycles.

The distance from the sun to the earth is 90,000,000 miles calculated from and to the ecliptic circuits and this distance corresponds to the space from the poles to the equator, and also from the meridian to the horizon.

In all the books of the Bible a description is given of strife and contention between two factions or elements, it is between the Jews and Gentiles and the Romans against the Christians. These contending elements consist of the twelve tribes of Israel, which were divided into the seven tribes of Israel and the five tribes of Judah. We find that the earth's ecliptic circuit has been divided into fourteen divisions of 72 degrees each, making 1008 degrees to a complete cycle. The seven tribes of Israel represent part of this circuit as a cycle of time, which were divided into the fourteen generations calculated by the precessions of the ecliptic. The earth has also been divided into five divisions located in opposite position and calculated in latitude. These five contain 72 degrees each, making 360 degrees to the cycle and the five distances of latitude represent the five tribes of Judah. From this we can see that the seven tribes represent the ecliptic circle in longitude of 504 degrees and that the distance calculated in opposition, represents latitude. The cycles of time are calculated by the precession in degrees and we also find that at the end of a given age that the children of Israel were numbered, when a conflict takes place and the population was destroyed. This is self explanatory and means, that at the end of a cycle in degrees of longitude a contention is encountered in the degrees of latitude. These distances were calculated in solar or sideral time in given number of degrees and the time, space and place were described to be located on earth as it were in the heavens. From this we can see that a cycle of time consists of 7 X 72 degrees or 504 degrees as years, which are calculated in longitude and that the contending degrees of latitude at the end of this ecliptic cycle killed the population before the new age began.

The meridian is calculated from Pisces and the North meridian is at Virgo. The ecliptic extends from Sagitarius to Gemini. The poles are located in 90-degree distances from the equator. The constellations of Aries and Libra are Polar signs and Capricorn and Cancer are Equatorial signs. Capricorn south and Cancer north which makes Sagitarius on the eastern and Gemini on the western horizon with the meridian in Pisces. This makes it very clear that astronomers have made a scientific error in calculating the horizon for the equator and the meridian for the poles.

There are two circles or belts of 24 degrees each extending from the poles and the equator. These polar belts have been called the Arctic circles and the equatorial belt, the Tropical circles of Cancer and Capricorn. The poles are at 90 degrees and 24 degrees distance from the poles gives the location of the Arctic circles at the 66th degree, that is, the south Arctic circle extends from 6 degrees of Pisces to 24 degrees in Aries with Aries 1 degree at the pole. The Arctic circle extends from Virgo 6 degrees to Libra 24 degrees with Libra 1 degree at the pole. The equatorial or tropical belt extends 24 degrees north and south of the equator. The 24 degrees located north of the equator is called the tropic of Cancer which extends to 24 degrees of Cancer in the west and 6 degrees of Sagitarius on the

Part VI—Chapter 49.   259

east. The 24 degrees south of the equator is called the tropic of Capricorn which extends to the 6 degrees of Gemini in the

PLATE No. 19—CONSTELLATIONS.

west and 24 degrees of Capricorn on the east. The equator is located at the first degree of Cancer and Capricorn.

The location of these zones represent the extent of the earth's rotary motion, giving the exact degree for the sun's position north and south of the equator and thereby locating the ecliptic circle.

We have described that there are belts or zones at the equator and at the poles extending 24 degrees in a circuit. We will next describe two other very important belts which encircle the earth from north to south and east to west. The belt from north to south is the meridian zone of 18 degrees in width encircling the earth and the heavens. It extends from 24 degrees Aquarius to 12 degrees Pisces in the south and in the north from 24 degrees Leo to 12 degrees Virgo. It means that the meridian path contains 18 degrees in width as a circuit around the earth. The other circuit is the ecliptic circle of 18 degrees in width encircling the earth east to west. It extends from 24 degrees Scorpio to 12 degrees Sagitarius in the east and in the west from 24 degrees Taurus to 12 degrees Gemini. This circircuit means that the ecliptic belt consists of 18 degrees in width encircling the earth. These belts are divided into three divisions of 6 degrees each, with the 6 degrees center described at the meridian and ecliptic. The meridian belt and the ecliptic circle forms a cross and corresponds to degrees of longitude and latitude, which were described as the tree of life and the tree of knowledge in the Bible and this is the cross all cycles or ages are crucified on. The extent of the ecliptic circle across the United States is 18 degrees, from Mexico to Canada. The 36-degree dividing line is the Mason and Dixon line and the equator of the earth at 30 degrees latitude is represented at the Mississippi river, and New Orleans, Louisiana.

We will briefly describe the ecliptic circle of the earth and the method of calculating the precession of the equinoxes in 90-degree cycles. The meridian is a circle passing from north to south directly overhead at 12 o'clock noon and corresponds to 0 degree of longitude. The horizon is the dividing point between two elevations and is the place on earth where the sun strikes the dividing degree between the northern and southern hemisphere. A belt or circuit around the earth located at this degree is called the ecliptic circle.

A cycle or age is calculated from the horizon in the east to the horizon in the west, and the center of the meridian directly overhead is called the Zenith. The length of time constituting an age is calculated in degrees of longitude and latitude meas-

Part VI—Chapter 49.

ured by the system known as the precession of the equinoxes. A complete age is calculated in four 90-degree distances from the place on earth where the sun's ray strikes the eastern horizon.

We have made the statement that the precession of the equinoxes are calculated from and on the ecliptic circle and not from the equator or the poles. We will now give the exact degree for the meridian and the horizon to prove that these statements are correct. In the first place the distinction should be made that there are four places to make calculations from. It is from the meridian, the poles, equator and the horizon. The method used at the present time is to calculate from the poles and the equator and the consequence is that fractions of years and days have to be used.

We have described a belt around the earth and called it the ecliptic belt and shown from the description given in the Bible that this belt was located at the 36th degree north latitude. We will now show that it was the ecliptic circle representing the horizon which was described at this degree on earth.

The degrees of latitude are calculated in 90-degree distances north and south of the equator and in order to get the horizon we must know how far north and south of the equator it is located. We have learned from the Bible that the ecliptic circle is located 36 degrees north of the equator and that 36 degrees on earth equals one-half degree in the heavens. In order to find the ecliptic circle we must know that it means to locate the center of the earth's rotary motion. The earth rotates on its axis so that its position to the sun extends 24 degrees north and south of the equator and the extremes of these degrees are called the tropics of Cancer and Capricorn. We have previously described the location of these tropics in degrees. If we take 24 degrees north of the equator we have 24 degrees of Cancer and 24 degrees south of the equator on the east we have 24 degrees Capricorn. From this can be seen that the center of the earth's rotary motion is at 48 degrees from the tropic of Cancer and 48 degrees from the tropic of Capricorn. The eastern horizon is, therefore, at Sagitarius 6 degrees and the western horizon at Gemini 6 degrees. After having located the eastern and western horizon it becomes an easy task to locate the meridian degrees. The meridian is located 90 degrees from the 6 degrees of Sagitarius and is at Pisces 6 degrees and Virgo 6 degrees. From this it will be seen that the northern and southern poles rotate in a circuit of 24 degrees which are the distances of the poles from the meridian and these circuits are called the Arctic circles.

The equatorial distance is the two tropical belts containing 48 degrees and the third belt at the meridian containing 18 degrees, which means that the distance of 90 degrees is divided into three belts of 48 degrees, 24 degrees and 18 degrees respectively. These three belts are again divided into separate parts, the equatorial belt of 48 degrees is divided into four parts of 12 degrees each, the Polar belt of 24 degrees is divided into three parts of 8 degrees each, and the meridian belt of 18 degrees contains three parts of 6 degrees each. When applying the location of these belts, to the ecliptic circle around the earth, the country is divided and time calculated accordingly. This principle can be readily understood and applied to the Pacific Coast States, which was divided into the separate divisions referred to. San Francisco is located at the dividing point and corresponds to the meridian in Pisces and the rest of the distances of 12 degrees, 8 degrees, and 6 degrees can be calculated in degrees of latitude from the location given in the book of Joshua.

We now realize that the horizon on the east is located at 6 degrees Sagitarius, that the meridian is located at 6 degrees Pisces and that the western horizon must be at 6 degrees Gemini with the northern meridian at 6 degrees Virgo.

The ecliptic on earth is located at 36 degrees north latitude and this circuit is divided into four 90-degree ages by the winter, spring, summer, and fall ecliptic or equinoxes. The winter equinox takes place about February 25th, when the sun is in the 6th degree of Pisces. The spring equinox about May 27th when the sun is in the 6th degree of Gemini. The summer equinox about August 29th when the sun is in the 6th degree of Virgo. The fall equinox about November 28th, when the sun is in the 6th degree of Sagitarius.

We will locate the ecliptic circle on earth as it is located in the heavens, and divide the four 90-degree distances from Greenwich and the meridian. The meridian corresponds to the 36th degree east longitude and crosses the ecliptic at the 36th degree north latitude near Palestine in Turkey. The Greenwich degree is calculated from the equator and is the first degree of Aries being 36 degrees west from the meridian degree of 6 degrees Pisces and crosses England and France. The 114th

Part VI—Chapter 49.

degree east longitude corresponds to 90 degrees from meridian at the location of Sagitarius 6 degrees and this is on the east

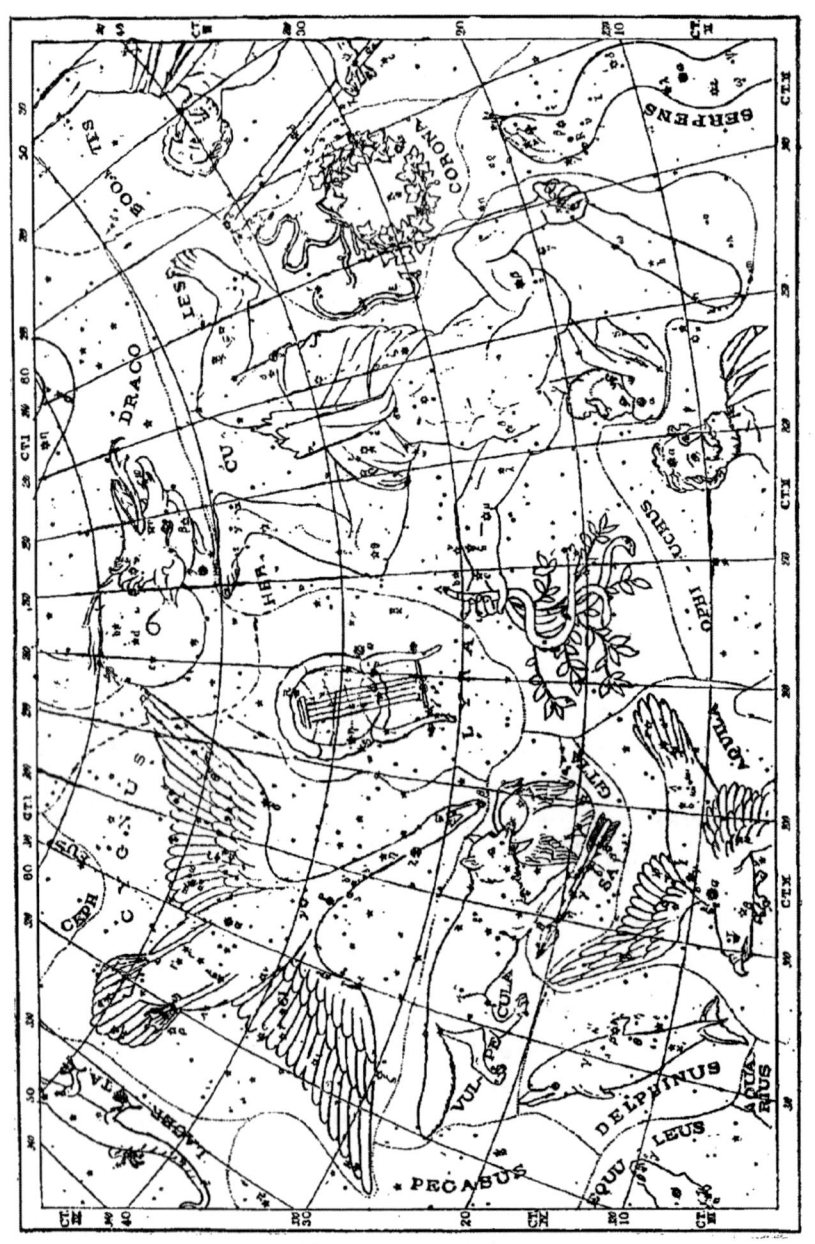

PLATE NO. 20—CONSTELLATIONS.

coast of China. The western horizon is 90 degrees west from Palestine, which is in the Atlantic Ocean east of the United

States. The north meridian degree of 6 degrees is located in the Pacific Ocean at 156 degrees west from Greenwich and is the opposite location to that described for Palestine.

It should be understood that it is the northern hemisphere of the earth which is described and that the degrees calculated for south of the ecliptic and equator is considered as the north and is described in latitude. The signs Leo and Virgo have been called a fiery furnace and it will be seen that they are located on the equator at the solstices.

In describing the circuit westward the Bible describes the distance of 90 degrees from Greenwich which is in the United States and to the sign Cancer, which again corresponds to the degrees west when the age is killed. In describing the circuit west of the 120 degrees longitude, in the Pacific Coast States, the circuit is changed and is then calculated in degrees of latitude northward. The 30th degree north latitude and 120th degree longitude represent the equator and Cancer. At this degree the age was destroyed by Noah when he crossed the ocean and also called Sodom and Gomorrah.

It will be seen that in describing the country north of the 30th degree on the Pacific Coast, that it is the beginning of a new cycle in the sign Leo and that the 36th degree at Mt. Whitney in California is the center for the tribe of Judah.

The location of the twelve tribes of Israel in the Pacific Coast States which is described in the book of Joshua, is so arranged in latitude in distances between the tribes that the country is divided into degrees and named in the same proportion as the location of the tribes around the heavens and earth. The locating and naming of these tribes northward to correspond to the ecliptic circuit is one of the greatest scientific problems of creation. The distance of 18 degrees from Mexico to British Columbia, which is from the 30th degree to the 48th degree of latitude, were given the names of the twelve signs of the heavens. The Pacific Coast States have been so arranged into the twelve tribes by locating them in latitude that the nature of the earth around the ecliptic circle corresponds to the nature of the land given in degrees. We have described the location of the tribes in another chapter and it will prove to be a study worth considering from a scientific standpoint.

We have described that astronomers use the Greenwich degree and think they are using the meridian and that this is a mistake of vital importance. The sign of Pisces has been

Part VI—Chapter 49.

ignored and the excuse made that it is drifted out of the heavens. Astronomical calculations can only be made one way in the heavens and this method is called right ascension, but if the calculation is made in the opposite direction the space is one hour or degree short. The reason we refer to this topic again is, that as it is in the heavens so is it on earth, and we find that the same mistake is made on earth as it was in the heavens. The nautical law is, that when traveling around the earth and in passing the 180th degree longitude, in the Pacific Ocean that time is set forward or backward one degree in order to correct the mistake that Greenwich is the meridian degree.

We have described that the ecliptic circle is the horizon in the heavens and that it divides the earth in two halves of equal distances north and south. The earth rotates on its axis in angles of 18 degrees, 24 degrees and 48 degrees calculated from the equator and the poles. In other words, the earth swings 12 degrees to one side and 24 degrees to the other side of the meridian. The center of the earth, therefore, is at the center of the rotating degree and not at the equator. From this it will be seen that the exact degree which divides the earth in two halves is at the 36th degree north latitude calculated from the meridian degree.

The earth's rotary motion causes it to dip east and west of the meridian so that 204 degrees remain south and 156 degrees north. In this dipping motion of the earth, the system known as the precession of the equinoxes is produced and each rotary dip is called an age. The earth makes fourteen dips to a complete cycle and this was termed fourteen generations in the Bible. The distance on earth of 204 degrees constitutes the seven tribes of Israel and the five tribes of Judah represent the 156 degrees as the opposition tribes; because they were located opposite as night is to day. For those familiar with astronomy the dipping motion of the earth and the calculations of time will be readily understood.

The Solar or heavenly cycle of time and space consists of 12 houses of 30 degrees which equals 360 degrees calculated as an ecliptic year for the sun, but the equatorial distance is 365 degrees or years and fractions. The reason why the space at the ecliptic circle is shorter is that it measures the earth at its center or middle of the ball, and the equatorial circuit makes a longer way around as it extends both north and south of the earth's center. It is like measuring the circumference of an egg. It makes no difference in the measurement of an egg whether it is held in an upright or slanting position, but if the measurement were taken at an angular position and extends on both sides of the center towards the ends, the distance will be longer. The prevailing system is to calculate the long way and this is called the equatorial or equinoctial distance. From this it will be seen that time and space calculated by the equinoctial method gives two measurements, a long and a short. It will also be seen that the center of these two extremes will be the center of the space called the ecliptic. This can be shown in the cycles calculated for the moon. The moon's equinoctial cycles consist of 27 and 29 degrees and fractions, but the moon's ecliptic time is 28 degrees or years without fractions.

Saturn's ecliptic time corresponds to the time given for the moon. Saturn remains 28 months or years in a sign, he makes the circuit of the 12 signs in 336 months or years; that is, Saturn makes 36 circuits of the 12 signs of 28 years each in 1008 years.

Uranus remains 7 years in a sign making the circuit of the 12 signs in 84 years and 12 revolutions of 84 years each equals 1008 years.

Neptune remains 14 years in each sign and travels the 12 houses in 168 years making 6 revolutions in 1008 years.

We have made the statement that the ecliptical cycles for the heavens and earth correspond, which means that all cycles begin and end at the same time and that all measurements are calculated from and on the ecliptic. From this statement it will be seen that we have precession of the ecliptic as well as precession of the equinox. The cycles for the sun, planets, and earth, in fact, all space of the heavens, are calculated from the precession on the ecliptic circuits. The beginning and ending of the cycles on earth correspond to the distances in space in the celestial and terrestrial heavens. The Bible shows that an age consists of 1008 years and we will describe these cycles as an example.

The solar and earth's ecliptic precession consists of 14 rotations of 72 degrees each making 1008 years.

The solar cycle consists of 864 years which are divided into 12 signs or houses containing 72 years each and these 12 signs are again divided into the two divisions containing 5 and 7 signs each. The 5 signs of 72 years each contain 360 years and 7 signs of 72 years each equals 504 years and the two together make the solar cycle of 864 years or thousands of years.

Part VI—Chapter 49.

There are six 1008-year cycles, making 6048 years, which are divided by the 84-year cycle of Uranus. There are 72 degrees to a cycle and 84 X 72 equals 6048 years as an age.

The comparative ages given in degrees in distance between the fixed stars and constellations correspond to the sun and earth's ecliptic cycles. The earth's cycle in relation to the sun is calculated in 360 degrees and corresponds to days. The 360 days are divided into 12 months of 30 days. The year is divided into the four equinoctial seasons of three months each or 90 days and are also divided into ecliptic seasons of four months each or 120 days. The months are divided into four weeks and the weeks into cycles of six days. The six working days are divided into 24 hours each which again is divided into two 12-hour divisions. The length of time for a day is 12 hours but a day extends from sunrise to sunset and contains approximately 14 hours, which leaves 10 hours of the 24 for night.

The days and nights are divided into well-known subdivisions of hours, minutes, and seconds, constituting a complete cycle. One day contains 24 hours, three days 72 hours and six days contain 144 hours. A day of 24 hours is divided into three 8-hour periods which is again divided into three parts and corresponds to the space given for the diameter of the sun. It is unnecessary to explain the comparative description between the hours as here given and the distances in the celestial heavens as it is the same figures in hours which is given in thousands of degrees and years in the heavens.

It will be seen that the twelve tribes of Israel correspond to the twelve hours of the day and that the opposition within the twelve tribes are the 5 hours during the night. The five tribes represent 5 of the 24 hours and are the five tribes of Judah. The time for the five tribes are from 9 o'clock to 4 o'clock at night, and as there are 24 hours to the cycles there are 10 tribes to represent this age. From this it will be seen that the seven tribes of Israel represent the time from sunrise to sunset and that the Judah tribes represent the hours of night. The system which we have described in days and hours is also applied to longitude and latitude as well as to the nations and man.

The Bible describes that six days constitute a working day with the Lord and that the seventh day is the Sabbath. The changing from a working day to Sunday is called the passover and a day of rest. "A day is as a year or a thousand years with the Lord."

We should realize that the entire universe moves in cycles and that the method of calculating space, distance and time, is in the precessions caused by the rotating and spinning motion of all the heavenly bodies in space. Our solar systems circuit is in the celestial heavens and we have learned that it makes its circuit in 2,592,000 years. The beginning of this year, cycle or age is at the 6th degree of Sagitarius, and we find that the pole star or ecliptic pole of the celestial heavens is in this location at the present time. From this can be seen that the pole of the celestial heavens is 90 degrees east of the meridian of the terrestrial heavens and that this position indicates the beginning of a new cycle for our solar system. In other words, the meridian 0 degree in the terrestrial heavens is in the center of the Milky Way and the celestial pole is on the ecliptic degree in Sagitarius which is the position of the earth to the sun at the beginning of all cycles.

It is very important to know that Sagitarius is the rising sign and that the 6th degree is located at the horizon; which we will explain. We have illustrated by the hours of the clock that the meridian corresponds to 12 o'clock at noon and the northern end of the meridian is at 12 o'clock at night, which means that there are 12 hours above and 12 hours below the horizon. The sun is in the southern hemisphere in the day and in the northern at night. The time then when the sun will pass from the north to the south will be 6 o'clock in the morning and the sunset will be 6 o'clock in the evening. The meridian degree is in Pisces being 12 o'clock and 6 signs east of the meridian is Sagitarius at the horizon, with Gemini at sunset in the west. The equator represents 4 o'clock in the morning and afternoon. The sun's ray extends over the earth 204 degrees which is the distance from the horizon in the east to the equator in the west and corresponds to the distance from the east coast of China to the 90th degree longitude in the United States. From this we see that the sun's rays extend from 6 degrees Sagitarius to 1 degree Cancer.

We have previously described that the celestial heavens are the circuit of our solar system and that the ecliptic pole of this circuit is calculated from the location of the pole star in Ursa Minor. The pole star is located in degree of longitude to correspond to the location of Sagitarius in 90-degree angles from the other pole stars.

We will next call attention to the Milky Way and its loca-

Part VI—Chapter 49. 269

tion in the universe. The Milky Way is located in the very path which we have described as the ecliptic circuit and extends from

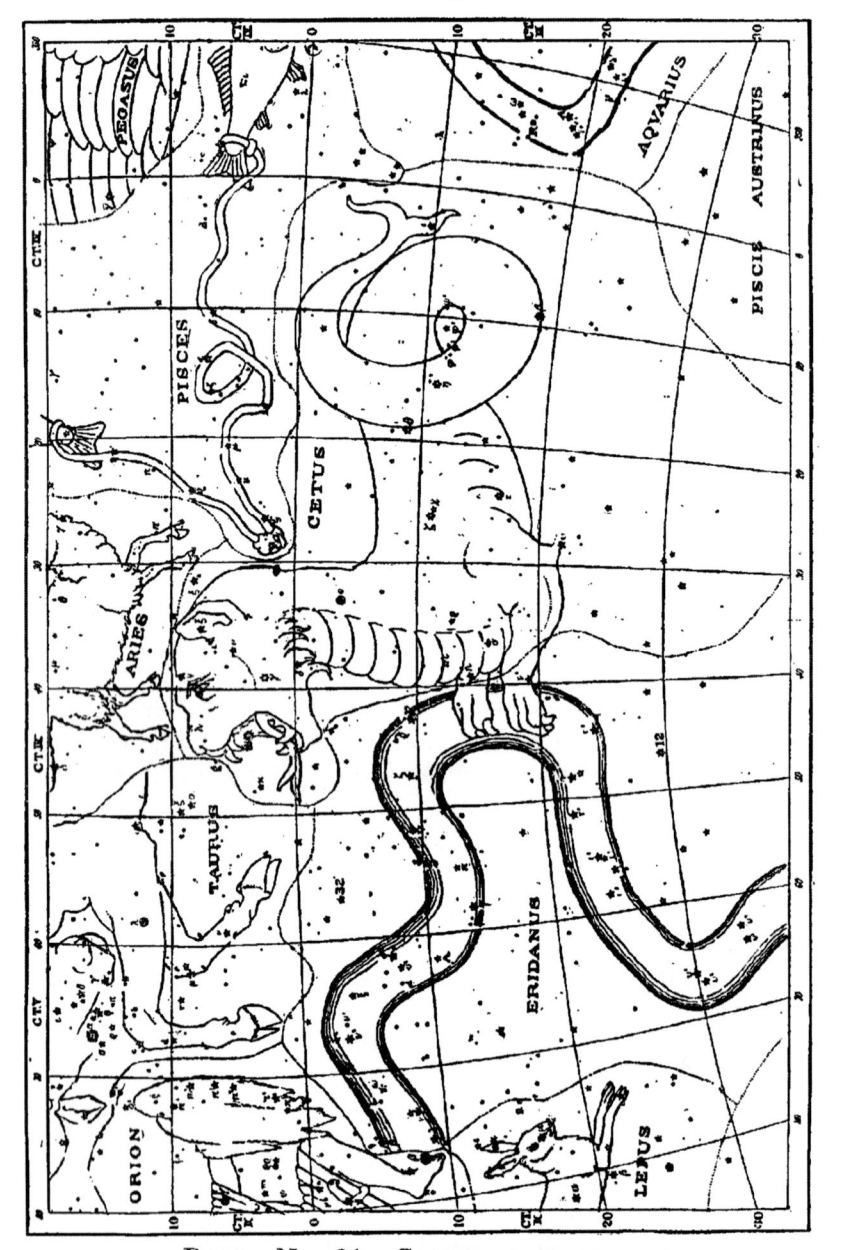

PLATE No. 21—CONSTELLATIONS.

Sagitarius in the east southward over the meridian in Casiopeia to Gemini in the west. This path or way is the ecliptic circuit for our solar system and is calculated the same in degrees and time as the ecliptic circle for the earth and sun.

The Milky Way extends in space 204 degrees and covers the distance from sunrise to sunset. It is located in the seven signs from Sagitarius in the east going over the meridian in the south and terminates in Gemini at the equator.

The meridian of the terrestrial heavens is the same to the celestial heavens as the sun's meridian is to the earth. It is the center of the circle from which to calculate time and space. The center or meridian of the universe is at the present time near Polaris, from which all calculations are made for the constellations.

The sun's meridian therefore, must correspond to the earth's meridian as both obtained its meridian from the same center. As an example, we will say that this method is like drawing three circles, one inside the other of 360 degrees, and that the 0 degree is at the same location for the three circles.

The universe as a whole and the terrestrial and celestial heavens including the sun can be considered as centers. The measurements for the sun and the heavens are calculated on the basis of 360 degrees regardless of whether the circuits are large or small. When the measurement of the sun and the length of time for its circuit is known, it can be used to base all other calculations on. We will describe this principle by comparing the measurement of the sun to the distances in the celestial and terrestrial heavens. The dimensions of the sun as a center compares to all space of the universe.

The diameter of the sun is 32 minutes which is divided into four parts of 8 minutes each. In order to get the circumference of the sun and the circuits, we multiply the 8 minutes X 3 which equals 24 minutes. From this it will be seen that the circumference of the sun is 24 minutes, which corresponds to the ecliptic circuits of the heavens, and that these circuits are made into 24 divisions. We have now made one great cycle of four parts into a smaller circle of 24 and this circle is again multiplied three times which equals 72 minutes. We have now the sun and the heavens divided into four quarters of 8 minutes each, making 72 minutes, and this is again multiplied by four, equalling 288, which is the circumference in minutes. There are 60 minutes to one hour so we will make the 288 minutes into hours and divide 288 by 60 which equals 48 hours. We have now made the circumference of the sun and the space of the three heavens as ecliptic circuits to contain 48 hours of solar time. If we reduce the circuit of 48 hours to the original one-quarter of the circle we have 12 hours for the quarter distance. One-fourth of the space containing 72 parts of 12 hours each and if we multiply the 12 X 72 it equals 864. From this it will be seen that one-fourth or 90 degrees consists of 864 degrees or thousands of degrees and that this circuit is the celestial heavens.

We will give the dimensions of the three planets to prove that all measurements of the heavens and earth correspond, and by referring to astronomical books these measurements can be verified.

The diameter of Uranus corresponds in proportion to the diameter of the sun which is 32 minutes. The diameter of Uranus is 32,000 miles. The diameter of Neptune is one-half degree or 36,000 miles.

The diameter of Saturn is 72,000 miles or one degree. Uranus has four moons and the distances of the moons in miles from Uranus corresponds to the ecliptic dimensions of the earth. Uranus' cycle of time is divided into four ages of 84 years each containing 336 years, which is one-third of a complete cycle of 1008 years.

We realize that the astrological system of calculating space in the heavens will not be understood by all, and some may condemn it before knowing that it is a system, but we know it is scientific and correct.

It is our mission to give the key to the secret of the heavens and let others explain the details.

The Bible gives us the information that the secrets and knowledge of the heavens, whether obtained from this book or not, will be generally understood within one year from the time it first becomes known.

We are living in the age described for the Apostle Paul and he was supposed to be a tentmaker by trade, at least the Bible is so translated that the profession of Paul was to build houses in the air as tents. The tenthouses Paul is described to build are the same kind of houses which are spoken of in this book and are houses in the heavens.

"In my father's house are many mansions if it were not so I would have told you."

272 *Key to Bible and Heaven.*

CHAPTER 50.

LOCATION OF SUNS AND STARS.

The following is a list of fixed Stars and Constellations copied from ancient records.

The six 1,000-year periods are illustrated in the six great constellations located nearest to the pole. They are Cassiopeia, Camelo Pardalis, Ursa Major, Ursa Minor, Draco, and Cepheus.

The twelve constellations pictured, located north of the Zodiac, represent the twelve hours of the great cycle. The first four are Andromeda, Persius, Auriga, and Lynx. The dividing degree begins at the 120th degree and contains the eight constellations of Leo Minor, Coma Berenices, Bootes, Hercules, Ophiuchus, Aquilla, Sygnus, and Pegasus. The other smaller constellations placed between the greater, illustrate the nature of the place in the heavens where they are located.

South of the twelve constellations are located what is known as the twelve houses of the Zodiac, beginning with Pisces as the first house, and ending with Aquarius, as the twelfth house.

South of the twelve houses of the Zodiac are located another set of constellations in the following order, beginning with Cetus south of Pisces, as the first house. Cetus, Eridanus, Orion, and Monoceros constituting the first four. The other eight constellations begin with the great Hydra and include Sextans, Crater, Corvus, Centaurus, S. Cross, Altair and Pisces Austrinus. There are also other southern constellations, as Canis Major and Minor, Argo, Lepus, and Columba, which include some very important stars.

The list we have given of constellations and fixed stars of the Zodiac are mostly copied from books published about 2,000 years ago, by Claudius Ptolemy. His books contain the scientific description of Astronomy and Astrology but do not describe the philosophy of life given in the Bible.

We have given the nearest degrees published by Ptolemy but have purposely left out the minutes and seconds as unimportant. It will be seen that the constellations and fixed stars are given to begin from Casiopeia and Diphta, in Cetus, which are from Pisces and that latitude and R. A. is given to begin with the first degree of Pisces on the ecliptic.

North of the Zodiac are located the following constellations: Cassiopeia, R. A. 12°°, Dec. 60°. Andromeda, R. A.

14, Dec. 30°. The Triangle, R. A. 27°. Dec. 32°°. Nebula of Perseus, R. A. 38°°, Dec. 39°. Perseus, R. A. 46°°, Dec. 45°°. Auriga, R. A. 75°°, Dec. 65°. Ursa Major, R. A. 153°°, Dec.

50°. Nebula in Ursa Major, R. A. 165, Dec. 56. Delphinus, R. A. 208°, Dec. 15°. Bootes, R. A. 212°, Dec. 20°. Arcturus, R. A. 213°, Dec. 20°. Ursa Minor, R. A 235°, Dec 75°. Corona,

Borealis, R. A. 235°, Dec. 30°. Serpens, R. A. 236° Dec. 16°. Hercules, R. A. 255°, Dec. 22°. Serpentarius, R. A. 260°, Dec. 13°. Draco, R. A. 270°, Dec. 66°°. Lyra, R. A. 283°°, Dec. 38° Aquilla, R. A. 295°, Dec. 8°. Sagitta R A. 398°, Dec. 18°. Cygnus, R. A. 308°, Dec. 42°. Cepheus, R. A. 238° Dec. 68°=. Pegasus, R. A. 340°, Dec. 14°.

South of Zodiac are located the following: Cetus, the Whale, R. A. 25°°, Dec. 12°. Hydrus, R. A. 28°, Dec. 66°=. Eridanus, R. A. 60°, Dec. 10°. Orion, R. A. 80°, Dec. 00°. Lepus, the Hare, R. A. 80°, Dec. 18°. Canis Minoris, R. A. 100°, Dec. 20°. Canis Majoris, R. A. 105°, Dec. 20°=. Argo Navis, R. A. 115°, Dec. 50. Corvus, the Crow, R. A. 185°°, Dec 15°°. Centaurus, R. A. 200°°, Dec. 50°. Lupus, the Wolf, R. A. 230°, Dec. 45°. Ara, the Altar, R. A. 255°, Dec. 55°. Coron Australis R. A. 280°, Dec. 40°. Pisces Australis, R. A. 335°, Dec. 30°.

EIGHTY FIXED STARS.

1. Diphda: Whale's tail, Citus, (south end). Lat. 21° s. Dec. 19°° s. R. A 10°; self destruction by brute force, sickness, disgrace, misfortune, compulsory change. 2. Algenib: Pegasi, Lat. 13° n. Dec. 15° n. R. A. 2°; dishonor, notoriety, violence, misfortune, the naked and poor professional beggar. 3. Andromeda: Caput Andro, Alpheratz. Lat. 26° n. Dec. 29°° n. R. A. 1°; independence, freedom, fortune, intellect, love, riches and honor. 4. Baten Kaitos: Whale's belly, Citus. Lat. 20° s. Dec. 11° s. R. A. 27°°; compulsory transportation, change or emigration, misfortune by accident or force, shipwreck with rescue. 5. Al Pherg. Al Muachher (Piscium); Head of Typhon. Lat. 5° n. Dec. 15°° n. R. A. 22°; preparedness, steadiness, determinedness, final success. 6. Andromeda Zona. Merach. Girdle of Andro. Lat. 26°° n. Dec. 35° n. R. A. 16°; love, beneficence, forgiveness and overcoming by kindness. 7. Sheritan. (Arietis). Ram's horn. Lat. 9° n. Dec. 20° n. R. A. 27°°; "cut off with a bloody wound," unscrupulously defeated, destroyed by fire, war or earthquake. 8. El Nath, El Natick, Ram's following horn. (Arietis). Lat. 10° n. Dec. 23°°=. R. A. 30; violence, brutishness, cruelty, premeditated crime, "the death wound." 9. Menkar, Whale's jaw, Citus. Lat. 12°° s. Dec. 4° n. R. A. 44°°; disease disgrace, ruin, injury from beasts. 10. Algol. Medusae's head, Persei. Lat. 22° n. Dec. 41° n. R. A. 45°; misfortune, violence, decapitation, hanging, electrocution, mob violence. 11. Alcyone, Pleiades, Bright Pleiad, Kesil, Karma, Kimah, "The central sun." Lat. 4° n. Dec. 24° n. R. A. 55°; "An immortal seal or type," love, blindness from fevers, accidents to the face. 12.

Part VI—Chapter 50.   275

Hyades, first star in Taurus near Aldebaren in bull's head. Lat. 6° s. Dec. 16°° n. R. A. 64°; tears, sudden events, violence, fierceness, poisoning, blindness, wounds or hurts to the head by in-

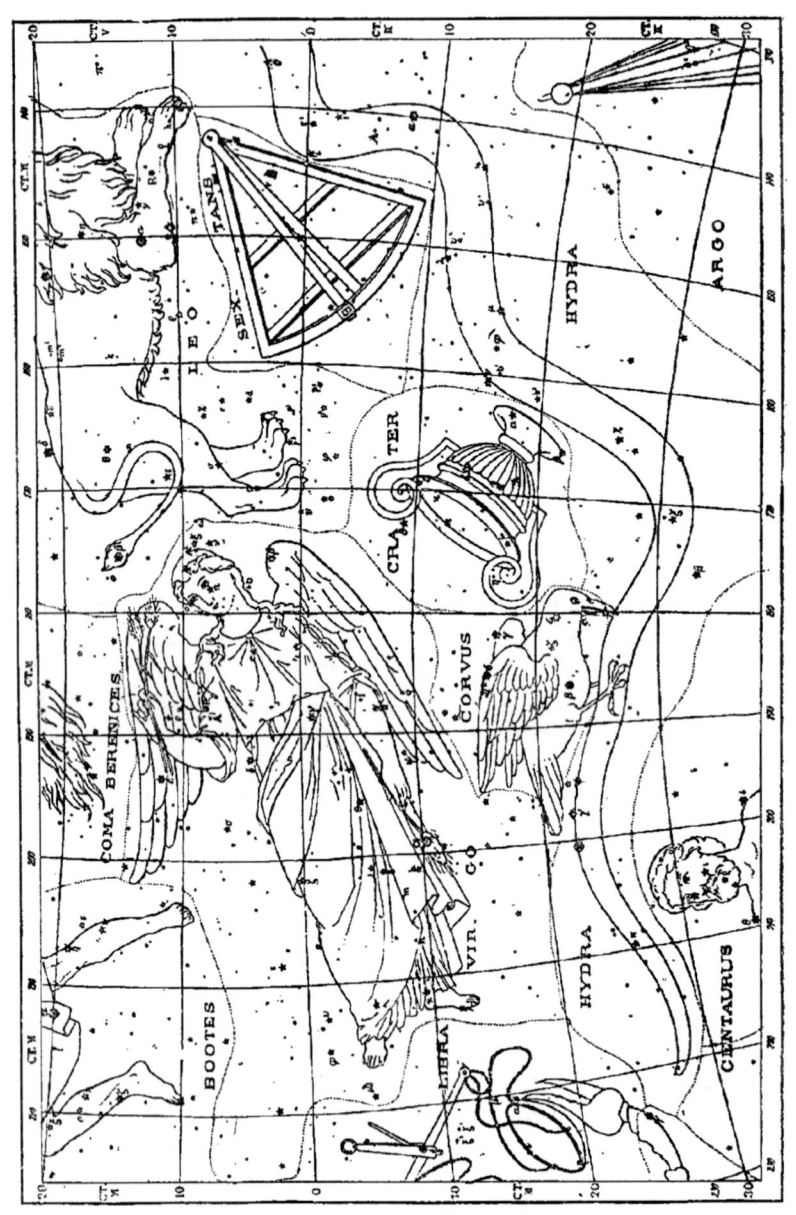

struments or fevers. 13. Aldebaren, Bull's south eye. Lat. 5° s. Dec. 16° n. R. A. 67°°; success in military occupation, honor, integrity, popularity, gain of power and wealth through others, "the subduing governor." 14. Rigel (nigel), Orion's left foot. Lat. 31°° s. Dec. 8° s. R. A. 77°°; benevolence, honor, riches and happiness. 15. Bellatrix, Orion's left shoulder. Lat. 16° s. Dec. 6° n. R. A. 78°; martial honor with sudden dishonor, subject to accidents causing ruin and blindness. 16. Capella, Auragia's left shoulder. Lat. 23° n. Dec. 46° n. R. A. 77°°; honor, wealth, friends, eminence, renown, public position of trust. 17. Phact. "Noah's dove," Columba. Lat. 57°° s. Dec. 34°° s. R. A. 84°; beneficence, good fortune, hopefulness. 18. Auriga. Bull's north horn; Lat. 5° n. Dec. 29° n. A. R. 80°; "the shepherd," neutrality for good or evil, fortune and eminence. 19. Alhecka, Heka, Bull's south horn; Lat. 1° s. Dec. 22° n. R. A. 82°; "the driver," violence, malevolence, danger by accident. 20. Betelguese, Orion's right shoulder; Lat. 16° s. Dec. 7° n. R. A. 87°°; martial honor, preferment and wealth. 21. Propus; Lat. 1° s. Dec. 23° n. R. A. 85°; strength, eminence and success. 22. Tejat, (Geminorum); Lat. 1° s. Dec. 22° n. R. A. 92°; violence, pride, overconfidence and shamelessness. 23. Gemini, forward foot, Dirah; Lat. 1° s. Dec. 23° n. R. A. 94°; protection, power and force, "the abused or beaten one." 24. Bright foot of Gemini, Alhena; Lat. 7° s. Dec. 16°° n. R. A. 98°°; liability to accidents of the feet, "the wound in the tendon Achiles." 25. Sirius, the dog star, Canis Majoris; 13°. Lat. 39° s. Dec. 16° s. R. A. 100°; honor, renown and wealth. 26. Canupis, Oar of Argo; Lat. 76° s. Dec. 53°° s. R. A. 95°; evil changed to good, piousness, conservativeness. 27. Wesat, (Geminorum); Lat. 1° s. Dec. 22°° n. R. A. 108°; violence, malevolence, chemical poison or gas, destructiveness as first principle. 28. Castor, Apollo, (Geminorum); Lat. 10° n. Dec. 32° n. R. A. 112°°; sudden changes in commerce for fame and honor, "a ruler yet to come." 29. Pollux, Hercules, (Geminorum); Lat. 7° n. Dec. 28°° n. R. A. 115°°; dignified malevolence, poison, "a heartless judge." 30. Procyon, Canis Minor; Lat. 16° s. Dec. 5° n. R. A. 113°°; activity, violence, malevolence, hydrophobia, causes elevation terminating in disaster. 31. Ascellus north, (Cancri) Baalam's Ass; Lat. 3°° n. Dec. 22° n. R. A. 129°; patience, beneficence, courage, a heroic defiant leader. 32. Proespe, Nebula, Crab's breast; Lat. 1° n. Dec. 20°° n. R. A. 128°; disease, disgrace, adventure, insolence, wantonness, brutality, blindness. 33. Ascellus south, (Cancri) Khan; Lat. 1° n. Dec. 18° n. R. A. 130°°; "a resting place," "the mare Ass," the ending or stop. 34. Acubens, Crab's claw, (Cancri); Lat. 5° s. Dec. 13° n. R. A. 134°; activity, malevolence, poison, liars and criminals. 35. Epsilon Leonis, Arych, the Lion's mouth; Lat. 10°° n. Dec. 24°° n. R. A. 145°°;

direfulness, cruelty, heartlessness, brutishness and destructiveness, "he who reads." 36. Alphard, Hydra's heart; Lat. 22° s. Dec. 8°° s. R. A. 141°°; death by drowning or poison, asphyxia-

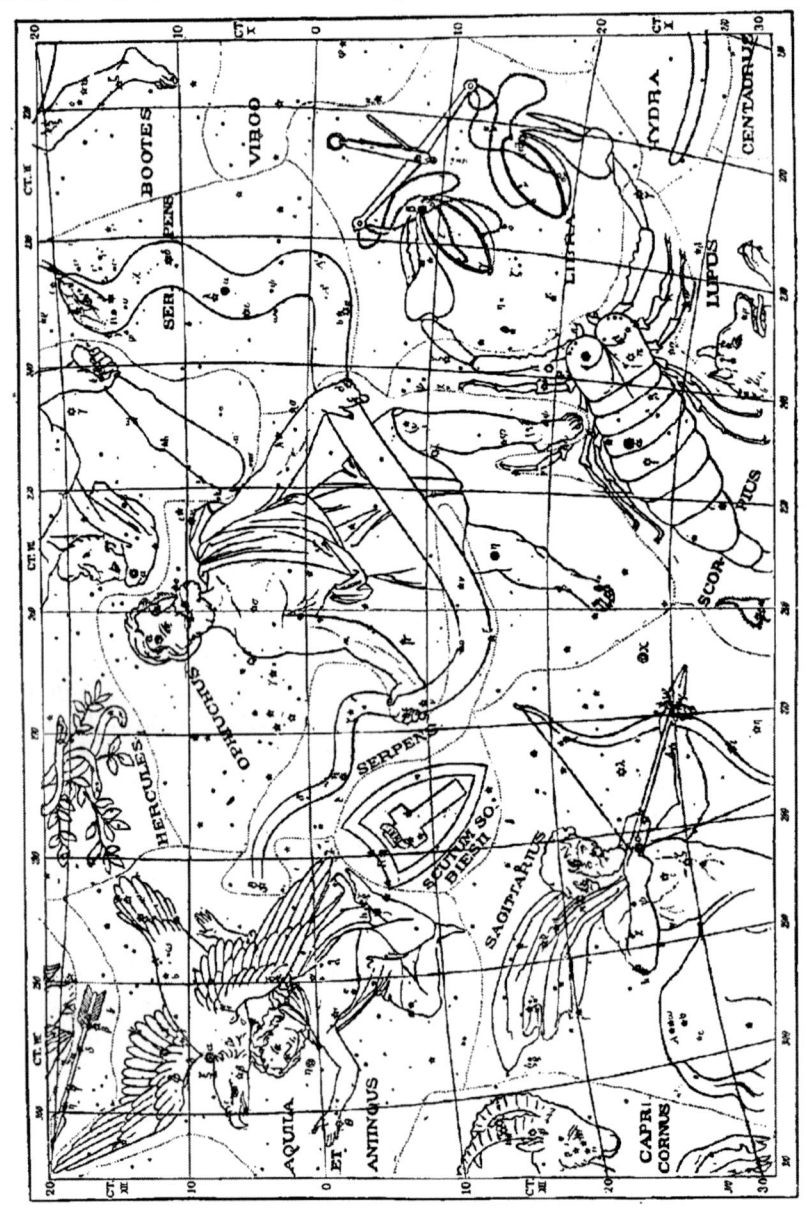

tion, sudden termination, immorality, revolting. 37. Regules, Lion's heart; Lat. 1° n. Dec. 12° n. R. A. 151°; "the crushing foot," violence, destructiveness, military honor of short duration with ultimate failure, imprisonment and death. 38. Phi Leonis, Al Serpha, Lion's belly. Lat. 1° n. Dec. 10° n. R. A. 157°°; "the funeral pyre," self destruction, acid poison, liquid explosive or fire, internal melting pot, lying, stealing, crime. 39. Zosma Lion's back; Lat. 14° n. Dec. 21° n. R. A. 167°; benefit by disgrace, selfishness, unreasonableness, egotism, immorality, meanness, shamelessness. 40, Deneboia, Denebola Lion's tail; Lat. 12° n. Dec. 15° n. R. A. 176°; "swift judgment," despair, regrets, public disgrace, misfortune from elements of nature, happiness turned to anger. 41. Zavijani; Lat. 1°° n. Dec. 5° n. R. A. 175°; "correct weighing," beneficence, force, strength, combative movements, destructiveness. 42. Crater. The Cup, Crateria, "Holy cup or grail;" Lat. 17°° s. Dec. 14° s. R. A. 169°; honors and riches in disgrace, the purifier unto salvation, ideality, psychic vision, intelligence. 43. Virgo, south wing; Lat. 1° n. Dec. 1° s. R. A. 184°; refinement, honor, congeniality, order, loveableness. 44. Vendemiatrix (Virginis); Lat. 16° n. Dec. 11° n. R. A. 194°; falsity, disgrace, stealing, wanton folly. 45. Caphir, Iclil, (Virginis); Lat. 3° n. Dec. 1° s. R. A. 189°; "an atonement offering," "the submissive one," a lovable character, courteous, refined. 46. Algorab, Corvus, in the crow or buzzard; Lat. 12° s. Dec. 16°° s=. R. A. 186; destruction, fiendishness, malevolence, repulsiveness, lying, the scavenger 47. Argus, the ship's stern; Lat. 59° s. Dec. 59°° s. R. A. 160°; peril usefulness, dignity, piousness, acquisitiveness. 48. Spica, Arista, (Virginis); Lat. 2° s. Dec. 10° s. R. A. 200°; unscrupulousness, success, renown, riches, "the seed of wheat.' 49. Arcturus, Arctophilax, Bootes; Lat. 31° n. Dec. 20° n. R. A. 213°; riches, honors, high renown, self-determination. 50. Virgo's left foot; Lat. 1° s. Dec. 13° s. R. A. 211°; swift violence, unreliability, argumentation, changeability. 51. Acrux, southern cross, Crucis, Roscroix; Lat. 53° s. Dec. 63° s. R. A. 185 °; religious ceremonial, magic, mystery, beneficence. 52. South scale of Libra, Zubenalgenubi; Lat. 1° n. Dec. 16° s. R. A. 221°; "the insufficient price," malevolence, obstruction, an unforgiving character, violent disease producing, lying crime. 53. North scale of Libra, Zubenalschemali; Lat. 9° n. Dec. 9° s. R. A. 228°; "the full price," beneficence, honor, riches, happiness, high ambition. 54. Agena, (Centauri); Lat. 44° s. Dec. 60° s. R. A. 209°; position, friendship, refinement, high morality, health, honor. 55. Bungula, (Centauri); Lat. 43° s. Dec. 60° s. R. A. 218°; beneficence, friends, position of honor, refinement. 56. Grafias, (Libra); Lat. 7° n. Dec. 11° s. R. A. 240°; extreme malevolence, mercilessness, fiendishness, repulsiveness, the criminal. 57. Isidis (Scorpii);

Lat. 2° s. Dec. 22° s. R. A. 239°; "sudden assault," malevolence, immorality, shamelessness. 58. Front of Scorpio; Lat. 1° n. Dec. 20° s. R. A. 240°; pestilence, contagious diseases, malice,

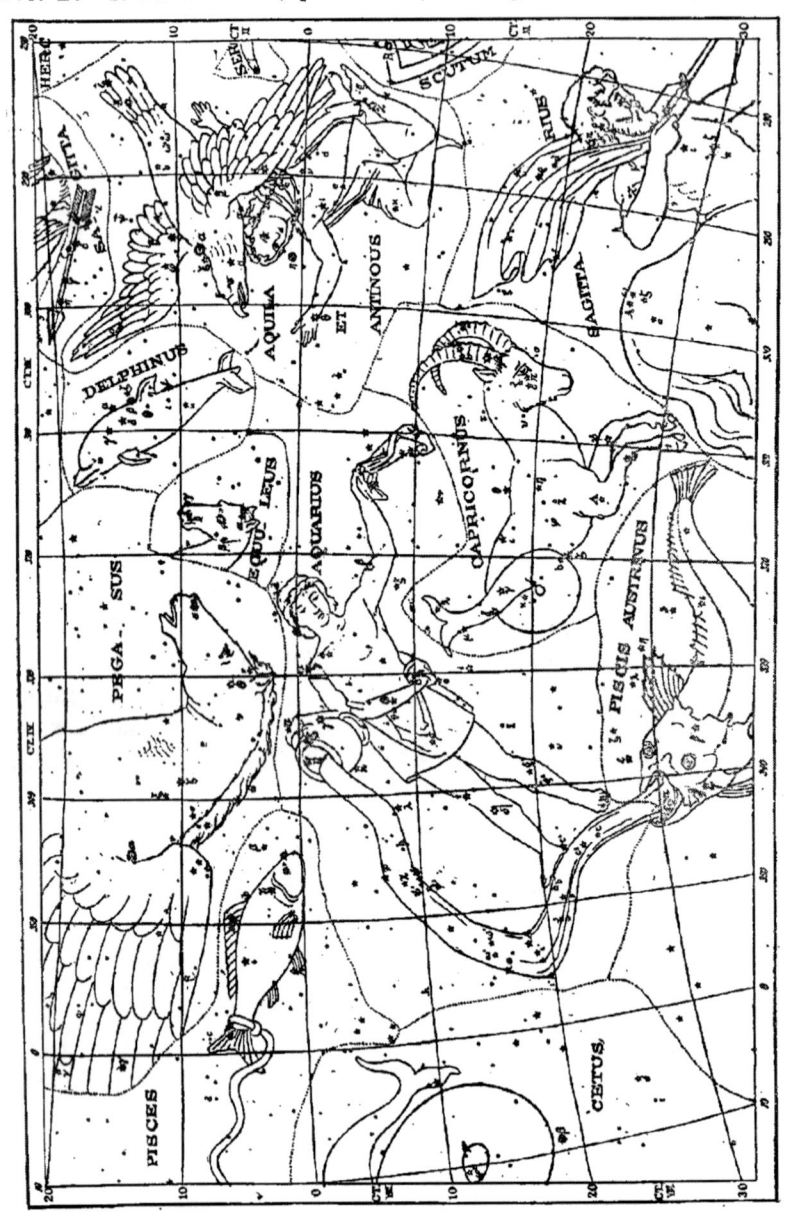

stealing, mercilessness, crime. 59. Antares, Shiloh, (Scorpi); Lat. 5° s. Dec. 26°° s. R. A. 246°; "it rends; tears," malevolence, destructiveness, liberality, broadmindedness. 60. Ophiuchu's knee, Ophinci, Serpentarius; Lat. 7° n. Dec. 16° s. R. A. 256°°; success in evil deeds, wastefulness, lost energy, perverted morals. 61. Rasalhagne, Head of Ophuchus, Ophinci; Lat. 36° n. Dec. 13° n. R. A. 263°; misfortune through woman, perverted tastes, mental depravity. 62. Lesuth, Scorpion's sting; Lat. 14° s. Dec. 36° s. R. A. 260°; malevolence, acid poison, danger, desperateness, low morals. 63. Yed, Ophuchi; Lat. 17° n. Dec. 3° s. R. A 242°; revolution, immorality, shamelessness 64. Archer's bow, (Sagitari); Lat. 3° n. Dec. 21° s. R. A. 272°; success, high ambition, martial desires, keen perception, domination. 65. Archer's fact, Nebula, (Sagitari); Lat. 1° n. Dec. 21°° s. R. A. 283°; blindness, explosives, fire, flaring heat, heroism, courage, defiance. 66. Vega Lyra; Lat. 62° n. Dec. 39° n. R. A. 278°°; beneficence, ideality, hopefulness, refinement, changeableness. 67. Eagle's tail, Aquilla; Lat. 36° n. Dec. 14° n. R. A. 285°; capability to command, liberality, success in war, beneficence. 68. Terrebellum, Archer's tail, (Sagitari); Lat. 5° s. Dec. 28° s. R. A. 293°°; a fortune but with regret and disgrace, cunning, a mercenary nature, repulsiveness. 69. Albireo, Swan's head, Cygni; Lat. 49° n. Dec. 28° n. R. A. 292°; "the song of the dying swan," beneficence in despair, a handsome person, neatness, lovableness. 70. Altair, Aquilla, Ara, Bird of Jove; Lat. 29° n. Dec. 9° n. R. A. 297°°; great and sudden material wealth, ambition, command, liberality. 71. Giedi, Goat's horn, (Capricorn); Lat. 7° n. Dec. 13°° n. R. A. 303°; "the slain kid," beneficence, sacrifice, offering. 72. Heart of Goat, (Capricorni); Lat. 3° s. Dec. 21°° s. R. A. 313°; disagreeableness, contemptibleness, instability, shamelessness. 73. Sea, Goat's belly, (Capricorni); Lat. 8° s. Dec. 24° s. R. A. 325°; malevolence, destructiveness, uncontrollable temper. 74. Deneb, Algedi, (Capricorni); Lat. 3° s. Dec. 18°° s. R. A. 323°; "the judicial point of the goat," beneficence and destructiveness, sorrow, happiness, life and death. 75. Sad Naschira, Goat's tail, (Capricorn); Lat. 3° s. Dec. 17° s. R. A. 326°; overcoming by evil which is turned to success. 76. El Melik, (Aquari); Lat. 11° n. Dec. 1° s. R. A. 330°; extreme and sudden destruction, persecution, lawsuits, death penalty. 77. Fomalhaut, South fish; Lat. 21° s. Dec. 30° s. R. A. 343°; change from a material to a spiritual form of expression. 78. Archernar, Fridani, Cherub and Sword; Lat. 60° s. Dec. 58° s. R. A. 324°; success in public office, beneficence, religion. 79. Markab, Wing of Pegasus; Lat. 20° n. Dec. 15° n. R. A. 345°°; honor riches, fortune, danger by fevers, violent death 80. Schet, Pegasi, Tail of western fish; Lat. 7° n. Dec. 7° n. R. A. 359°; extreme misfortune, suicide, drowning, murder.